Washington Irving's
LIFE OF MOHAMMED

Portrait of Washington Irving painted in London in 1820 by his friend Charles Robert Leslie, R. A. (1794-1859). (In the collection of the New York Public Library. Irving was appointed a trustee of the predecessor Astor Library by the will of John Jacob Astor, and served as the Library's first president until his death in 1859.)

WASHINGTON IRVING'S LIFE OF MOHAMMED

With an Introduction by
RAPHAEL PATAI

Edited by
CHARLES GETCHELL

THE IPSWICH PRESS
Ipswich, Massachusetts

ACKNOWLEDGMENTS

The editor gratefully acknowledges his indebtedness to the following sources of illustration and decoration in this volume:

For the frontispiece portrait of Washington Irving by Charles Robert Leslie, R.A. (1794-1859), oil on canvas, painted in London in 1820: Collection of The New York Public Library, Astor, Lenox and Tilden Foundations.

For the chapter headings, a photograph of a panel of nine tiles from Turkey, second half of the 16th century (the inscription beginning within verse 255 of the second chapter of the Koran, and continuing into verse 256): the al-Sabah Collection in the Kuwait National Museum.

For the map of the Arabian peninsula: Charles A. Pearsall (1924).

Published by
THE IPSWICH PRESS
Box 291
Ipswich, Massachusetts 01938

ISBN 0-938864-12-2

Contents

Editor's Foreword

Recent events have brought many of us to reflect on how poorly informed we in the West are about the origins of Islam and the lifework of the prophet Mohammed in implanting the foundations of that faith—which now claims more than half a billion followers around the world. Any reduction in the general level of ignorance can only be counted as a benefit in the current state of relations among nations and cultures. So we are emboldened to hope that this reappearance in paperback of the first volume of Washington Irving's two-volume *Mahomet and His Successors* (long out of print except in prohibitively expensive facsimile editions) will be welcomed by a multitude of new readers, interested in learning more about one of the most influential leaders in history.

Americans may be surprised to discover that such a knowledgeable and thorough treatment of this subject was accomplished a century and a half ago by one of their compatriots, who is far better remembered for his folk tales of old New York.

Ours is not by any means a definitive edition of this book. For that, readers are referred to the scholarly edition of the complete two-volume work published in 1970 by The University of Wisconsin Press, under the able editorship of Henry A. Pochmann and E. N. Feltskog, with Historical Note, Textual Commentary, Adopted Readings, and Emendations (part of the series "The Complete Works of Washington Irving").

Not being bound by academic strictures, we have, on the other hand, felt at liberty to make a few changes of our own. We have presumed to treat the author as though he were still at work today: that is to say, we have imagined that he might be willing to accept the advice of an admiring editor to suppress his occasional dangling participles, update some of his verb forms ("digged," "spake"), turn around inversions that jar us now as quaint ("exclaimed she"), simplify the structure of a handful of his sentences, and bring his use of commas and semicolons in line with current styles. (Wherever there was a risk of an essential rhythm or sound being lost, though, we kept hands off.) While "Mahomet" was a common spelling in the nineteenth century, we have throughout adopted "Mohammed," which is now the more familiar English-language form. We have also replaced the antiquated "Mahometan," "Mahometanism" and "Islamism" with "Moslem," "Islamic" or "Islam." We would like to think that these small touches have rendered Irving's book more accessible to a wider range of contemporary readers, without unsettling his ghost.

The subject matter itself, of course, is linked to profound sensibilities in today's world, so the idea of a mild bowdlerization not unnaturally crossed our mind. We recognized in particular that the concept of "the sword as an instrument of faith," discussed by Irving in Chapter 16 and elsewhere, is a highly controversial interpretation unacceptable to most Moslems. (It has been suggested that quotations of the prophet purporting to advocate such a policy are from spurious additions to the Ḥadīth, or "tradition," made by adversaries of Islam.) Equally unorthodox are Irving's suggestions here and there that Mohammed may have acted as more than a messenger of God—that indeed he may sometimes have phrased the received texts of the Koran to suit his own purposes—and that he may occasionally have disingenuously disavowed the actions of his followers.

But we rejected the notion of making substantive changes in the text as offensive to the intelligence of our readers and to the memory of Washington Irving. By any measure, his study of Mohammed is on the whole sympathetic and fair-minded, and whatever debatable conjectures and conclusions may be found in it are put in their proper historical and social perspective through the Introduction provided by the distinguished cultural anthropologist Raphael Patai. We are indebted to Dr. Patai not only for his Introduction and for the list of Transliteration Equivalents at the end of the volume, but also for his wise counsel during the preparation of this new edition of a long-overlooked classic.

—*Charles Getchell*

Introduction

by Raphael Patai

Washington Irving (1783-1859), the first native American to become a successful, and, more than that, a highly acclaimed writer, began his literary career as a satirist, while in his later writing the satirical vein was largely overshadowed by a gentler humor and sentimentalism. His *Knickerbocker's History of New York* (published in 1809), a work of crude power and complex humor presented as a facetious mock history of the colony of "New Netherlands," brought him instant success. His subsequent *Sketch Book of Geoffrey Crayon, Gent.* (1819-20), *Bracebridge Hall* (1822), and *Tales of a Traveller* (1824), written in a similar vein, secured him a lasting place in American literature, and his short stories "Rip Van Winkle" and "The Legend of Sleepy Hollow" (both published in the *Sketch Book*) have become recognized as masterpieces. As late as in 1975 Charles Neider still found them "masterly, bewitching, magical, with a great aptness of phrase and metaphor, and with the subtle, delicate, delicious irony that marks Irving's best work."[1]

In 1804, when he was twenty-one, Irving sailed for Europe, and spent eighteen months in France, Germany, Italy, the Netherlands, and England. After his return to America he was briefly engaged to Matilda Hoffman, but she died of consumption, and Irving never married. In May 1815, the 32-year-old Irving, by then the famous author of *Knickerbocker's History*, again embarked for Europe to work in the Liverpool office of his family's hardware trading business. He stayed in England for five years, then went on to Paris and Germany, and in February 1826 joined the American legation in Madrid. He was to remain in Spain for nearly four years.

In Madrid Irving spent several hours almost daily in the library of the Jesuits' Convent of San Isidro, and became entranced by the romance of the country's medieval history. "What a deep-felt, quiet luxury there is," he wrote in 1827 to Prince Dolgorouki, a young attaché at the Russian legation, "in delving into the rich ore of these old, neglected volumes!" When, travelling to Granada, he first caught sight of the Alhambra, he wrote to Antoinette Bollviller: "But Granada, *bellissima* Granada! Think what must have been our delight when . . . we turned a promontory . . . and Granada with its towers, its Alhambra, and its snowy mountains burst upon our sight! . . . The more I contemplate these places, the more my admiration is awakened for the elegant habits and delicate taste of the Moorish monarchs."

The years Irving spent in Spain and subsequently in England were one of the most fruitful periods in his life. He wrote *The Life and Voyages of Christopher Columbus* (published in 1828), and while serving as secretary in the American legation in London (1829-32) he completed *The Chronicle of the Conquest of Granada* (1829), *The Voyages and Discoveries of the Companions of Columbus* (1831), and *The Alhambra* (1832), which soon became almost as popular as the Hudson River tales in his *Sketch Book*. These books earned Irving impressive royalties (for the English edition of his *Columbus* he got £3,150, a huge amount at the time), and brought him great literary acclaim, including an LL. D. from Oxford University and a gold medal of the Royal Society of Literature.

Even prior to his Spanish sojourn Irving had taken an interest in Arab legend and history. As early as in November 1823 he wrote to his British publisher John Murray, proposing a collection of Arabian tales—but it was only after his arrival in Spain that he became attracted to the Arabian prophet himself. He started making notes on a "Legendary Life of Mahomet," and, from November 1827 on, his diaries contain entries such as "All day writing legend of Mahomet." In 1829 he proposed to John Murray a "life of Mahomet," in 1831 he revised and enlarged the manuscript, and in September of that year he announced to Murray that his "Legendary Life of Mahomet" would be ready to go to the printer in a few days. A month later he actually mailed twenty-one chapters of this book to Colonel Thomas Aspinwall, his colleague at the American legation, and wrote to Murray that the full volume would contain about seventy chapters.

In the event, Irving and Murray were unable to reach an agreement on the publication of *Mahomet*, and the manuscript remained unpublished for nearly two decades. From 1842 to 1846 Irving served as U. S. minister to Spain, and it was only after his return to America that he completed his *Mahomet and His Successors*. The two-volume work was published in December 1849 by Putnam in New York.

Today Mohammed is probably the most thoroughly researched and best documented figure among all the great religious founders of old. There are several reasons for this. Firstly, Mohammed lived much later than Abraham (17th century B.C.) and Moses (13th century B.C.), the semi-legendary founders of Judaism; than Buddha, Confucius, and Lao Tzu (6th-5th centuries B.C.), the great, likewise semi-legendary founders of the major South and Southeast Asian religions; or Jesus and Paul, the founders of Christianity. Secondly, in contrast to the others, Mohammed's own words were carefully memorized and written down by several of his early followers and disciples at the very time he uttered them. Thirdly, the veneration of the Prophet gave rise, very soon after his death, to a huge corpus of literature, the so-called *Ḥadīth* ("tradition"), in which every act and word attributed to Mohammed was meticulously recorded. And fourthly, within a very few decades after his death Arab historians, characterized by scholarly acumen and firm belief in the divine mission of the Prophet, began to write Mohammed biographies. In modern times this rich material came to serve as the basis for a steadily increasing number of studies by both Western and Moslem scholars. In fact, the interest in the life, work, and personality of the Arabian prophet has increased in recent decades to such an extent that the computer catalog of the New York Public Library lists no less than three hundred titles of Mohammed studies published since 1971.

In the 1820's, when Irving first turned his attention to the life of Mohammed, very little of the Arabic writings on the life of the Prophet was available in a European translation. One of them was a 14th-century compilation by Shams ul-Din al-Tibrizi, titled (in modern scholarly transliteration) *Mishkāt ul-Maṣābīḥ*, that is, "Niche of the Lamps," an English translation of which was published in 1809[2]. Irving quotes two brief passages from this work (on page   21 of the present edition). Another Arab author to whom Irving refers is Aḥmad ibn Yūsuf al-Jannābī al-Qaramānī, a 16th-century historian, whose book *Akhbār al-Duwal wa-athār al-Uwal* ("Histories of the Times and Traces of the Ancients") is a history of the eighty-two Moslem dynasties in various parts of the world.

The Arab author who served as Irving's main source, and whom he duly credits in his Preface, is "Abulfeda," that is, Ismāīl ibn 'Alī Abu 'l-Fidā (1273-1331), whose magnum opus, the *Mukhtaṣar Ta'rīkh al-Bashar* ("Concise History of Man") covers the pre-Islamic period and Islamic history down to 1329. The section dealing with the life of Mohammed is short: it comprises about 13,000 words in the original Arabic. This part of the *Mukhtaṣar* was published in 1723 with a Latin translation and copious notes by Jean Gagnier, professor of Oriental languages at Oxford, under the title *Ismael Abu'l-Feda, De vita et rebus Mohammedis . . . Ex Codice MSto Procockiano Bibliothecae Bodleinae Textum Arabicum primus edidit, Latinae vertit, Prefatione & Notis illustravit Joannes Gagnier, A. M. Oxoniae: e Theatro Sheldoniano, A. D. 1723.* The publication of this book, and even more so that of the later multivolume French work of Gagnier[3]—which appeared just in time for Irving to utilize it for his last revision and expansion of his *Mahomet*—were milestones in the Western Mohammed research.

The few Western writings about Mohammed antedating Gagnier were in many cases seriously blemished either by an anti-Mohammed, or an apologetically pro-Mohammed tendency. One of the former, referred to, and censured by, Irving (page 73) was titled *The true Nature of Imposture, fully displayed in the Life of Mahomet.* It was written by Humphrey Prideaux (1648-1724), and its first American edition was printed in Fairhaven, Vermont, in 1798. The contrary view was represented by Henry Stubbe (1632-1676), as indicated by the title of his book, *An Account of the rise and progress of Mahometanism: with the life of Mahomet and a vindication of him and his religion from the calumnies of the Christians.*[4] Another early pro-Mohammed biography was that of Henri Comte de Boulainvilliers (1658-1722), whose *Vie de Mahomet* was translated and published in London in 1731. Irving quotes neither of these two books, but it is quite likely that he was familiar with them.

The one scholarly source to which Irving acknowledges his indebtedness, in addition to Abulfeda-Gagnier, is the Mohammed biography of Gustav Weil (1808-1889) published in Stuttgart in 1843 and entitled *Mohammed der Prophet, sein Leben und seine Lehre* ("Mohammed the Prophet: His Life and Teachings"). While this work impressed Irving as being "industrious researches and able disquisitions" (see his Preface), in Abulfeda he found a kindred spirit despite his differing religious premises. Abulfeda, as a 13th-14th-century believing Moslem, considered Mohammed the last and greatest of the prophets and the Koran the literal record of the words Allah addressed to him through the intermediacy of the angel Gabriel. Moreover, for Abulfeda all the details transmitted by Arab tradition about the life, acts, and sayings of the Prophet that were found authentic by the authoritative *Hadith* collections were all indubitably true. Although Irving could not share this unquestioning approach to the life of Mohammed, it nevertheless had an intrinsic appeal for the author, many of whose writings had taken the form of retelling or reconstructing old legends, and presenting them in an attractive literary form interspersed here and there with a few guarded disavowals of belief in the literal truth of this or that detail. Likewise, without commiting himself to the historicity of the stories about Mohammed, Irving presented them in a style that from the very outset was calculated to lull the reader into a willing suspension of disbelief at which point the question of the legends' veracity becomes entirely irrelevant.

Irving's *Mahomet* opens with a brief account of the Arabs' traditions about their remote ancestors, both Biblical and native Arabian. Absorbing these old Arab stories, one becomes instantly enveloped in the atmosphere of that particular culture of which Mohammed was at first the product and then the chief molder and shaper. In telling the life story of Mohammed, Irving again proves himself a master in weaving together historical data and pious Moslem traditions. For example, when speaking of Mohammed's father Abdallah who married Amina, he adds: "So remarkable was Abdallah for personal beauty and those qualities which win the affections of women, that, if Moslem traditions are to be credited, on the night of his marriage with Amina, two hundred virgins of the tribe of Koreish died of broken hearts" (p.11). Irving's critical mind told him that this can be nothing but a legend (hence the clause "if Moslem traditions are to be credited"), but at the same time the mention of this "tradition" suffices to give the reader a whiff of the old Arab folk life and folk belief breathed by Mohammed.

Similarly, legendary or marvelous accounts of Mohammed's birth and childhood, quoted by Irving (on pp. 11-13), build up in the reader's mind the image of the Prophet as it appeared to the eyes of the believers. Irving keeps a historian's distance from these traditions by stating repeatedly, "according to similar traditions," "we are assured," "say the authorities," etc., yet as a master storyteller he realtes these fables because he senses that for an understanding of Mohammed's impact on the Arab world the presentation of these legends is more important than would be a painstaking tracking down of the actual events in the life of the Prophet. It is that image, presented in the legends, that shaped Arab history and culture, and ultimately influenced the history of all mankind.

Irving handles with considerable tact and restraint the supernatural occurences related in the Koran in connection with the life and work of Mohammed. When, for instance, discussing the Moslem tradition about the night journey of Mohammed from Mecca to Jerusalem, and from there to the seventh heaven (based on Koran 17:1), Irving calls it a "vision or revelation," and asserts that he "will endeavor to seize upon its most essential features" (p. 58). Thereupon he proceeds to tell the story of that famous journey in all its novelistic amplitude, devoting to it no less than nine pages (pp. 58-66), which seem to be an abridgement of the ninety-two pages Gagnier gives to the subject in his *Vie de Mahomet.* But then, as if to reassert his position of scholarly skepticism, Irving concludes his fascinating rendering of that legend by saying that it "rests almost entirely upon tradition, though some of its circumstances are vaguely alluded to in the Koran. The whole may be a fanciful superstructure of Moslem fanatics on one of these visions or ecstasies to which Mohammed was prone. . ." (p. 66).

Irving shared the Western scholarly view that the success of Mohammed's life work was due more to his exceptional personal qualities than to divine election; yet he did not repress his critical acumen in painting the character of the Arabian prophet. Thus, when he refers to Mohammed's Moslem biographers who "would fain persuade us his high destiny was clearly foretold in his childhood by signs and prodigies," he adds that in fact Mohammed's "education appears to have been as much neglected as that of ordinary Arab children, for we find that he was not taught either to read or to write" (p. 17). Likewise, while Irving leaves us in no doubt about his sympathy for the Prophet, and manifests a considerable capacity for empathy with his beliefs, motivations, and aims, yet, being a child of his day and age, he cannot help but view the life and work of Mohammed from a typical 19th-century Western, Christian point of view. This is apparent in Irving's presentation of Mohammed's metamorphosis from the prophet that he was in the pre-Hegira Meccan days to the statesman and army commander he became after the Hegira to Medina. This, for Irving, was a fall from grace, a divergence "from the celestial spirit of the Christian [!] doctrines," and an inability of "maintaining the sublime forbearance he had hitherto inculcated." From that time on, as Irving sees it, although "zeal for religious reform . . . was still [the Prophet's] predominant motive," his "sudden access of power" awakened in him "human passions and mortal resentments" (pp. 84-85). Thus Mohammed's originally pure religious fervor became, in Irving's eyes, compromised by "that wordly alloy which at times was debasing his spirit, now that he had become the Apostle of the Sword" (p. 123).

In Irving's view Mohammed was indebted to Judaism and its sacred religious sourcebooks—the Bible, the Mishna (Irving spells it "Mishnu"), and the Talmud—and, above all, to Christianity. He refers to Mohammed's "reverence for the Jewish faith," but adds that "the system laid down in the Koran, however, was essentially founded on Christian doctrines inculcated in the New Testament" (p. 36). This assertion can be interpreted as manifesting either Irving's pro-Christian bias, or his insufficient scrutiny of the relationship between the Koran and the Bible. For the easily ascertainable fact is that the Koran contains no less than some three dozen longer or shorter references to Old Testament figures, as against the mention of only three New Testament characters (John, Jesus and Mary).[5]

To flesh out the story of the Prophet, Irving used several of the studies published shortly before he completed his last revision of *Mahomet.*, in which he found background information for his book. Traces of this work are found in his footnotes in which we encounter the names of some of the great 18th- and 19th-century Orientalists, such as Burckhardt, Lane,

Niebuhr, and Layard.[6] Nor is a passing reference to Gibbon missing.[7] That Irving also used additional sources, not appearing in his text of Mahomet, becomes clear from a cursory perusal of the "Memoranda" he prepared for the book, which are preserved in the Berg Collection of the New York Public Library.

As indicated above, Irving's *Mahomet* is a mixture of historical narrative and novelistic or dramatized retelling of conversations that supposedly took place between the Prophet and his contemporaries. Occasionally Irving presents dialogues as quotes from "the legend," *e.g.*, the spirited conversation between Mohammed and Abu Sofian (p. 145). He is at his best when describing dramatic scenes, such as the encounter between the Prophet and the powerful Bedouin chieftain Amir ibn Tufiel (p. 165). It is these dialogues, interspersed among the dramatic passages, that give Irving's *Mahomet* the vivacity lacking in many of the later and more scholarly lives of Mohammed.

Another feature that makes Irving's *Mahomet* as attractive today as it was at the time of its publication is the naive directness and unhesitating expression with which he describes Mohammed's personality. When he finds in his sources something he likes about Mohammed, he says so; and when he finds traits or acts which he, from his 19th-century point of view, must condemn, he again says so. The result is that Irving's *Mahomet* paints a picture of the Arabian prophet that is totally human; as we proceed reading it we get acquainted with a man who, like all men, was both good and bad, who went through periods of life in which he was the self-abnegating Messenger of God, convinced that he was commanded from on high to speak and act, and who obeyed that command whatever the consequences for himself; and then reached a stage in which he was forced by circumstances to act and to move as a ruthless political and military leader, and to use his prophetic reputation for pursuing a calculated course of action in which it is difficult to distinguish between service to the great eternal cause of Allah, and the advancement of the small temporal interests of the Messenger.

A third characteristic of Irving's book that endows it with lasting value is one that was pointed out as early as in January 1850 by the *United States Magazine*: it tells its story "with a perspicuity and grace which has seldom been equalled"[8]—a judgment that holds good today as it did then.

More than in any other part of his book, Irving's view of Mohammed finds its clear expression in the brief concluding chapter titled "Person and Character of Mohammed and Speculations on His Prophetic Career" (pp. 197-206).[9] From this chapter it becomes evident that, viewing Mohammed's *persona* in its totality, Irving had considerable admiration for him. This is attested by statements such as these: "[Mohammed's] intellectual qualities were undoubtedly of an extraordinary kind." He had "a quick apprehension, a retentive memory, a vivid imagination, and an inventive genius." He had "a voice musical and sonorous." "He was sober and abstemious in his diet . . . indulged in no magnificence of apparel." He was characterized by "extreme cleanliness." ". . . he was just." "In the intercourse of domestic life he was kind and tolerant." "He disdained all miracles excepting the Koran" (pp. 197-99).

In this chapter Irving recapitulates Mohammed's life and divides it into "two grand divisions." (p. 201). In the first, Mohammed's prophetic claims and revelations earned him only scorn, ridicule and persecution. Throughout this period he could have been motivated to persist in his mission only by "his enthusiastic and visionary spirit gradually wrought up by solitude, fasting, prayer, and meditation . . . into a state of temporary delirium in which he fancies he receives a revelation from heaven, and is declared a prophet of the Most High" (p. 202). Continuing in this psychologizing vein, Irving concludes that Mohammed must have been fully convinced that he was chosen by God "to go forth and preach the faith" (p. 202). Although Irving calls the state of mind of Mohammed until the Hegira "that of an enthusiast acting under a species of mental delusion," yet he recognizes that there was "something striking and sublime in the luminous path which his enthusiastic spirit struck out for itself . . . the pure and spiritual worship of the one true God, which he sought to substitute for the blind idolatry of his childhood" (p. 202). In sum, he characterizes Mohammed as "a man of great genius and a suggestive imagination" (p. 203).

Irving's psychological analysis of Mohammed's personality after the flight to Medina reveals to him that, after that milestone in the Prophet's career, "a signal change . . . took place" in him. From that time on, Mohammed was increasingly prompted by "worldly passions and worldly schemes" (p. 203), or, as we would prefer to put it, he became more and more preoccupied with the problems and tasks of governing the rapidly growing body of his followers and of subduing by force of arms those who continued to oppose him. While Irving admires the pre-Hegira Mohammed, he becomes rather critical when contemplating Mohammed after he achieved a position of power in Medina. At that point in time, Mohammed "proclaimed the religion of the sword," inspired his followers with a "fanatic zeal" (p. 204), and "had occasionally to avail himself of his supernatural machinery as a prophet" in order to achieve what he believed was his mission (p. 204). Still, even when speaking of Mohammed in Medina, Irving recognizes that Mohammed did not aspire to military triumphs for selfish purposes, that he maintained even "in the time of his greatest power . . . the same simplicity of manners and appearance as in the days of his adversity" (p. 204), that he did not want testimonials of respect, and aimed at universal dominion not for himself or his family, but for the faith. He did not accumulate riches, he continued in a "perfect abnegation of self, and, whatever worldly power he acquired, "the early aspirations of his spirit continually returned and bore him above all earthly things" (p. 205). Prayer remained "his constant practice," and trust in God the lodestone of his existence. Even in his "dying hour . . . he still breathed the same religious devotion, and the same belief in his apostolic mission" (p. 205). Passages such as these attest to Irving's admiration for Mohammed, which is only partially obscured by his somewhat ingenuous attempt at a psychologizing explanation of Mohammed's character given in the concluding paragraph of Chapter 39:

". . . we find no other satisfactory mode of solving the enigma of his character and conduct, than by supposing that the ray of mental hallucination which flashed upon his enthusiastic spirit during his religious ecstasies in the midnight cavern of Mount Hara, continued more or less to bewilder him with a species of monomania to the end of his career, and that he died in the delusive belief of his mission as a prophet" (p. 206).

Spoken, we may add, as a true son of the 19th-century West for whom any belief in the prophetic mission of a non-Biblical or non-Christian religious leader could simply be nothing else but a delusion. Yet, within the limitations imposed upon him by his upbringing, age, and environment, Irving painted a most prepossessing picture of Mohammed—a picture that even today, a century and a half later, we can still find attractive, instructive, and more appealing than many of the modern, more detailed, more scholarly, and more factual biographies of the Arabian prophet.

RAPHAEL PATAI

Forest Hills, New York
June 1989

Author's Preface

Some apology may seem necessary for presenting a life of Mohammed at the present day, when no new fact can be added to those already known concerning him. Many years since, during a residence in Madrid, the author projected a series of writings illustrative of the domination of the Arabs in Spain. These were to be introduced by a sketch of the life of the founder of the Islam Faith, and the first mover of Arabian conquest. Most of the particulars for this were drawn from Spanish sources, and from Gagnier's translation of the Arabian historian Abulfeda, a copy of which the author found in the Jesuits' Library of the Convent of St. Isidro, at Madrid.

Not having followed out, in its extent, the literary plan devised, the manuscript life lay neglected among the author's papers until the year 1831, when he revised and enlarged it for the Family Library of Mr. John Murray. Circumstances prevented its publication at that time, and it was again thrown aside for years.

During his last residence in Spain, the author beguiled the tediousness of a lingering indisposition by again revising the manuscript, profiting in so doing by recent lights thrown on the subject by different writers, and particularly Dr. Gustav Weil, the very intelligent and learned librarian of the University of Heidelberg, to whose industrious researches and able disquisitions he acknowledges himself greatly indebted. (*Mohammed der Prophet, sein Leben und seine Lehre*, Stuttgart, 1843.)

Such is the origin of the work now given to the public, on which the author lays no claim to novelty of fact nor profundity of research. It still bears the type of a work intended for a Family Library, in constructing which the whole aim of the writer has been to digest into an easy, perspicuous and flowing narrative the admitted facts concerning Mohammed, together with such legends and traditions as have been wrought into the whole system of oriental literature; and at the same time to give such a summary of his faith as might be sufficient for the more general reader. Under such circumstances, he has not thought it worthwhile to encumber his pages with a scaffolding of references and citations, nor depart from the old English nomenclature of oriental names.

W. I.

SUNNYSIDE, 1849

"A Voice Out of the Depths of the Wilderness . . . "

In a review of the first edition of this book, in February of 1850, the editors of The Athenæum *of London wrote: "As a piece of literary work we can award high praise to this Life of Mohammed." But they regretted in passing that Washington Irving had not provided a global historical perspective for his study. They then went on to fill the gap they had noted, and their brief survey can profitably be revived here as a prologue to this edition:*

Had Europe, by some strange anachronism, produced in the seventh century of our era a man gifted with the power of reading the signs of the times, we can fancy with what an utter absence of faith in the future he would have looked around him. On every side the clouds were gathering fast. Gradually but surely the darkness which seemed to cover the whole world—to blot out all the past, to menace all the future—had come down. The long and dismal night of history had set in. Nowhere was there a gleam of hope on which the mind could seize. Intellectually, socially, politically, it was the same; in every one of those great spheres in which the human spirit in its day of free and vigorous youth loves to develop, multiply, and reproduce itself, there reigned the one type of moral paralysis. There were no living arts, sciences or literature—nothing but a few monuments and traditions, of which the beauty was unfelt and the value unknown. With the exceptions of Isidore of Seville and the Alexandrian chronicler—pitiful exceptions at best—those hundred years did not produce a single author, properly so called. This one fact is a history in itself. The only department of letters which received a partial cultivation was that of dogmatic controversy—and even that was below contempt.

The politics of the period looked quite as desperate as its literature. The Roman empire had fallen into fragments. A magnificent piece of the ruin yet lay on the shores of the Bosphorus—but it was not the old empire, not supported by the old spirit, very partially governed by the same laws. The Goths had fixed their barbarism in Spain. The Langobards had settled on the fertile plains of Italy. North and west the barbarian hordes had seated themselves on the wrecks of a civil system infinitely more advanced and more corrupt than that which they had brought with them from their native steppes and forests. But the greatest danger of all lay in the East, whence the Parthian Khosru the Second threatened to over whelm with his warlike idolaters not only the Eastern Empire, but with it Christianity and whatever remained of the antique civilization. This mighty chieftain had recently renewed the days of Cyrus. Advancing against the Grecian emperor, he conquered Armenia, Cappadocia and Palestine—made himself master of Jerusalem, and carried off the Holy Cross to his Persian capital. He invaded Africa with similar success, added Egypt and Libya to his mighty empire, and carried his victorious standard into the neighborhood of Carthage. These conquerors were of a haughty and intractable race, barbarians and idolaters; but what was still worse, the germs of a vigorous life were not in them. They had reached the apex of their power; and their overgrown empire, held together only by the sword, was already threatening to dissolve of itself.

In the other half of the world society was far advanced in the earlier stages of decomposition. The canker had seized on every part of the body politic. Vices and luxuries of which the modern world can barely form a conception reigned in the court, the camp, and the city of Constantine. Whatever remnants of the old arts, manners, politeness existed, were used for the servile purposes of adulation. Vain and preposterous titles were invented to conceal the absence of true merit:—nothing less than "your magnificence," "your illustrious highness," "your sublime and wonderful magnitude," would content the pettiest magistrate who prided himself on being the countryman of Pericles or of Scipio. Courtesans and murderers sat on the throne of the Caesars. Crime and immorality, baseness and treachery, were the royal roads to eminence. The Church was nearly as far gone in corruption as the Court:—simony, avarice, worldly pride, the lusts of the flesh, a vain and disputatious spirit, disgraced its ministers. Under new names, the people were returning to the pantheism of their early forefathers. The saints and angels had become to them the inferior deities of the old Olympus, and the Christian God was but the chief personage in the celestial hierarchy. The Eastern and Western Churches had alike returned—in spirit, if not in name—to the rites of Paganism. The man who stood apart and discerned the signs of the times—had there been such a man—might well have despaired for virtue, for morality, for civilization itself.

It was into the midst of a world thus decaying and dissolving in all its parts, that a voice came out of the depths of the wilderness of Arabia, saying in a strange tone, "There is no God but God—and Mohammed is the prophet of God." The men who bore this message appeared in the two rival courts in the self-same year. Heraclius, who had never heard of Mohammed and knew very little of Arabia, treated the messengers with the grave respect due from a polite Greek to such strangers—made them handsome presents,—and sent them home—having no distinct notion of what they or their master meant. Khosru received the messengers in a different manner, but one equally characteristic. At the head of his victorious Golden Lances, in his day of success, they brought him a letter. The warrior called his interpreter to read it. "In the name of the most merciful God; Mohammed, son of Abdallah, and apostle of God, to Khosru, King of Persia,"—thus it began. "What!" cried the proud Barbarian, "does my slave dare to put his name before mine?" Then, he seized the letter, and tore it into fragments. The answer was sent to his lieutenant in Yemen, instead of Medina: "I am told there is in Medina a madman, of the tribe of Koreish, who pretends to be a prophet. Restore him to his senses. If you cannot, send me his head." When the messenger of Mohammed returned to Medina, and told him that the great monarch had torn up his letter without reading it, his master simply replied, "Even so shall Allah rend his empire in pieces." And these few words spoke the oracle of destiny. In less than ten years from the scornful tearing of that letter by Khosru, the lieutenants of the unknown "madman" ruled in Jerusalem, Alexandria and Damascus, as well as in Mecca and Medina.

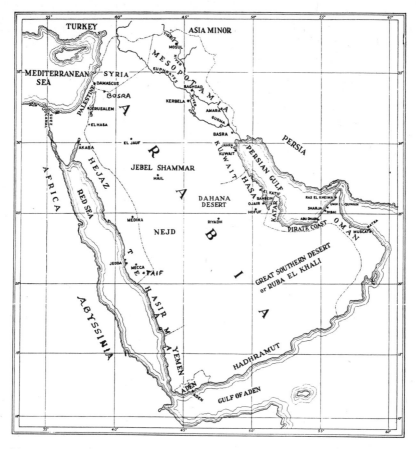

Map of the Arabian peninsula, drawn by Charles A. Pearsall (1924). Scale: 1 inch = 490 miles. The area of the Kingdom of Saudi Arabia is about 927,000 sq. mi., nearly one-third the size of the "lower 48" of the United States. The region in which Mohammed lived was the Hejaz, the west-central province bordering on the Red Sea. The coastal slope consists mainly of a long and rugged mountain range, which drops abruptly to the sea. Elevations approach 7,000 feet in the north and 10,000 feet in the south, descending toward the middle to 2,000 feet around Mecca. The upper slopes of the mountains south of Mecca are terraced to make good use of the annual rainfall of some 20 inches, and since early times fruits, vegetables, grain and coffee have been grown there. Mohammed's youthful journeys with the trading caravans (Chapters 4 and 5) took him north to Bosra, near Damascus, and south to Yemen ("Arabia Felix"). So far as is known, he never traveled beyond the Arabian peninsula himself, although in the fifth year of his mission he dispatched his daughter and son-in-law and a few other fugitive disciples across the Red Sea to Abyssinia (now Ethiopia), where they found safety under the protection of Nestorian Christians ("the first Hegira", Chapter 9).

1

Arabia and the Arabs

During a long succession of ages, extending from the earliest period of recorded history down to the seventh century of the Christian era, that great chersonese or peninsula formed by the Red Sea, the Euphrates, the Gulf of Persia, and the Indian Ocean, and known by the name of Arabia, remained unchanged and almost unaffected by the events which convulsed the rest of Asia, and shook Europe and Africa to their centre. While kingdoms and empires rose and fell; while ancient dynasties passed away; while the boundaries and names of countries were changed, and their inhabitants were exterminated or carried into captivity, Arabia, though its frontier provinces experienced some vicissitudes, preserved in the depths of its deserts its primitive character and independence, nor had its nomadic tribes ever bent their haughty necks to servitude.

The Arabs carry back the traditions of their country to the highest antiquity. It was peopled, they say, soon after the deluge, by the progeny of Shem the son of Noah, who gradually formed themselves into several tribes, the most noted of which are the Adites and Thamudites. All these primitive tribes are said to have been either swept from the earth in punishment of their iniquities, or obliterated in subsequent modifications of the races, so that little remains concerning them but shadowy traditions and a few passages in the Koran. They are occasionally mentioned in oriental history as the "old primitive Arabians"—the "lost tribes."

The primitive population of the peninsula is ascribed, by the same authorities, to Kahtan or Joctan, a descendant in the fourth generation from Shem. His posterity spread over the southern part of the peninsula and along the Red Sea. Yarab, one of his sons, founded the kingdom of Yemen, where the territory of Arabs was called after him; whence the Arabs derive the names of themselves and their country. Jurham, another son, founded the kingdom of Hedjaz, over which his descendants bore sway for many generations. Among these people Hagar and her son Ishmael were kindly received, when exiled from their home by the patriarch Abraham. In the process of time Ishmael married the daughter of Modâd, a reigning prince of the line of Jurham, and thus a stranger and a Hebrew became grafted on the original Arabian stock. It proved a vigorous graft. Ishmael's wife bore him twelve sons, who acquired dominion over the country, and whose prolific race, divided into twelve tribes, expelled or overran and obliterated the primitive stock of Joctan.

Such is the account given by the peninsular Arabs of their origin[1] and Christian writers cite it as containing the fulfillment of the covenant of God with Abraham, as recorded in Holy Writ: "And Abraham said unto God, O that Ishmael might live before thee. And God said, As for Ishmael, I have heard thee. Behold, I have blessed him, and will make him fruitful, and will multiply him exceedingly: twelve princes shall he beget, and I will make him a great nation." (Genesis, xvii, 18, 20.)

These twelve princes with their tribes are further spoken of in the Scriptures (Genesis, xxv, 18) as occupying the country "from Havilah unto Shur, that is before Egypt, as thou goest towards Assyria," a region identified by sacred geographers with part of Arabia. The description of them agrees with that of the Arabs of the present day. Some are mentioned as holding towns and castles, others as dwelling in tents, or having villages in the wilderness. Nebaioth and Kedar, the two first-born of Ishmael, are most noted among the princes for their wealth in flocks and herds, and for the fine wool of their sheep. From Nebaioth came the Nebaithai who inhabited Stony Arabia, while the name of Kedar is occasionally given in Holy Writ to designate the whole Arabian nation. "Woe is me," says the Psalmist, "that I sojourn in Mesech, that I dwell in the tents of Kedar." Both appear to have been the progenitors of the wandering or pastoral Arabs, the free rovers of the desert. "The wealthy nation," says the prophet Jeremiah, "that dwelleth without care; which have neither gates nor bars, which dwell alone."

A strong distinction grew up in the earliest times between the

Arabs who "held towns and castles," and those who "dwelt in tents." Some of the former occupied the fertile wadies, or valleys, scattered here and there among the mountains, where these towns and castles were surrounded by vineyards and orchards, groves of palm trees, fields of grain, and well-stocked pastures. They were settled in their habits, devoting themselves to the cultivation of the soil and the breeding of cattle.

Others of this class gave themselves up to commerce, having ports and cities along the Red Sea, the southern shores of the peninsula and the Gulf of Persia, and carrying on foreign trade by means of ships and caravans. Such especially were the people of Yemen, or Arabia the Happy, that land of spices, perfumes, and frankincense; the Sabaea of the poets; the Sheba of the sacred Scriptures. They were among the most active mercantile navigators of the eastern seas. Their ships brought to their shores the myrrh and balsams of the opposite coast of Berbera, with the gold, the spices, and other rich commodities of India and tropical Africa. These, with the products of their own country, were transported by caravans across the deserts to the semi-Arabian states of Ammon, Moab, and Edom or Idumea, to the Phoenician ports of the Mediterranean, and thence distributed to the western world.

The camel has been termed the ship of the desert; the caravan may be termed its fleet. The caravans of Yemen were generally fitted out, manned, conducted, and guarded by the nomadic Arabs, the dwellers in tents, who, in this respect, might be called the navigators of the desert. They furnished the innumerable camels required, and also contributed to the freight by the fine fleeces of their countless flocks. The writings of the prophets show the importance, in Scriptural times, of this inland chain of commerce, by which the rich countries of the south—India, Ethiopia, and Arabia the Happy—were linked with ancient Syria.

Ezekiel, in his lamentations for Tyre, exclaims, "Arabia and all the princes of Kedar, they occupied with thee in lambs, and rams, and goats; in these were they thy merchants. The merchants of Sheba and Raamah occupied in thy fairs with chief of all spices, and with all precious stones and gold. Haran, and Canneh, and Eden,[2] the merchants of Sheba, Asshur, and Chelmad, were thy merchants." And Isaiah, speaking to Jerusalem, says: "The multitude of camels shall cover thee; the dromedaries of Midian and Ephah; all they from Sheba shall come; they shall bring gold and incense. . . . .All the flocks of Kedar shall be gathered together unto thee; the rams of Nebaioth shall minister unto thee." (Isaiah, lx, 6, 7.)

The agriculturing and trading Arabs, however, the dwellers in towns and cities, have never been considered the true type of the race. They became softened by settled and peaceful occupations, and lost much of their original stamp by an intercourse with strangers. Yemen, too, being more accessible than the other parts of Arabia, and offering greater temptation to the spoiler, had been repeatedly invaded and subdued.

It was among the other class of Arabs, the rovers of the desert, the "dwellers in tents," by far the most numerous of the two, that the national character was preserved in all its primitive force and freshness. Nomadic in their habits, pastoral in their occupations, and acquainted by experience and tradition with all the hidden resources of the desert, they led a wandering life, roaming from place to place in quest of those wells and springs which had been the resort of their forefathers since the days of the patriarchs; encamping wherever they could find date trees for shade, and sustenance and pasturage for their flocks, and herds, and camels; and shifting their abode whenever the temporary supply was exhausted.

These nomadic Arabs were divided and subdivided into innumerable petty tribes or families, each with its Sheikh or Emir, the representative of the patriarch of yore, whose spear, planted beside his tent, was the ensign of command. His office, however, though continued for many generations in the same family, was not strictly hereditary, but depended upon the good will of the tribe. He might be deposed, and another of a different line elected in his place. His power, too, was limited, and depended upon his personal merit and the confidence reposed in him. His prerogative consisted in conducting negotiations of peace and war; in leading his tribe against the enemy; in choosing the place of encampment; and in receiving and entertaining strangers of note. Yet, even in these and similar privileges, he was controlled by the opinions and inclinations of his people.[3]

However numerous and minute might be the divisions of a tribe, the links of affinity were carefully kept in mind by the several sections. All the Sheikhs of the same tribe acknowledge a common chief called the Sheikh of Sheikhs, who, whether ensconced in a rockbuilt castle, or encamped amid his flocks and herds in the desert, might assemble under his standard all the scattered branches on any emergency affecting the common weal.

The multiplicity of these wandering tribes, each with its petty prince and petty territory, but without a national head, produced frequent collisions. Revenge, too, was almost a religious principle among them. To avenge a relative slain was the duty of his family, and often involved the honor of his tribe; and these debts of blood sometimes remained unsettled for generations, producing deadly feuds.

The necessity of being always on the alert to defend his flocks and herds made the Arab of the desert familiar from his infancy with the exercise of arms. None could excel him in the use of the bow, the lance, and the scimitar, and the adroit and graceful management of the horse. He was a predatory warrior also; for though at times he was engaged in the service of the merchant, furnishing him with camels and guides and drivers for the transportation of his merchandise, he was more apt to lay contributions on the caravan, or plunder it outright in its toilful progress through the desert. All this he regarded as a legitimate exercise of arms; looking down upon the gainful sons of traffic as an inferior race, debased by sordid habits and pursuits.

Such was the Arab of the desert, the dweller in tents, in whom was fulfilled the prophetic destiny of his ancestor Ishmael: "He will be a wild man; his hand will be against every man, and every man's hand against him." (Genesis, xvi, 12). Nature had fitted him for his destiny. His form was light and meagre, but sinewy and active, and capable of sustaining great fatigue and hardship. He was temperate and even abstemious, requiring but little food, and that of the simplest kind. His mind, like his body, was light and agile. He eminently possessed the intellectual attributes of the Semitic race: penetrating sagacity, subtle wit, a ready conception, and a brilliant imagination. His sensibilities were quick and acute, though not lasting; a proud and daring spirit was stamped on his sallow visage and flashed from his dark and kindling eye. He was easily aroused by the appeals of eloquence, and charmed by the graces of poetry. Speaking a language copious in the extreme, the words of which have been compared to gems and flowers, he was naturally an orator; but he delighted in proverbs and apothegms, rather than in sustained flights of declamation, and was prone to convey his ideas in the oriental style, by apologue and parable.

Though a restless and predatory warrior, he was generous and hospitable. He delighted in giving gifts; his door was always open to the wayfarer, with whom he was ready to share his last morsel; and his deadliest foe, having once broken bread with him, might repose securely beneath the inviolable sanctity of his tent.

In religion the Arabs, in what they term the Days of Ignorance, partook largely of the two faiths, the Sabean and the Magian, which at that time prevailed over the eastern world. The Sabean, however, was the one to which they most adhered. They pretended to derive it from Sabi the son of Seth, who, with his father and his brother Enoch, they supposed to be buried in the pyramids. Others derive the name from the Hebrew word, Saba, or the stars, and trace the origin of the faith to the Assyrian shepherds, who as they watched their flocks by night on their level plains, and beneath their cloudless skies, noted the aspects and movements of the heavenly bodies, and formed theories of their good and evil influences on human affairs—vague notions which the Chaldean philosophers and priests reduced to a system, supposed to be more ancient even than that of the Egyptians.

By others it is derived from still higher authority, and claimed to be the religion of the antediluvian world. It survived, say they, the Deluge, and was continued among the patriarchs. It was taught by Abraham, adopted by his descendants, the children of Israel, and sanctified and confirmed in the tablets of the law delivered unto Moses, amid the thunder and lightning of Mount Sinai.

In its original state the Sabean faith was pure and spiritual, inculcating a belief in the unity of God, the doctrine of a future state of rewards and punishments, and the necessity of a virtuous and holy life to obtain a happy immortality. So profound was the reverence of the Sabeans for the Supreme Being, that they never mentioned his name, nor did they venture to approach him, but through intermediate intelligences or angels. These were supposed to inhabit and animate the heavenly bodies in the same way as the human body is inhabited and animated by a soul. They were placed in their respective spheres to supervise and govern the universe in subserviency to the Most High. In addressing themselves to the stars and other celestial luminaries, therefore, the Sabeans did not worship them as deities, but sought only to propitiate their angelic occupants as intercessors with the Supreme Being, looking up through these created things to God the great Creator.

By degrees this religion lost its original simplicity and purity, and became obscured by mysteries, and degraded by idolatries. The Sabeans, instead of regarding the heavenly bodies as the habitations of intermediate agents, worshipped them as deities; set up graven images in honor of them, in sacred groves and in the gloom of forests; and at length enshrined these idols in temples, and worshipped them as if instinct with divinity. The Sabean faith too underwent changes and modifications in the various countries through which it was diffused. Egypt has long been accused of reducing it to the most abject state of degradation; the statues, hieroglyphics, and painted sepulchres of that mysterious country being considered records of the worship, not merely of celestial intelligences, but of the lowest order of created beings, and even of inanimate objects. Modern investigation and research, however, are gradually rescuing the most intellectual nation of antiquity from this aspersion, and as they slowly lift the veil of mystery which hangs over the tombs of Egypt, are discovering that all these apparent objects of adoration were but symbols of the varied attributes of the one Supreme Being, whose name was too sacred to be pronounced by mortals. Among the Arabs the Sabean faith became mingled with wild superstitions, and degraded by gross idolatry. Each tribe worshipped its particular star or planet, or set up its particular idol. Infanticide mingled its horrors with their religious rites. Among the nomadic tribes the birth of a daughter was considered a misfortune, her sex rendering her of little service in a wandering and predatory life, while she might bring disgrace upon her family by misconduct or captivity. Motives of unnatural policy, therefore, may have mingled with their religious feelings, in offering up female infants as sacrifices to their idols, or in burying them alive.

The rival sect of Magians or Guebres (fire worshippers), which, as we have said, divided the religious empire of the East, took its rise in Persia, where, after a while, its oral doctrines were reduced to writing by its great prophet and teacher Zoroaster, in his volume of the Zend-avesta. The creed, like that of the Sabeans, was originally simple and spiritual, inculcating a belief in one supreme and eternal God, in whom and by whom the universe exists; that he produced, through his creating word, two active principles, Ormusd, the principle or angel of light or good, and Ahriman, the principle or angel of darkness or evil: that these formed the world out of a mixture of their opposite elements, and were engaged in a perpetual contest in the regulation of its affairs. Hence the vicissitudes of good and evil, accordingly as the angel of light or darkness has the upper hand: this contest would continue until the end of the world, when there would be a general resurrection and a day of judgment; the angel of darkness and his disciples would then be banished to an abode of woeful gloom, and their opponents would enter the blissful realms of enduring light.

The primitive rites of this religion were extremely simple. The Magians had neither temples, altars, nor religious symbols of any kind, but addressed their prayers and hymns directly to the Deity, in what they conceived to be his residence, the sun. They reverenced this luminary as being his abode, and as the source of the light and heat of which all the other heavenly bodies were composed; and they kindled fires upon the mountain tops to supply light during its absence. Zoroaster first introduced the use of temples, wherein sacred fire, pretended to be derived from heaven, was kept perpetually alive through the guardianship of priests, who maintained a watch over it night and day.

In process of time this sect, like that of the Sabeans, lost sight of the Divine principle in the symbol, and came to worship light or fire, as the real Deity, and to abhor darkness as Satan or the devil. In their fanatic zeal the Magians would seize upon unbelievers and offer them up in the flames to propitiate their fiery deity.

To the tenets of these two sects reference is made in that beautiful text of the "Wisdom of Solomon:" "Surely vain are all men by nature who are ignorant of God, and could not, by considering the work, acknowledge the work-master; but deemed either fire, or wind, or the swift air, or the circle of the stars, or the violent water, or the lights of heaven, to be gods which govern the world."

Of these two faiths the Sabean, as we have observed, was much the most prevalent among the Arabs; but in an extremely degraded form, mingled with all kinds of abuses and varying among the various tribes. The Magian faith prevailed among those tribes which, from their frontier position, had frequent intercourse with Persia; while other tribes partook of the superstitions and idolatries of the nations on which they bordered.

Judaism had made its way into Arabia at an early period, but very vaguely and imperfectly. Still many of its rites and ceremonies, and fanciful traditions, became implanted in the country. At a later day, however, when Palestine was ravaged by the Romans, and the city of Jerusalem taken and sacked, many of the Jews took refuge among the Arabs. They became incorporated with the native tribes, formed themselves into communities, acquired possession of fertile tracts, built castles and strongholds, and rose to considerable power and influence.

The Christian religion had likewise its adherents among the Arabs. St. Paul himself declares in his Epistle to the Galatians, that soon after he had been called to preach Christianity among the heathens, he "went into Arabia." The dissensions, also, which rose in the Eastern church, in the early part of the third century, breaking it up into sects, each persecuting the others as it gained the ascendency, drove many into exile into remote parts of the East, filled the deserts of Arabia with anchorites, and planted the Christian faith among some of the principal tribes.

The foregoing circumstances, physical and moral, may give an idea of the causes which maintained the Arabs for ages in an unchanged condition. While their isolated position and their vast deserts protected them from conquest, their internal feuds, and their want of a common tie, political or religious, kept them from being formidable as conquerors. They were a vast aggregation of distinct parts, full of individual vigor but wanting coherent strength. Although their nomadic life rendered them hardy and active, and the greater part of them were warriors from their infancy, yet their arms were only wielded against each other, excepting some of the frontier tribes, which occasionally engaged as mercenaries in external wars. While, therefore, the other nomadic races of Central Asia, possessing no greater aptness for warfare, had, during a course of ages, successively overrun and conquered the civilized world, this warrior race, unconscious of its power, remained disjointed and harmless in the depths of its native deserts.

The time at length arrived when its discordant tribes were to be united in one creed, and animated by one common cause; when a mighty genius was to arise, who should bring together these scattered limbs, animate them with his own enthusiastic and daring spirit, and lead them forth, a giant of the desert, to shake and overturn the empires of the earth.

2

*Birth and parentage of Mohammed - His infancy
and childhood*

Mohammed, the great founder of the faith of Islam, was born in
Mecca, in April, in the year 569 of the Christian era. He was of
the valiant and illustrious tribe of Koreish, of which there were
two branches, descended from two brothers, Haschem and Abd
Schems. Haschem, the progenitor of Mohammed, was a great
benefactor of Mecca. This city is situated in the midst of a
barren and stony country, and in former times was often subject
to scarcity of provisions. At the beginning of the sixth century
Haschem established two yearly caravans, one in the winter to
South Arabia or Yemen, the other in the summer to Syria. By
these means abundant supplies were brought to Mecca, as well as
a great variety of merchandise. The city became a commercial
mart, and the tribe of Koreish, which engaged largely in these
expeditions, became wealthy and powerful. Haschem, at this
time, was the guardian of the Caaba, the great shrine of Arabian
pilgrimage and worship, the custody of which was confided to
none but the most honorable tribes and families, in the same
manner, as in old times, the temple of Jerusalem was entrusted
only to the care of the Levites. In fact the guardianship of the
Caaba was connected with civil dignities and privileges, and
gave the holder of it the control of the sacred city.

On the death of Haschem, his son, Abd al Motâlleb,
succeeded to his honors, and inherited his patriotism. He
delivered the holy city from an invading army of troops and
elephants, sent by the Christian princes of Abyssinia, who at that
time held Yemen in subjection. These signal services rendered
by father and son confirmed the guardianship of the Caaba in

the line of Haschem, to the great discontent and envy of the line of Abd Schems.

Abd al Motâlleb had several sons and daughters. Those of his sons who figure in history were Abu Taleb, Abu Lahab, Abbas, Hamza and Abdallah. The last named was the youngest and best beloved. He married Amina, a maiden of a distant branch of the same illustrious stock of Koreish. So remarkable was Abdallah for personal beauty and those qualities which win the affections of women, that, if Moslem traditions are to be credited, on the night of his marriage with Amina two hundred virgins of the tribe of Koreish died of broken hearts.

Mohammed was the only fruit of the marriage thus sadly celebrated. His birth, according to similar traditions with the one just cited, was accompanied by signs and portents announcing a child of wonder. His mother suffered none of the pangs of travail. At the moment of his coming into the world, a celestial light illumined the surrounding country, and the newborn child, raising his eyes to heaven, exclaimed: "God is great ! There is no God but God, and I am his prophet."

Heaven and earth, we are assured, were agitated at his advent. The Lake Sawa shrank back to its secret springs, leaving its borders dry, while the Tigris, bursting its bounds, overflowed the neighboring lands. The palace of Khosru, the King of Persia, shook to its foundations, and several of its towers were toppled to the earth. In that troubled night the Kadhi, or Judge of Persia, beheld, in a dream, a ferocious camel conquered by an Arabian courser. He related his dream in the morning to the Persian monarch, and interpreted it to portend danger from the quarter of Arabia.

In the same eventful night the sacred fire of Zoroaster, which, guarded by the Magi, had burned without interruption for upwards of a thousand years, was suddenly extinguished, and all the idols in the world fell down. The demons, or evil genii, which lurk in the stars and the signs of the zodiac, and exert a malignant influence over the children of men, were cast forth by the pure angels, and hurled, with their arch-leader, Eblis, or Lucifer, into the depths of the sea.

The relatives of the newborn child, say the like authorities, were filled with awe and wonder. His mother's brother, an astrologer, cast his nativity, and predicted that he would rise to vast power, found an empire, and establish a new faith among men. His grandfather, Abd al Motâlleb, gave a feast to the principal Koreishites, the seventh day after his birth, at which he presented this child as the dawning glory of their race, and gave him the name of Mohammed (Mahomet or Muhamed), indicative of his future renown.

Such are the marvelous accounts given by Moslem writers of the infancy of Mohammed, and we have little else than similar fables about his early years. He was scarcely two months old when his father died, leaving him no other inheritance than five camels, a few sheep, and a female slave of Ethiopia, named Barakat. His mother, Amina, had hitherto nurtured him, but care and sorrow dried the fountains of her breast, and the air of Mecca being unhealthy for children, she sought a nurse for him among the females of the neighboring Bedouin tribes. These were accustomed to come to Mecca twice a year, in spring and autumn, to foster the children of its inhabitants; but they looked for the offspring of the rich, where they were sure of ample recompense, and turned with contempt from this heir of poverty. At length Halêma, the wife of a Saadite shepherd, was moved to compassion, and took the helpless infant to her home. It was in one of the pastoral valleys of the mountains.[1]

Many were the wonders related by Halêma of her infant charge. On the journey from Mecca, the mule which bore him became miraculously endowed with speech, and proclaimed aloud that he bore on his back the greatest of prophets, the chief of ambassadors, the favorite of the Almighty. The sheep bowed to him as he passed; as he lay in his cradle and gazed at the moon, it stooped to him in reverence.

The blessing of heaven, say the Arabian writers, rewarded the charity of Halêma. While the child remained under her roof, everything around her prospered. The wells and springs were never dried up; the pastures were always green; her flocks and herds increased tenfold; a marvelous abundance reigned over her fields, and peace prevailed in her dwelling.

The Arabian legends go on to extol the almost supernatural powers, bodily and mental, manifested by this wonderful child at a very early age. He could stand alone when three months old, run abroad at seven months, and at ten months could join other children in their sports with bows and arrows. At eight months he could speak so as to be understood, and in the course of another month could converse with fluency, displaying a wisdom astonishing to all who heard him.

At the age of three years, while he was playing in the fields with his foster brother, Masroud, two angels in shining apparel appeared before them. They laid Mohammed gently upon the ground, and Gabriel, one of the angels, opened his breast, but without inflicting any pain. Then taking forth his heart, he cleansed it from all impurity, wringing from it those black and bitter drops of original sin, inherited from our forefather Adam, and which lurk in the hearts of the best of his descendants, inciting them to crime. When he had thoroughly purified it, he filled it with faith and knowledge and prophetic light, and replaced it in the bosom of the child. Now, we are assured by the same authorities, began to emanate from his countenance that mysterious light which had continued down from Adam, through the sacred line of prophets, till the time of Isaac and Ishmael; but which had lain dormant in the descendants of the latter until it thus shone forth with renewed radiance from the features of Mohammed.

At this supernatural visitation, it is added, was impressed between the shoulders of the child the seal of prophecy, which continued throughout life the symbol and credential of his divine mission (though unbelievers saw nothing in it but a large mole, the size of a pigeon's egg).

When the marvelous visitation of the angel was related to Halêma and her husband, they were alarmed lest some misfortune should be impending over the child, or that his supernatural visitors might be of the race of evil spirits or genii, which haunt the solitudes of the desert, wreaking mischief on the children of men. His Saadite nurse, therefore, carried him back to Mecca, and delivered him to his mother, Amina.

He remained with his parent until his sixth year, when she took him with her to Medina, on a visit to her relatives of the tribe of Adij; but on her journey homeward she died, and was buried at Abwa, a village between Medina and Mecca. Her grave, it will be found, was a place of pious resort and tender recollection to her son, at the latest period of his life.

The faithful Abyssinian slave Barakat now acted as a mother to the orphan child, and conducted him to his grandfather Abd al Motâlleb, in whose household he remained for two years, treated with care and tenderness. Abd al Motâlleb was now well stricken in years, having outlived the ordinary term of human existence. Finding his end approaching, he called to him his eldest son Abu Taleb, and bequeathed Mohammed to his special protection. The good Abu Taleb took

3

Traditions concerning Mecca and the Caaba

When Adam and Eve were cast forth from Paradise, say
Arabian traditions, they fell in different parts of the earth:
Adam on a mountain of the island of Serendib, or Ceylon, Eve in
Arabia on the borders of the Red Sea, where the port of Jeddah is
now situated. For two hundred years they wandered separate
and lonely about the earth, until, in consideration of their
penitence and wretchedness, they were permitted to come
together again on Mount Arafat, not far from the present city of
Mecca. In the depth of his sorrow and repentance, Adam, it is
said, raised his hands and eyes to heaven, and implored the
clemency of God, entreating that a shrine might be vouchsafed to
him similar to that at which he had worshipped when in
Paradise, and round which the angels used to move in adoring
processions.

The supplication of Adam was effectual. A tabernacle or
temple formed of radiant clouds was lowered down by the hands
of angels, and placed immediately below its prototype in the
celestial paradise. Towards this heaven-descended shrine,
Adam thenceforth turned when in prayer, and round it he daily
made seven circuits in imitation of the rites of the adoring
angels.

At the death of Adam, say the same traditions, the tabernacle
of clouds passed away, or was again drawn up to heaven; but
another, of the same form and in the same place, was built of
stone and clay by Seth, the son of Adam. This was swept away by
the deluge. Many generations afterwards, in the time of the
patriarchs, when Hagar and her child Ishmael were near
perishing with thirst in the desert, an angel revealed to them a

spring or well of water, near to the ancient site of the tabernacle. This was the well of Zem Zem, held sacred by the progeny of Ishmael to the present day. Shortly afterwards two individuals of the gigantic race of the Amalekites, in quest of a camel which had strayed from their camp, discovered this well, and, having slaked their thirst, brought their companions to the place. Here they founded the city of Mecca, taking Ishmael and his mother under their protection. They were soon expelled by the proper inhabitants of the country, among whom Ishmael remained. When grown to man's estate, he married the daughter of the ruling prince, by whom he had a numerous progeny, the ancestors of the Arabian people. In process of time, by God's command he undertook to rebuild the Caaba, on the precise site of the original tabernacle of clouds. In this pious work he was assisted by his father Abraham. A miraculous stone served Abraham as a scaffold, rising and sinking with him as he built the walls of the sacred edifice. It still remains there as an inestimable relic, and the print of the patriarch's foot is clearly to be perceived on it by all true believers.

While Abraham and Ishmael were thus occupied, the angel Gabriel brought them a stone, about which traditional accounts are a little at variance. By some it is said to have been one of the precious stones of Paradise, which fell to the earth with Adam and was afterwards lost in the slime of the deluge, until retrieved by the angel Gabriel. The more received tradition is that it was originally the guardian angel appointed to watch over Adam in Paradise, but changed into a stone and ejected thence with him at his fall, as a punishment for not having been more vigilant. This stone Abraham and Ishmael received with proper reverence, and inserted it in a corner of the exterior wall of the Caaba, where it remains to the present day, devoutly kissed by worshippers each time they make a circuit of the temple. When first inserted in the wall it was, we are told, a single jacinth of dazzling whiteness, but became gradually blackened by the kisses of sinful mortals. At the resurrection it will recover its angelic form, and stand forth a testimony before God in favor of those who have faithfully performed the rites of pilgrimage.

Such are the Arabian traditions which rendered the Caaba and the well of Zem Zem objects of extraordinary veneration from the remotest antiquity among the people of the East, and especially the descendants of Ishmael. Mecca, which encloses these sacred objects within its walls, was a holy city many ages before the rise of Islam, and was the resort of pilgrims from all parts of Arabia. So universal and profound was the religious feeling respecting this observance, that four months in every year were devoted to the rites of pilgrimage, and held sacred from all violence and warfare. Hostile tribes then laid aside their arms; took the heads from their spears; traversed the late dangerous deserts in security; thronged the gates of Mecca clad in the pilgrim's garb; made their seven circuits round the Caaba in imitation of the angelic host; touched and kissed the mysterious black stone; drank and made ablutions at the well Zem Zem in memory of their ancestor Ishmael; and having performed all the other primitive rites of pilgrimage returned home in safety, again to resume their weapons and their wars.

Among the religious observances of the Arabs in these their "days of ignorance"—that is to say, before the promulgation of the Moslem doctrines—fasting and prayer had a foremost place. They had three principal fasts within the year: one of seven, one of nine, and one of thirty days. They prayed three times each day; about sunrise, at noon, and about sunset, turning their faces in the direction of the Caaba, which was their kebla or point of adoration. They had many religious traditions, some of them acquired in early times from the Jews, and they are said to have nurtured their devotional feelings with the book of Psalms, and with a book said to be by Seth, and filled with moral discourses.

As Mohammed was brought up in the house of the guardian of the Caaba, the ceremonies and devotions connected with the sacred edifice may have given an early bias to his mind, and inclined it to those speculations in matters of religion by which it eventually became engrossed. Though his Moslem biographers would fain persuade us his high destiny was clearly foretold in his childhood by signs and prodigies, yet his education appears to have been as much neglected as that of ordinary Arab children, for we find that he was not taught either to read or write. He was a thoughtful child, however, quick to observe, prone to meditate on all that he observed, and possessed of an imagination fertile, daring and expansive. The yearly influx of pilgrims from distant parts made Mecca a receptacle for all kinds of floating knowledge, which he appears to have imbibed with eagerness and retained in a tenacious memory; and as he increased in years, a more extended sphere of observation was gradually opened to him.

4

First journey of Mohammed with the caravan to Syria

Mohammed was now twelve years of age, but he had an intelligence far beyond his years. The spirit of inquiry was awake within him, quickened by intercourse with pilgrims from all parts of Arabia. His uncle Abu Taleb, too, beside his sacerdotal character as guardian of the Caaba, was one of the most enterprising merchants of the tribe of Koreish, and had much to do with those caravans set on foot by his ancestor Haschem, which traded to Syria and Yemen. The arrival and departure of those caravans, which thronged the gates of Mecca and filled its streets with pleasing tumult, were exciting events to a youth like Mohammed, and carried his imagination to foreign parts. He could no longer repress the ardent curiosity thus aroused; but once, when his uncle was about to mount his camel to depart with the caravan for Syria, clung to him, and entreated to be permitted to accompany him. "For who, O my uncle," said he, "will take care of me when thou art away?" The appeal was not lost upon the kindhearted Abu Taleb. He realized, too, that the youth was of an age to enter upon the active scenes of Arab life, and of a capacity to render essential service in the duties of the caravan. He readily, therefore, granted Mohammed's prayer, and took him with him on the journey to Syria.

The route lay through regions fertile in fables and traditions, which it is the delight of the Arabs to recount in the evening halts of the caravan. The vast solitudes of the desert, in which that wandering people pass so much of their lives, are prone to engender superstitious fancies. They have accordingly peopled them with good and evil genii, and clothed them with tales of enchantment, mingled up with wonderful events which happened in days of old. In these evening halts of the caravan, the youthful mind of Mohammed doubtless imbibed many of those superstitions of the desert which ever afterwards dwelt in his memory, and had a powerful influence over his imagination. We may especially note two traditions which he must have heard at this time, and which we find recorded by him in after years in the Koran. One related to the mountainous district of Hedjar. Here, as the caravan wound its way through silent and deserted valleys, caves were pointed out in the sides of the mountains once inhabited by the Beni Thamud, or children of Thamud, one of the "lost tribes" of Arabia; and this was the tradition concerning them.

They were a proud and gigantic race, existing before the time of the patriarch Abraham. As they had fallen into blind idolatry, God sent a prophet of the name of Saleh to restore them to the right way. They refused, however, to listen to him, unless he should prove the divinity of his mission by causing a camel, big with young, to issue from the entrails of a mountain. Saleh accordingly prayed, and lo! a rock opened, and a female camel came forth, which soon produced a foal. Some of the Thamudites were convinced by the miracle, and were converted by the prophet from their idolatry; the greater part, however, remained in unbelief. Saleh left the camel among them as a sign, warning them that a judgment from heaven would fall on them, should they do her any harm. For a time the camel was suffered to feed quietly in their pastures, going forth in the morning, and returning in the evening. It is true, that when she bowed her head to drink from a brook or well, she never raised it until she had drained the last drop of water; but then in return she yielded milk enough to supply the whole tribe. As, however, she frightened the other camels from the pasture, she became an object of offense to the Thamudites, who hamstrung and slew her. Upon this there was a fearful cry from heaven, and great claps of thunder, and in the morning all the offenders were found lying on their faces dead. Thus the whole race was swept from the earth, and their country was laid for ever afterward under the ban of heaven.

This story made a powerful impression on the mind of Mohammed, insomuch that, in after years, he refused to let his people encamp in the neighborhood, but hurried them away from it as an accursed region.

Another tradition, gathered on this journey, related to the city of Eyla, situated near the Red Sea. This place, he was told, had been inhabited in old times by a tribe of Jews, who lapsed into idolatry and profaned the Sabbath, by fishing on that sacred day; whereupon the old men were transformed into swine, and the young men into monkeys.

We have noted these two traditions especially, because they are both cited by Mohammed as instances of divine judgment on the crime of idolatry, and evince the bias his youthful mind was already taking on that important subject.

Moslem writers tell us, as usual, of wonderful circumstances which attended the youth throughout this journey, giving evidence of the continual guardianship of heaven. At one time, as he traversed the burning sands of the desert, an angel hovered over him unseen, sheltering him with his wings (a miracle, however, which evidently does not rest on the evidence of an eyewitness). At another time he was protected by a cloud which hung over his head during the noontide heat; and on another occasion, as he sought the scanty shade of a withered tree, it suddenly put forth leaves and blossoms.

After skirting the ancient domains of the Moabites and the Ammonites, often mentioned in the sacred Scriptures, the caravan arrived at Bosra, or Bostra, on the confines of Syria, in the country of the tribe of Manasseh, beyond the Jordan. In Scripture days it had been a city of the Levites, but now was inhabited by Nestorian Christians. It was a great mart, annually visited by the caravans; and here our wayfarers came to a halt, and encamped near a convent of Nestorian monks.

By this fraternity Abu Taleb and his nephew were entertained with great hospitality. One of the monks, by some called Sergius, by others Bahira[1], on conversing with Mohammed, was surprised at the precocity of his intellect, and interested by his eager desire for information, which appears to have had reference principally to matters of religion. They had frequent conversations together on such subjects, in the course of which the efforts of the monk must have been mainly directed against that idolatry in which the youthful Mohammed had hitherto been educated; for the Nestorian Christians were strenuous in condemning not merely the worship of images, but even the casual exhibition of them. Indeed, so far did they carry their scruples on this point that even the cross, that general emblem of Christianity, was in a great degree included in this prohibition.

Many have ascribed Mohammed's knowledge of the principles and traditions of the Christian faith, which he displayed later in his life, to those early conversations with this monk. It is probable, however, that he had further encounters with the latter in the course of subsequent visits which he made to Syria.

Moslem writers contend that the interest taken by the monk in the youthful stranger, arose from his having accidentally perceived between his shoulders the seal of prophecy. He warned Abu Taleb, they say, when he was about to set out on his return to Mecca, to take care that his nephew did not fall into the hands of the Jews, foreseeing with the eye of prophecy the trouble and opposition he was to encounter from that people.

It required no miraculous sign, however, to interest a sectarian monk, anxious to make proselytes, in an intelligent and inquiring youth, nephew of the guardian of the Caaba, who might carry back with him to Mecca the seeds of Christianity sown in his tender mind; and it was natural that the monk should be eager to prevent his hoped-for convert, in the present unsettled state of his religious opinions, from being beguiled into the Jewish faith.

Mohammed returned to Mecca, his imagination teeming with the wild tales and traditions picked up in the desert, and his mind deeply impressed with the doctrines imparted to him in the Nestorian convent. He seems ever afterwards to have entertained a mysterious reverence for Syria, probably from the religious impressions received there. It was the land whither Abraham the patriarch had repaired from Chaldea, taking with him the primitive worship of the one true God. "Verily," he used to say in after years, "God has ever maintained guardians of his word in Syria; forty in number; when one dies another is sent in his room; and through them the land is blessed." And again: "Joy be to the people of Syria, for the angels of the kind God spread their wings over them."[2]

5

Commercial occupations of Mohammed - His marriage with Cadijah

Mohammed was now completely launched in active life, accompanying his uncles in various expeditions. At one time, when he was about sixteen years of age, we find him with his uncle Zobier, journeying with the caravan to Yemen; at another time acting as armor-bearer to the same uncle, who led a warlike expedition of Koreishites in aid of the Kenanites against the tribe of Hawazan. This is cited as Mohammed's first essay in arms, though he did little else than supply his uncle with arrows in the heat of the action, and shield him from the darts of the enemy. It is stigmatized among Arabian writers as al Fadjar, or the impious war, having been carried on during the sacred months of pilgrimage.

As Mohammed advanced in years, he was employed by different persons as commercial agent or factor in caravan journeys to Syria, Yemen, and elsewhere; all of which tended to enlarge the sphere of his observation, and to give him a quick insight into character and a knowledge of human affairs.

He was a frequent attender of fairs also, which, in Arabia, were not always mere resorts of traffic, but occasionally scenes of poetical contests between different tribes, where prizes were adjudged to the victors, and their prize poems treasured up in the archives of princes. Such, especially, was the case with the fair of Ocadh; and seven of the prize poems adjudged there were hung up as trophies in the Caaba. At these fairs, also, were recited the popular traditions of the Arabs, and inculcated the various religious faiths which were afloat in Arabia. From oral sources of this kind, Mohammed gradually accumulated much of that varied information as to creeds and doctrines which he afterwards displayed.

There was at this time residing in Mecca a widow, named Cadijah (or Khadijah), of the tribe of Koreish. She had been twice married. Her last husband, a wealthy merchant, had recently died, and the extensive concerns of the house were in need of a conductor. A nephew of the widow, named Chuzima, had become acquainted with Mohammed in the course of his commercial expeditions, and had noticed the ability and integrity with which he acquitted himself on all occasions. He pointed him out to his aunt as a person well qualified to be her factor. The personal appearance of Mohammed may have strongly seconded this recommendation, for he was now about twenty-five years of age, and extolled by Arabian writers for his manly beauty and engaging manners. So desirous was Cadijah of securing his services that she offered him double wages to conduct a caravan which she was on the point of sending off to Syria. Mohammed consulted his uncle Abu Taleb, and by his advice accepted the offer. He was accompanied and aided in the expedition by the nephew of the widow, and by her slave Maïsara, and so highly satisfied was Cadijah with the way in which he discharged his duties, that, on his return, she paid him double the amount of his stipulated wages. She afterwards sent him to the southern parts of Arabia on similar expeditions, in all which he gave like satisfaction.

Cadijah was now in her fortieth year, a woman of judgment and experience. The mental qualities of Mohammed rose more and more in her estimation, and her heart began to yearn toward the fresh and comely youth. According to Arabian legends, a miracle occurred most opportunely to confirm and sanctify the bias of her inclinations. She was one day with her handmaids, at the hour of noon, on the terraced roof of her dwelling watching the arrival of a caravan conducted by Mohammed. As it approached, she beheld, with astonishment, two angels overshadowing him with their wings to protect him from the sun. Turning with emotion to her handmaids, she said, "Behold! the beloved of Allah, who sends two angels to watch over him!"

Whether or not the handmaidens looked forth with the same eyes of devotion as their mistress, and likewise discerned the angels, the legend does not mention. Suffice it to say that the widow was filled with a lively faith in the superhuman merits of her youthful steward, and forthwith commissioned her trusty slave, Maïsara, to offer him her hand. The negotiation is recorded with simple brevity. "Mohammed," demanded Maïsara, "why dost thou not marry?" "I have not the means," replied Mohammed. "Well, but if a wealthy dame should offer thee her hand: one also who is handsome and of high birth? " "And who is she?" "Cadijah!" " How is that possible?" "Let me manage it." Maïsara returned to his mistress and reported what had passed. An hour was appointed for an interview, and the affair was brought to a satisfactory arrangement with that promptness and sagacity which had distinguished Mohammed in all his dealings with the widow. The father of Cadijah made some opposition to the match, on account of the poverty of Mohammed, following the common notion that wealth should be added to wealth. But the widow wisely considered her riches only as the means of enabling her to follow the dictates of her heart. She gave a great feast, to which were invited her father and the rest of her relatives, and Mohammed's uncles Abu Taleb and Hamza, together with several other of the Koreishites. At this banquet wine was served in abundance, and soon diffused good humor round the board. The objections to Mohammed's poverty were forgotten; speeches were made by Abu Taleb on the one side, and by Waraka, a kinsman of Cadijah, on the other, in praise of the proposed nuptials; the dowry was arranged, and the marriage formally concluded.

Mohammed then caused a camel to be killed before his door, and the flesh to be distributed among the poor. The house was thrown open to all comers; the female slaves of Cadijah danced to the sound of timbrels, and all was revelry and rejoicing. Abu Taleb, forgetting his age and his habitual melancholy, made merry on the occasion. He had paid down from his purse a dower of twelve and a half okes of gold, equivalent to twenty young camels. Halêma, who had nursed Mohammed in his infancy, was summoned to rejoice at his nuptials, and was presented with a flock of forty sheep, with which she returned, enriched and contented, to her native valley, in the desert of the Saadites.

6

Conduct of Mohammed after his marriage - Becomes anxious for religious reform - His habits of solitary abstraction - The vision of the cave - His annunciation as a prophet

The marriage with Cadijah placed Mohammed among the most wealthy of his native city. His moral worth also gave him great influence in the community. Allah, says the historian Abulfeda, had endowed him with every gift necessary to accomplish and adorn an honest man. He was so pure and sincere, so free from every evil thought, that he was commonly known by the name of Al Amin or The Faithful.

The great confidence reposed in his judgment and probity caused him to be frequently referred to as arbiter in disputes between his townsmen. An anecdote is given as illustrative of his sagacity on such occasions. The Caaba, having been injured by fire, was undergoing repairs, in the course of which the sacred black stone was to be replaced. A dispute arose among the chiefs of the various tribes, as to which was entitled to perform so august an office, and they agreed to abide by the decision of the first person who should enter by the gate Al Harâm. That person happened to be Mohammed. Upon hearing their different claims, he directed that a great cloth should be spread upon the ground, and the stone laid thereon; and that a man from each tribe should take hold of the border of the cloth. In this way the sacred stone was raised equally and at the same time by them all to a level with its allotted place, in which Mohammed fixed it with his own hands.

Four daughters and one son were the fruit of the marriage with Cadijah. The son was named Kasim, whence Mohammed was occasionally called Abu Kasim, or the father of Kasim, according to Arabian nomenclature. This son, however, died in his infancy.

For several years after his marriage he continued in commerce, visiting the great Arabian fairs, and making distant journeys with the caravans. His expeditions were not as profitable as in the days of his stewardship, and the wealth acquired with his wife diminished, rather than increased in the course of his operations. That wealth, in fact, had raised him above the necessity of toiling for subsistence, and given him leisure to indulge the original bias of his mind—a turn for reverie and religious speculation, which he had evinced from his earliest years. This had been fostered in the course of his journeyings by his intercourse with Jews and Christians, originally fugitives from persecution, but now gathered into tribes, or forming part of the population of cities. The Arabian deserts too, rife as we have shown them with fanciful superstitions, had nourished his enthusiastic reveries. Since his marriage with Cadijah, also, he had a household oracle to influence him in his religious opinions. This was his wife's cousin Waraka, a man of speculative mind and flexible faith; originally a Jew, subsequently a Christian, and withal a pretender to astrology. He is worthy of note as being the first on record to translate parts of the Old and New Testament into Arabic. From him Mohammed is supposed to have derived much of his information respecting those writings, and many of the traditions of the Mishnu and the Talmud, on which he draws so copiously in his Koran.

The knowledge thus variously acquired and treasured up in an uncommonly retentive memory was in direct hostility to the gross idolatry prevalent in Arabia, and practiced at the Caaba. That sacred edifice had gradually become filled with and surrounded by idols, to the number of three hundred and sixty, being one for every day of the Arab year. Hither had been brought idols from various parts, the deities of other nations, the chief of which, Hobal, was from Syria, and supposed to have the power of giving rain. Among these idols, too, were Abraham and Ishmael, once revered as prophets and progenitors, now represented with divining arrows in their hands, symbols of magic.

Mohammed became more and more sensible of the grossness and absurdity of this idolatry, as his intelligent mind contrasted it with the spiritual religions which had been the subject of his inquiries. Various passages in the Koran show the ruling idea which gradually sprang up in his mind, until it engrossed his thoughts and influenced all his actions. That idea was a religious reform. It had become his fixed belief, deduced from all that he had learned and meditated, that the only true religion had been revealed to Adam at his creation, and been promulgated and practiced in the days of innocence. That religion inculcated the direct and spiritual worship of one true and only God, the Creator of the universe.

It was his belief, furthermore, that this religion, so elevated and simple, had repeatedly been corrupted and debased by man, and especially outraged by idolatry; wherefore a succession of prophets, each inspired by a revelation from the Most High, had been sent from time to time, and at distant periods, to restore it to its original purity. Such was Noah, such was Abraham, such was Moses, and such was Jesus Christ. By each of these, the true religion had been reinstated upon earth, but had again been vitiated by their followers. The faith, as taught and practiced by Abraham when he came out of the land of Chaldea, seems especially to have formed a religious standard in his mind, from his veneration for the patriarch as the father of Ishmael, the progenitor of his race.

It appeared to Mohammed that the time for another reform was again arrived. The world had once more lapsed into blind idolatry. It needed the advent of another prophet, authorized by a mandate from on high, to restore the erring children of men to the right path, and to bring back the worship of the Caaba to what it had been in the days of Abraham and the patriarchs. The probability of such an advent, with its attendant reforms, seems to have taken possession of his mind, and produced habits of reverie and meditation incompatible with the ordinary concerns of life and the bustle of the world. We are told that he gradually absented himself from society, and sought the solitude of a cavern on Mount Hara, about three leagues north of Mecca, where, in emulation of the Christian anchorites of the desert, he would remain days and nights together, engaged in prayer and meditation. In this way he always passed the month of Ramadhan, the holy month of the Arabs. Such intense occupation of the mind on one subject, accompanied by fervent enthusiasm of spirit, could not but have a powerful effect upon his frame. He became subject to dreams, to ecstasies, and trances. For six months successively, according to one of his historians, he had constant dreams bearing on the subject of his waking thoughts. Often he would lose all consciousness of surrounding objects, and lie upon the ground as if insensible. Cadijah, who was sometimes the faithful companion of his solitude, beheld these paroxysms with anxious solicitude, and entreated to know the cause; but he evaded her inquiries, or answered them mysteriously. Some of his adversaries have attributed them to epilepsy, but devout Moslems declare them to have been the workings of prophecy; for already, they say, the intimations of the Most High began to dawn, though vaguely, on his spirit; and his mind labored with conceptions too great for mortal thought. At length, they say, what had hitherto been shadowed out in dreams was made apparent and distinct by an angelic apparition and a divine annunciation.

It was in the fortieth year of his age that this famous revelation took place. Accounts are given of it by Moslem writers as if received from his own lips, and it is alluded to in certain passages of the Koran. He was passing, as was his wont, the month of Ramadhan in the cavern of Mount Hara, endeavoring by fasting, prayer, and solitary meditation to elevate his thoughts to the contemplation of divine truth. It was on the night called by Arabs Al Kader, or the Divine Decree; a night in which, according to the Koran, angels descend to earth, and Gabriel brings down the decrees of God. During that night there is peace on earth, and a holy quiet reigns over all nature until the rising of the morn.

As Mohammed, in the silent watches of the night, lay wrapped in his mantle, he heard a voice calling upon him. He uncovered his head, and a flood of light broke upon him of such intolerable splendor that he swooned away. On regaining his senses, he beheld an angel in a human form, which, approaching from a distance, displayed a silken cloth covered with written characters. "Read!" said the angel.

"I know not how to read!" replied Mohammed.

"Read!" repeated the angel, "in the name of the Lord, who has created all things; who created man from a clot of blood. Read, in the name of the Most High, who taught man the use of the pen; who sheds on his soul the ray of knowledge, and teaches him what before he knew not."

Upon this Mohammed instantly felt his understanding illumined with celestial light, and read what was written on the cloth, which contained the decrees of God, as afterwards promulgated in the Koran. When Mohammed had finished the perusal, the heavenly messenger announced, "O Mohammed, of a verity, thou art the prophet of God! and I am his angel Gabriel."

Mohammed, we are told, came trembling and agitated to Cadijah in the morning, not knowing whether what he had heard and seen was indeed true, and that he was a prophet decreed to effect that reform so long the object of his meditations; or whether it might not be a mere vision, a delusion of the senses, or worse than all, the apparition of an evil spirit.

Cadijah, however, saw everything with the eye of faith, and the credulity of an affectionate woman. She saw in it the fruition of her husband's wishes, and the end of his paroxysms and privations. "Joyful tidings dost thou bring!" she exclaimed. "By him, in whose hand is the soul of Cadijah, I will henceforth regard thee as the prophet of our nation. Rejoice," she added, seeing him still cast down. "Allah will not suffer thee to fall to shame. Hast thou not been loving to thy kinsfolk, kind to thy neighbors, charitable to the poor, hospitable to the stranger, faithful to thy word, and ever a defender of the truth? "

Cadijah hastened to communicate what she had heard to her cousin Waraka, the translator of the Scriptures; who, as we have shown, had been a household oracle of Mohammed in matters of religion. He caught at once, and with eagerness, at this miraculous annunciation. "By him in whose hand is the soul of Waraka," he exclaimed, "thou speakest true, O Cadijah! The angel who has appeared to thy husband is the same who, in days of old, was sent to Moses the son of Amram. His annunciation is true. Thy husband is indeed a prophet!"

The zealous concurrence of the learned Waraka is said to have had a powerful effect in fortifying the dubious mind of Mohammed.

7

*Mohammed inculcates his doctrines secretly and slowly -
Receives further revelations and commands -
Announcement to his kindred - Manner in which it was
received - Enthusiastic devotion of Ali - Christian
portents*

For a time Mohammed confided his revelations merely to his
own household. One of the first to avow himself a believer was
his servant Zeid, an Arab of the tribe of Kalb. This youth had
been captured in childhood by a freebooting party of Koreishites,
and had come by purchase or lot into the possession of
Mohammed. Several years afterwards his father, hearing of his
being in Mecca, repaired thither and offered a considerable sum
for his ransom. "If he chooses to go with thee," said Mohammed,
"he shall go without ransom: but if he chooses to remain with
me, why should I not keep him?" Zeid preferred to remain,
having ever, he said, been treated more as a son than as a slave.
Upon this, Mohammed publicly adopted him, and he had ever
since remained with him in affectionate servitude. Now, on
embracing the new faith, he was set entirely free, but it will be
found that he continued through life that devoted attachment
which Mohammed seems to have had the gift of inspiring in his
followers and dependents.

The early steps of Mohammed in his prophetic career were
perilous and doubtful, and taken in secrecy. He had hostility to
apprehend on every side: from his immediate kindred, the
Koreishites of the line of Haschem, whose power and prosperity
were identified with idolatry; and still more from the rival line
of Abd Schems, who had long looked with envy and jealousy on
the Haschemites, and would eagerly raise the cry of heresy and

impiety to dispossess them of the guardianship of the Caaba. At the head of this rival branch of Koreish was Abu Sofian, the son of Harb, grandson of Omeya, and great-grandson of Abd Schems. He was an able and ambitious man, of great wealth and influence, and will be found one of the most persevering and powerful opponents of Mohammed.[1]

Under these adverse circumstances the new faith was propagated secretly and slowly, so that for the first three years the number of converts did not exceed forty. These, too, for the most part, were young persons, strangers, and slaves. Their meetings for prayer were held in private, either at the house of one of the initiated, or in a cave near Mecca. Their secrecy, however, did not protect them from outrage. Their meetings were discovered; a rabble broke into their cavern and a scuffle ensued. One of the assailants was wounded in the head by Saad, an armorer, thenceforth renowned among the faithful as the first of their number who shed blood in the cause of Islam.

One of the bitterest opponents of Mohammed was his uncle Abu Lahab, a wealthy man, of proud spirit and irritable temper. His son Otha had married Mohammed's third daughter, Rokaia, so that they were doubly allied. Abu Lahab, however, was also allied to the rival line of Koreish, having married Omm Jemil, sister of Abu Sofian, and he was greatly under the control of his wife and his brother-in-law. He reprobated what he termed the heresies of his nephew, as calculated to bring disgrace upon their immediate line, and to draw upon it the hostilities of the rest of the tribe of Koreish. Mohammed was keenly sensible of the rancorous opposition of this uncle, which he attributed to the instigations of his wife, Omm Jemil. He especially deplored it as he saw that it affected the happiness of his daughter Rokaia, whose inclination to his doctrines brought on her the reproaches of her husband and his family.

These and other causes of solicitude preyed upon his spirits, and increased the perturbation of his mind. He became worn and haggard, and subject more and more to fits of abstraction. Those of his relatives who were attached to him noticed his altered mien, and dreaded attack of illness. Others scoffingly accused him of mental hallucination, and the foremost among these scoffers was his uncle's wife, Omm Jemil, the sister of Abu Sofian.

The result of this disordered state of mind and body was another vision, or revelation, commanding him to "arise, preach, and magnify the Lord." He was now to announce, publicly and boldly, his doctrines, beginning with his kindred and tribe. Accordingly, in the fourth year of what is called his mission, he summoned all the Koreishites of the line of Haschem to meet him on the hill of Safa, in the vicinity of Mecca, when he would unfold matters important to their welfare. They assembled there, accordingly, and among them came Mohammed's hostile uncle Abu Lahab, and with him his scoffing wife, Omm Jemil. Scarcely had the prophet begun to discourse of his mission, and to impart his revelations, when Abu Lahab started up in a rage, reviled him for calling them together on so idle an errand, and catching up a stone, would have hurled it at him. Mohammed turned upon him a withering look, cursed the hand thus raised in menace, and predicted his doom to the fire of Jehennam, with the assurance that his wife, Omm Jemil, would bear the bundle of thorns with which the fire would be kindled.

The assembly broke up in confusion. Abu Lahab and his wife, exasperated at the curse dealt out to them, compelled their son, Otha, to repudiate his wife, Rokaia, and sent her back weeping to Mohammed. She was soon indemnified, however, by having a husband of the true faith, being eagerly taken to wife by Mohammed's zealous disciple, Othman Ibn Affan.

Nothing discouraged by the failure of his first attempt, Mohammed called a second meeting of the Haschemites at his own house, where, having regaled them with the flesh of a lamb, and given them milk to drink, he stood forth and announced, at full length, his revelations received from heaven, and the divine command to impart them to those of his immediate line.

"O children of Abd al Motâlleb," he cried with enthusiasm, "to you, of all men, has Allah vouchsafed these most precious gifts. In his name I offer you the blessings of this world, and endless joys hereafter. Who among you will share the burden of my offer? Who will be my brother, my lieutenant, my vizier?"

All remained silent, some wondering, others smiling with incredulity and derision. At length Ali, starting up with youthful zeal, offered himself to the service of the prophet, though modestly acknowledging his youth and physical weakness.[2] Mohammed threw his arms around the generous youth, and pressed him to his bosom. "Behold my brother, my vizier, my vicegerent," he exclaimed; "let all listen to his words, and obey him."

The outburst of such a stripling as Ali, however, was answered by scornful laughter from the Koreishites, who taunted Abu Taleb, father of the youthful proselyte, with having to bow down before his son, and yield him obedience.

But though the doctrines of Mohammed were thus ungraciously received by his kindred and friends, they found favor among the people at large, especially among the women, who are ever prone to befriend a persecuted cause. Many of the Jews, also, followed him for a time but when they found that he permitted his disciples to eat the flesh of the camel, and of other animals forbidden by their law, they drew back and rejected his religion as unclean.

Mohammed now threw off all reserve, or rather was inspired with increasing enthusiasm, and went about openly and earnestly proclaiming his doctrines, and giving himself out as a prophet, sent by God to put an end to idolatry, and to mitigate the rigor of the Jewish and the Christian law. The hills of Safa and Kubeis, sanctified by traditions concerning Hagar and Ishmael, were his favorite places of preaching, and Mount Hara was his Sinai, whither he retired occasionally, in fits of excitement and enthusiasm, to return from its solitary cave with fresh revelations of the Koran.

The good old Christian writers, on treating of the advent of one whom they denounce as the Arab enemy of the church, make superstitious record of divers prodigies which occurred about this time— awful forerunners of the troubles about to agitate the world. In Constantinople, at that time the seat of the Christian empire, there were several monstrous births and prodigious apparitions, which struck dismay into the hearts of all beholders. In certain religious processions in that neighborhood, the crosses suddenly moved by themselves, and were violently agitated, causing astonishment and terror.

The Nile, too, that ancient mother of wonders, gave birth to two hideous forms, seemingly man and woman, which rose out of its waters, gazed about them for a time with terrific aspect, and sank again beneath the waves. For a whole day the sun appeared to be diminished to one third of its usual size, shedding pale and baleful rays. During a moonless night a furnace light glowed throughout the heavens, and bloody lances glittered in the sky.

All these, and sundry other like marvels, were interpreted as signs of coming troubles. The ancient servants of God shook their heads mournfully, predicting the reign of antichrist at hand; with vehement persecution of the Christian faith, and great desolation of the churches; and to such holy men who have passed through the trials and troubles of the faith, adds the venerable Padre Jayme Bleda, it is given to understand and explain these mysterious portents, which forerun disasters of the church; even as it is given to ancient mariners to read in the signs of the air, the heavens and the deep, the coming tempest which is to overwhelm their bark.

Many of these sainted men were gathered to glory before the completion of their prophecies. There, seated securely in the empyreal heavens, they may have looked down with compassion upon the troubles of the Christian world, as men on the serene heights of mountains look down upon the tempests which sweep the earth and sea, wrecking tall ships, and rending lofty towers.

Outlines of the Islamic religion

Though it is not intended in this place to go fully into the doctrines promulgated by Mohammed, yet it is important to the right appreciation of his character and conduct, and of the events and circumstances set forth in the following narrative, to give their main features.

It must be particularly borne in mind that Mohammed did not profess to set up a new religion, but to restore that derived in the earliest times from God himself. "We follow," says the second chapter of the Koran, "the religion of Abraham the orthodox, who was no idolater. We believe in God and that which hath been sent down to us, and that which hath been sent down unto Abraham and Ishmael, and Isaac and Jacob and the tribes, and that which was delivered unto Moses and Jesus, and that which was delivered unto the prophets from the Lord: we make no distinction between any of them, and to God we are resigned."

The Koran (derived from the Arabic word *Kora*, to read or teach), which was the great book of Mohammed's faith, was delivered in portions from time to time, according to the excitement of his feelings, or the exigency of circumstances. It was not given as his own work, but as divine revelation, as the very words of God. The Deity is supposed to speak in every instance. "We have sent thee down the book of truth, confirming the scripture which was revealed before it, and preserving the same its purity" (*Koran*, ch. v).

The law of Moses, it was said, had for a time been the guide and rule of human conduct. At the coming of Jesus Christ it was superseded by the Gospel. Both were now to give place to the

Koran, which was more full and explicit than the preceding codes, and intended to reform the abuses which had crept into them through the negligence or the corruptions of their professors. It was the completion of the Law; after it there would be no more divine revelations. Mohammed was the last, as he was the greatest, of the line of prophets sent to make known the will of God.

The unity of God was the cornerstone of this reformed religion. "There is no God but God," was its leading dogma. Hence it received the name of the religion of Islam, an Arabian word implying submission to God.[1] To this leading dogma was added, "Mohammed is the prophet of God"—an addition authorized, it was maintained, by the divine annunciation, and important to procure a ready acceptation of his revelations.

Beside the unity of God, a belief was inculcated in his angels or ministering spirits; in his prophets; in the resurrection of the body; in the last judgment and a future state of rewards and punishments, and in predestination. Much of the Koran may be traced to the Bible, the Mishnu and the Talmud of the Jews,[2] especially its wild though often beautiful traditions concerning the angels, the prophets, the patriarchs, and the good and evil genii. Mohammed had at an early age imbibed a reverence for the Jewish faith, his mother, it is suggested, having been of that religion.

The system laid down in the Koran, however, was essentially founded on the Christian doctrines inculcated in the New Testament, as they had been expounded to Mohammed by the Christian sectarians of Arabia. Our Saviour was to be held in the highest reverence as an inspired prophet, the greatest that had been sent before the time of Mohammed, to reform the Law. But all idea of his divinity was rejected as impious, and the doctrine of the Trinity was denounced as an outrage on the unity of God. Both were pronounced errors and interpolations of the expounders; and this, it will be observed, was the opinion of some of the Arabian sects of Christians.

The worship of saints, and the introduction of images and paintings representing them, were condemned as idolatrous lapses from the pure faith of Christ, and such, we have already observed, were the tenets of the Nestorians with whom Mohammed is known to have had much communication.

All pictures representing living things were prohibited.

Mohammed used to say that the angels would not enter a house in which there were such pictures, and that those who made them would be sentenced in the next world to find souls for them, or be punished.

Most of the benignant precepts of our Saviour were incorporated in the Koran. Frequent alms-giving was enjoined as an imperative duty, and the immutable law of right and wrong, "Do unto another, as thou wouldst he should do unto thee," was given for the moral conduct of the faithful.

"Deal not unjustly with others," says the Koran, "and ye shall not be dealt with unjustly. If there be any debtor under a difficulty of paying his debt, let his creditor wait until it be easy for him to do it; but if he remit it in alms, it will be better for him."

Mohammed inculcated a noble fairness and sincerity in dealing. "O merchants!" he would say, "falsehood and deception are apt to prevail in traffic, purify it therefore with alms; give something in charity as an atonement, for God is incensed by deceit in dealing, but charity appeases his anger. He who sells a defective thing, concealing its defect, will provoke the anger of God and the curses of the angels."

"Take not advantage of the necessities of another to buy things at sacrifice; rather relieve his indigence."

"Feed the hungry, visit the sick, and free the captive if confined unjustly."

"Look not scornfully upon thy fellow man; neither walk the earth with insolence, for God loveth not the arrogant and vainglorious. Be moderate in thy pace, and speak with a moderate tone, for the most ungrateful of all voices is the voice of asses."[3]

Idolatry of all kinds was strictly forbidden; indeed it was what Mohammed held in most abhorrence. Many of the religious usages, however, prevalent since time immemorial among the Arabs, to which he had been accustomed from infancy, and which were not incompatible with the doctrine of the unity of God, were still retained. Such was the pilgrimage to Mecca, including all the rites connected with the Caaba, the well of Zem Zem, and other sacred places in the vicinity, apart from any worship of the idols by which they had been profaned.

The old Arabian rite of prayer, accompanied or rather preceded by ablution, was still continued. Prayers indeed were enjoined at certain hours of the day and night; they were simple in form and phrase, addressed directly to the Deity with certain inflections, or at times a total prostration of the body, and with the face turned towards the Kebla, or point of adoration.

At the end of each prayer, the following verse from the second chapter of the Koran was recited. It is said to have great beauty in the original Arabic, and is engraved on gold and silver ornaments, and on precious stones worn as amulets: "God! There is no God but He, the living, the ever living; he sleepeth not, neither doth he slumber. To him belongeth the heavens, and the earth, and all that they contain. Who shall intercede with him unless by his permission? He knoweth the past and the future, but no one can comprehend anything of his knowledge but that which he revealeth. His sway extendeth over the heavens and the earth, and to sustain them both is no burthen to him. He is the High, the Mighty!"

Mohammed was strenuous in enforcing the importance and efficacy of prayer. "Angels," said he, "come among you both by night and day, after which those of the night ascend to heaven, and God asks them how they left his creatures. We found them, they say, at their prayers, and we left them at their prayers."

The doctrines in the Koran respecting the resurrection and final judgment were in some respects similar to those of the Christian religion, but were mixed up with wild notions derived from other sources; while the joys of the Moslem heaven, though partly spiritual, were clogged and debased by the sensualities of earth, and infinitely below the ineffable purity and spiritual blessedness of the heaven promised by our Saviour.

Nevertheless, the description of the last day, as contained in the eighty-first chapter of the Koran, and which must have been given by Mohammed at the outset of his mission at Mecca as one of the first of his revelations, partakes of the sublime:

"In the name of the all merciful God! a day shall come when the sun will be shrouded, and the stars will fall from the heavens.

"When the camels about to foal will be neglected, and wild beasts will herd together through fear.

"When the waves of the ocean will boil, and the souls of the dead again be united to the bodies.

"When the female infant that has been buried alive will demand, For what crime was I sacrificed? and the eternal books will be laid open.

"When the heavens will pass away like a scroll, and hell

will burn fiercely, and the joys of paradise will be made manifest.

"On that day shall every soul make known that which it hath performed.

"Verily, I swear to you by the stars which move swiftly and are lost in the brightness of the sun, and by the darkness of the night, and by the dawning of the day, these are not the words of an evil spirit, but of an angel of dignity and power, who possesses the confidence of Allah, and is revered by the angels under his command. Neither is your companion, Mohammed, distracted. He beheld the celestial messenger in the light of the clear horizon, and the words revealed to him are intended as an admonition unto all creatures."

9

Ridicule cast on Mohammed and his doctrines - Demand for miracles - Conduct of Abu Taleb - Violence of the Koreishites - Mohammed's daughter Rokaia, with her husband Othman and a number of disciples, take refuge in Abyssinia - Mohammed in the house of Orkham - Hostility of Abu Jahl and his punishment

The greatest difficulty with which Mohammed had to contend at the outset of his prophetic career was the ridicule of his opponents. Those who had known him from his infancy—who had seen him as a boy about the streets of Mecca, and afterwards occupied in all the ordinary concerns of life—scoffed at his assumption of the apostolic character. They pointed with a sneer at him as he passed, exclaiming, "Behold the grandson of Abd al Motâlleb, who pretends to know what is going on in heaven!" Some who had witnessed his fits of mental excitement and ecstasy considered him insane; others declared that he was possessed of a devil, and some charged him with sorcery and magic.

When he walked the streets he was subject to those jeers, and taunts, and insults which the vulgar are apt to vent upon men of eccentric conduct and unsettled mind. If he attempted to preach, his voice was drowned by discordant noises and ribald songs: even dirt was thrown upon him when he was praying in the Caaba.

Nor was it the vulgar and ignorant alone who thus insulted him. One of his most redoubtable assailants was a youth named Amru; and as he subsequently made a distinguished figure in the history of Islam, we would impress the circumstances of this, his first appearance, upon the mind of the reader. He was the son of a courtesan of Mecca, who seems to have rivaled in fascination the Phrynes and Aspasias of Greece, and to have numbered some of the noblest of the land among her lovers. When she gave birth to this child, she mentioned several of the tribe of Koreish who had equal claims to the paternity. The infant was declared to have most resemblance to Aass, the oldest of her admirers, whence, in addition to his name of Amru, he received the designation of Ibn Aass, the son of Aass.

Nature had lavished her choicest gifts upon this natural child, as if to atone for the blemish of his birth. Though young, he was already one of the most popular poets of Arabia, and equally distinguished for the pungency of his satirical effusions and the captivating sweetness of his serious lays.

When Mohammed first announced his mission, this youth assailed him with lampoons and humorous madrigals which, falling in with the poetic taste of the Arabs, were widely circulated, and proved greater impediments to the growth of Islamism than the bitterest persecution.

Those who were more serious in their opposition demanded of Mohammed supernatural proofs of what he asserted. "Moses, and Jesus, and the rest of the prophets," said they, "wrought miracles to prove the divinity of their missions. If thou art indeed a prophet, greater than they, work the like miracles."

The reply of Mohammed may be gathered from his own words in the Koran. "What greater miracle could they have than the Koran itself; a book revealed by means of an unlettered man; so elevated in language, so incontrovertible in argument, that the united skill of men and devils could compose nothing comparable. What greater proof could there be that it came from none but God himself? The Koran itself is a miracle."

They demanded, however, more palpable evidence, miracles addressed to the senses: that he should cause the dumb to speak, the deaf to hear, the blind to see, the dead to rise; or that he should work changes in the face of nature; cause fountains to gush forth; change a sterile place into a garden, with palm trees, and vines, and running streams; cause a palace of gold to rise, decked with jewels and precious stones; or ascend by a ladder into heaven in their presence. Or, if the Koran did indeed, as he affirmed, come down from heaven, that they might see it as it descended, or behold the angel who brought it; and then they would believe.

Mohammed replied sometimes by arguments, sometimes by

denunciations. He claimed to be nothing more than a man sent by God as an apostle. Had angels, said he, walked familiarly on earth, an angel would assuredly have been sent on this mission; but woeful had been the case of those who, as in the present instance, doubted his word. They would not have been able, as with him, to argue and dispute, and take time to be convinced; their perdition would have been instantaneous. "God," he added, "needs no angel to enforce my mission. He is a sufficient witness between you and me. Those whom he shall dispose to be convinced, will truly believe; those whom he shall permit to remain in error, will find none to help their unbelief. On the day of resurrection they will appear blind, and deaf, and dumb, and groveling on their faces. Their abode will be in the eternal flames of Jehennam. Such will be the reward of their unbelief.

"You insist on miracles. God gave to Moses the power of working miracles. What was the consequence? Pharaoh disregarded his miracles, accused him of sorcery, and sought to drive him and his people from the land. But Pharaoh was drowned, and with him all his host. Would ye tempt God to miracles, and risk the punishment of Pharaoh? "

It is recorded by Al Maalem, an Arabian writer, that some of Mohammed's disciples at one time joined with the multitude in this cry for miracles, and besought him to prove, at once, the divinity of his mission, by turning the hill of Safa into gold. Being thus closely urged, he betook himself to prayer; and having finished, assured his followers that the angel Gabriel had appeared to him and informed him that, should God grant his prayer and work the desired miracle, all who disbelieved it would be exterminated. In pity to the multitude, therefore, who appeared to be a stiff-necked generation, he would not expose them to destruction: so the hill of Safa was permitted to remain in its pristine state.

Other Moslem writers assert that Mohammed departed from his self-prescribed rule, and wrought occasional miracles, when he found his hearers unusually slow of belief. Thus we are told that, at one time, in presence of a multitude, he called to him a bull, and took from his horns a scroll containing a chapter of the Koran, just sent down from heaven. At another time, while he was discoursing in public, a white dove hovered over him, and, alighting on his shoulder, appeared to whisper in his ear, being, as he said, a messenger from the Deity. On another occasion he ordered the earth before him to be opened, when two jars were found, one filled with honey, the other with milk, which he pronounced emblems of the abundance promised by heaven to all who should obey his law.

Christian writers have scoffed at these miracles, suggesting that the dove had been tutored to its task, and sought grains of wheat which it had been accustomed to find in the ear of Mohammed; that the scroll had previously been tied to the horns of the bull, and the vessels of milk and honey deposited in the ground. The true course would be to discard these miraculous stories altogether, as fables devised by mistaken zealots, and such they have been pronounced by the ablest of the Moslem commentators.

There is no proof that Mohammed descended to any artifices of the kind to enforce his doctrines or establish his apostolic claims. He appears to have relied entirely on reason and eloquence, and to have been supported by religious enthusiasm in this early and dubious stage of his career. His earnest attacks upon the idolatry which had vitiated and superseded the primitive worship of the Caaba began to have a sensible effect, and alarmed the Koreishites. They urged Abu Taleb to silence his nephew or to send him away; but finding their entreaties unavailing, they informed the old man that if this pretended prophet and his followers persisted in their heresies, they should pay for them with their lives.

Abu Taleb hastened to inform Mohammed of these menaces, imploring him not to provoke against himself and his family such numerous and powerful foes.

The enthusiastic spirit of Mohammed kindled at the words. "O my uncle!" he exclaimed, "though they should array the sun against me on my right hand, and the moon on my left, yet, until God should command me, or should take me hence, would I not depart from my purpose."

He was retiring with dejected countenance when Abu Taleb called him back. The old man was as yet unconverted, but he was struck with admiration of the undaunted firmness of his nephew, and declared that, preach what he might, he would never abandon him to his enemies. Feeling that of himself he could not yield sufficient protection, he called upon the other descendants of Haschem and Abd al Motâlleb to aid in shielding their kinsman from the persecution of the rest of the tribe of Koreish; and so strong is the family tie among the Arabs that, though it was protecting him in what they considered a dangerous heresy, they all consented excepting his uncle Abu Lahab.

The animosity of the Koreishites became more and more virulent, and proceeded to personal violence. Mohammed was assailed and nearly strangled in the Caaba, and was rescued with difficulty by Abu Beker, who himself suffered personal injury in the affray. His immediate family became objects of hatred, especially his daughter Rokaia and her husband Othman Ibn Affan. Those of his disciples who had no powerful friends to protect them were in peril of their lives. Full of anxiety for their safety, Mohammed advised them to leave his dangerous companionship for the present, and take refuge in Abyssinia. The narrowness of the Red Sea made it easy to reach the African shore. The Abyssinians were Nestorian Christians, elevated by their religion above their barbarous neighbors. Their najashee or king was reputed to be tolerant and just. With him Mohammed trusted his daughter and his fugitive disciples would find refuge.

Othman Ibn Affan was the leader of this little band of Moslems, consisting of eleven men and four women. They took the way by the seacoast to Jeddah, a port about two days' journey to the east of Mecca, where they found two Abyssinian vessels at anchor, in which they embarked, and sailed for the land of refuge.

This event, which happened in the fifth year of the mission of Mohammed, is called the first Hegira or Flight, to distinguish it from the second Hegira, the flight of the prophet himself from Mecca to Medina. The kind treatment experienced by the fugitives induced others of the same faith to follow their example, until the number of Moslem refugees in Abyssinia amounted to eighty-three men and eighteen women, besides children.

The Koreishites, finding that Mohammed was not to be silenced and was daily making converts, passed a law banishing all who should embrace his faith. Mohammed retired before the storm, and took refuge in the house of a disciple named Orkham, situated on the hill of Safa. This hill, as has already been mentioned, was renowned in Arabian tradition as the one on which Adam and Eve were permitted to come once more together, after the long solitary wandering about the earth which followed their expulsion from paradise. It was likewise connected in tradition with the fortunes of Hagar and Ishmael.

Mohammed remained for a month in the house of Orkham, continuing his revelations and drawing to him sectaries from various parts of Arabia. The hostility of the Koreishites followed him to his retreat. Abu Jahl, an Arab of that tribe, sought him out, insulted him with opprobrious language, and even personally maltreated him. The outrage was reported to Hamza, an uncle of Mohammed, as he returned to Mecca from hunting. Hamza was no proselyte to Islam, but he was pledged to protect his nephew. Marching with his bow unstrung in his hand to an assemblage of the Koreishites, where Abu Jahl was vaunting his recent triumph, he dealt the boaster a blow over the head, inflicting a grievous wound. The kinfolk of Abu Jahl rushed to his assistance, but the brawler stood in awe of the vigorous arm and fiery spirit of Hamza, and sought to pacify him. "Let him alone," he said to his kinfolk. "In truth I have treated his nephew very roughly." He alleged in palliation of his outrage the apostasy of Mohammed, but Hamza was not to be appeased. "Well!" he cried, fiercely and scornfully, "I also do not believe in your gods of stone; can you compel me?" Anger produced in his bosom what reasoning might have attempted in vain. He forthwith declared himself a convert, took the oath of adhesion to the prophet, and became one of the most zealous and valiant champions of the new faith.

10

Omar Ibn Al Khattâb, nephew of Abu Jahl, undertakes to revenge his uncle by slaying Mohammed - His wonderful conversion to the faith - Mohammed takes refuge in a castle of Abu Taleb - Abu Sofian at the head of the rival branch of Koreishites persecutes Mohammed and his followers - Obtains a decree of non-intercourse with them - Mohammed leaves his retreat and makes converts during the month of pilgrimage - Legend of the conversion of Habib the Wise

The hatred of Abu Jahl to the prophet was increased by the severe punishment received at the hands of Hamza. He had a nephew named Omar Ibn al Khattâb, twenty-six years of age, of gigantic stature, prodigious strength and great courage. His savage aspect appalled the bold, and his very walking staff struck more terror into beholders than another man's sword. Such are the words of the Arabian historian, Abu Abdallah Mohamed Ibn Omal Alwakedi, and the subsequent feats of this warrior prove that they were scarce chargeable with exaggeration.

Instigated by his uncle Abu Jahl, this fierce Arab undertook to penetrate to the retreat of Mohammed, who was still in the house of Orkham, and to strike a poniard to his heart. The Koreishites are accused of having promised him one hundred camels and one thousand ounces of gold for this deed of blood; but this is improbable, nor did the vengeful nephew of Abu Jahl need a bribe.

As he was on his way to the house of Orkham he met a Koreishite, to whom he imparted his design. The Koreishite was a secret convert to Islamism, and sought to turn him from his bloody errand. "Before you slay Mohammed," he said, "and draw upon yourself the vengeance of his relatives, see that your own are free from heresy." "Are any of mine guilty of backsliding?" demanded Omar with astonishment. "Even so," was the reply; "thy sister Amina and her husband Seid."

Omar hastened to the dwelling of his sister and, entering it abruptly, found her and her husband reading the Koran. Seid attempted to conceal it, but his confusion convinced Omar of the truth of the accusation, and heightened his fury. In his rage he struck Seid to the earth, placed his foot upon his breast, and would have plunged his sword into it, had not his sister interposed. A blow on the face bathed her visage in blood. "Enemy of Allah!" sobbed Amina, "dost thou strike me thus for believing in the only true God? In despite of thee and thy violence, I will persevere in the true faith. Yes," added she with fervor, "'There is no God but God, and Mohammed is his prophet.' And now, Omar, finish thy work!"

Omar paused, repented of his violence, and took his foot from the bosom of Seid.

"Show me the writing," said he. Amina, however, refused to let him touch the sacred scroll until he had washed his hands. The passage which he read is said to have been the twentieth chapter of the Koran, which begins thus:

"In the name of the most merciful God! We have not sent down the Koran to inflict misery on mankind, but as a monitor, to teach him to believe in the true God, the creator of the earth and the lofty heavens.

"The All Merciful is enthroned on high, to him belongeth whatsoever is in the heavens above, and in the earth beneath, and in the regions under the earth.

"Dost thou utter thy prayers with a loud voice? Know that there is no need. God knoweth the secrets of thy heart; yea, that which is most hidden.

"Verily, I am God; there is none beside me. Serve me, serve none other. Offer up thy prayer to none but me."

The words of the Koran sank deep into the heart of Omar. He read farther, and was more and more moved, but when he came to the parts treating of the resurrection and of judgment, his conversion was complete.

He pursued his way to the house of Orkham, but with an altered heart. Knocking humbly at the door, he craved admission. "Come in, son of al Khattâb," exclaimed Mohammed, " what brings thee hither?"

"I come to enroll my name among the believers of God and his prophet." So saying, he made the Moslem profession of faith.

He was not content until his conversion was publicly known. At his request, Mohammed accompanied him instantly to the Caaba, to perform openly the rites of Islam. Omar walked on the left hand of the prophet, and Hamza on the right, to protect him from injury and insult, and they were followed by upwards of forty disciples. They passed in open day through the streets of Mecca, to the astonishment of its inhabitants. Seven times did they make the circuit of the Caaba, touching each time the sacred black stone, and complying with all the other ceremonials. The Koreishites regarded this procession with dismay, but dared not approach nor molest the prophet, being deterred by the looks of those terrible men of battle, Hamza and Omar, who, it is said, glared upon them like two lions that had been robbed of their young.

Fearless and resolute in everything, Omar went by himself the next day to pray as a Moslem in the Caaba, in open defiance of the Koreishites. Another Moslem who entered the temple was interrupted in his worship, and rudely treated; but no one molested Omar, because he was the nephew of Abu Jahl. Omar repaired to his uncle. "I renounce thy protection," said he. "I will not be better off than my fellow-believers." From that time he cast his lot with the followers of Mohammed, and was one of his most strenuous defenders.

Such was the wonderful conversion of Omar, afterwards the most famous champion of the Islamic faith. So exasperated were the Koreishites by this new triumph of Mohammed that his uncle Abu Taleb feared they might attempt the life of his nephew, either by treachery or open violence. At his earnest entreaties, therefore, the latter, accompanied by some of his principal disciples, withdrew to a kind of castle, or stronghold, belonging to Abu Taleb, in the neighborhood of the city.

The protection thus given by Abu Taleb, the head the Haschemites, and by others of his line, to Mohammed and his followers, although differing from them in faith, drew on them the wrath of the rival branch of the Koreishites, and produced a schism in the tribe. Abu Sofian, the head of that branch, availed himself of the heresies of the prophet to throw discredit, not merely upon such of his kindred as had embraced his faith, but upon the whole line of Haschem, which, though dissenting from his doctrines, had, through mere clannish feelings, protected him. It is evident the hostility of Abu Sofian arose, not merely from personal hatred or religious scruples, but from the family feud. He was ambitious of transferring to his own line the honors of the city so long engrossed by the Haschemites. The latest measure of the kind-hearted Abu Taleb, in placing Mohammed beyond the reach of persecution and giving him a castle as a refuge, was seized upon by Abu Sofian and his adherents as a pretext for a general ban of the rival line. They accordingly issued a decree forbidding the rest of the tribe of Koreish from intermarrying, or holding any intercourse, even of bargain or sale, with the Haschemites, until they should deliver up their kinsman, Mohammed, for punishment. This decree, which took place in the seventh year of what is called the mission of the prophet, was written on parchment and hung up in the Caaba. It reduced Mohammed and his disciples to great straits, and they were almost famished at times in the stronghold in which they had taken refuge. The fortress was also beleaguered occasionally by the Koreishites, to enforce the ban in all its rigor, and to prevent the possibility of supplies.

The annual season of pilgrimage, however, when hosts of pilgrims repair from all parts of Arabia to Mecca, brought transient relief to the persecuted Moslems. During that sacred season, according to immemorial law and usage among the Arabs, all hostilities were suspended, and warring tribes met in temporary peace to worship at the Caaba. At such times Mohammed and his disciples would venture from their stronghold and return to Mecca. Protected also by the immunity of the holy month, Mohammed would mingle among the pilgrims and preach and pray, propound his doctrines, and proclaim his revelations. In this way he made many converts, who, on their return to their several homes, carried with them the seeds of the new faith to distant regions. Among these converts were occasioually the princes or heads of tribes, whose example had an influence on their adherents. Arabian legends give a pompous and extravagant account of the conversion of one of these princes, which, as it was attended by some of the most noted miracles recorded of Mohammed, may not be unworthy of an abbreviated insertion.

The prince in question was Habib Ibn Malec, surnamed the Wise on account of his vast knowledge and erudition; for he is represented as deeply versed in magic and the sciences, and acquainted with all religions, to their very foundations, having read all that had been written concerning them, and also acquired practical information, for he had belonged to them all by turns, having been Jew, Christian, and one of the Magi. It is true, he had had more than usual time for his studies and experience, having, according to Arabian legend, attained to the age of one hundred and forty years. He now came to Mecca at the head of a powerful host of twenty thousand men, bringing with him a youthful daughter, Satiha, whom he must have begotten at a ripe old age, and for whom he was putting up prayers at the Caaba, she having been struck dumb, and deaf, and blind, and deprived of the use of her limbs.

Abu Sofian and Abu Jahl, according to the legend, thought the presence of this very powerful, very idolatrous, and very wise old prince, at the head of so formidable a host, a favorable opportunity to effect the ruin of Mohammed. They accordingly informed Habib the Wise of the heresies of the pretended prophet, and prevailed upon the venerable prince to summon Mohammed into his presence, at his encampment in the Valley of Flints, there to defend his doctrines, in the hope that his obstinacy in error would draw upon him banishment or death.

The legend gives a magnificent account of the issuing forth of the idolatrous Koreishites, in proud array, on horseback and on foot, led by Abu Sofian and Abu Jahl, to attend the grand inquisition in the Valley of Flints, and of the oriental state in which they were received by Habib the Wise, seated under a tent of crimson, on a throne of ebony, inlaid with ivory and sandalwood and covered with plates of gold.

Mohammed was in the dwelling of Cadijah when he received a summons to this formidable tribunal. Cadijah was loud in her expressions of alarm, and his daughters hung about his neck, weeping and lamenting, for they thought he was going to certain death. But he gently rebuked their fears, and bade them trust in Allah.

Unlike the ostentatious state of his enemies, Abu Sofian and Abu Jahl, Mohammed approached the scene of trial in simple guise, clad in a white garment, with a black turban, and a mantle which had belonged to his grandfather, Abd al Motâlleb, and was made of the stuff of Aden. His hair floated below his shoulders, the mysterious light of prophecy beamed from his countenance, and though he had not anointed his beard, nor used any perfumes, excepting a little musk and camphor for the hair of his upper lip, yet wherever he passed a bland odor diffused itself around, being, say the Arabian writers, the fragrant emanations from his person.

He was preceded by the zealous Abu Beker, clad in a scarlet vest and white turban, with his mantle gathered up under his arms, so as to display his scarlet slippers.

A silent awe, continues the legend, fell upon the vast assemblage as the prophet approached. Not a murmur, not a whisper was to be heard. The very brute animals were charmed to silence, and the neighing of the steed, the bellowing of the camel, and the braying of the ass were mute.

The venerable Habib received him graciously. His first question was to the point: "They tell thou dost pretend to be a prophet sent from God? Is it so? "

"Even so," replied Mohammed. "Allah has sent me to proclaim the veritable faith."

"Good," rejoined the wary sage, "but every prophet has given proof of his mission by signs and miracles. Noah had his rainbow; Solomon his mysterious ring; Abraham the fire of the furnace, which became cool at his command; Isaac the ram, which was sacrificed in his stead; Moses his wonder-working rod; and Jesus brought the dead to life, and appeased tempests with a word. If, then, thou art really a prophet, give us a miracle in proof."

The adherents of Mohammed trembled for him when they heard this request, and Abu Jahl clapped his hands, and extolled the sagacity of Habib the Wise. But the prophet rebuked him with scorn. "Peace! dog of thy race!" he exclaimed, "disgrace of thy kindred, and of thy tribe." He then calmly proceeded to execute the wishes of Habib.

The first miracle demanded of Mohammed was to reveal what Habib had within his tent, and why he had brought it to Mecca.

Upon this, says the legend, Mohammed bent toward the earth and traced figures upon the sand. Then, raising his head, he replied, "O Habib! thou hast brought hither thy daughter, Satiha, deaf and dumb, and lame and blind, in the hope of obtaining relief of Heaven. Go to thy tent; speak to her, and hear her reply, and know that God is all-powerful."

The aged prince hastened to his tent. His daughter met him with light step and extended arms, perfect in all her faculties, her eyes beaming with joy, her face clothed with smiles, and more beauteous than the moon in an unclouded night.

The second miracle demanded by Habib was still more difficult. It was that Mohammed should cover the noontide heaven with supernatural darkness, and cause the moon to descend and rest upon the top of the Caaba.

The prophet performed this miracle as easily as the first. At his summons, a darkness blotted out the whole light of day. The moon was then seen straying from her course and wandering about the firmament. By the irresistible power of the prophet, she was drawn from the heavens and rested on the top of the Caaba. She then performed seven circuits about it, after the manner of the pilgrims, and having made a profound reverence to Mohammed, stood before him with lambent, wavering motion, like a flaming sword, giving him the salutation of peace, and hailing him as a prophet.

Not content with this miracle, pursues the legend, Mohammed compelled the obedient luminary to enter by the right sleeve of his mantle, and go out by the left; then to divide into two parts, one of which went towards the east, and the other towards the west, and meeting in the centre of the firmament reunited themselves into a round and glorious globe.

It is needless to say that Habib the Wise was convinced, and converted by these miracles, as were also four hundred and seventy of the inhabitants of Mecca. Abu Jahl, however, was hardened in unbelief, exclaiming that all was illusion and enchantment produced by the magic of Mohammed.[1]

11

*The ban of non-intercourse mysteriously destroyed -
Mohammed enabled to return to Mecca - Deaths of Abu
Taleb and of Cadijah - Mohammed betroths himself to
Ayesha - Marries Sawda - The Koreishites renew their
persecution - Mohammed seeks an asylum in Taif - His
expulsion from there - Visited by genii in the desert of
Naklah*

Three years had elapsed since Mohammed and his disciples
took refuge in the castle of Abu Taleb. The ban or decree still
existed in the Caaba, cutting them off from all intercourse with
the rest of their tribe. The sect, as usual, increased under
persecution. Many joined it in Mecca; murmurs arose against
the unnatural feud engendered among the Koreishites, and Abu
Sofian was made to blush for the lengths to which he had carried
his hostility against some of his kindred.

All at once it was discovered that the parchment in the
Caaba, on which the decree had been written, was so
substantially destroyed that nothing of the writing remained but
the initial words, "In thy name, O Almighty God!" The decree
was therefore declared to be annulled, and Mohammed and his
followers were permitted to return to Mecca unmolested. The
mysterious removal of this legal obstacle has been considered
by pious Moslems as another miracle wrought by supernatural
agency in favor of the prophet, though unbelievers have
surmised that the document, which was becoming
embarrassing in its effects to Abu Sofian himself, was secretly
destroyed by mortal hands.

The return of Mohammed and his disciples to Mecca was
followed by important conversions, both of inhabitants of the city
and of pilgrims from afar. The chagrin experienced by the
Koreishites from the growth of this new sect was soothed by

tidings of victories of the Persians over the Greeks, by which they conquered Syria and a part of Egypt. The idolatrous Koreishites exulted in the defeat of the Christian Greeks, whose faith, being opposed to the worship of idols, they assimilated to that preached by Mohammed. The latter replied to their taunts and exultations by producing the thirtieth chapter of the Koran, opening with these words: "The Greeks have been overcome by the Persians, but they shall overcome the latter in the course of a few years."

The zealous and believing Abu Beker made a wager of ten camels that this prediction would be accomplished within three years. "Increase the wager, but lengthen the time," whispered Mohammed. Abu Beker staked one hundred camels, but made the time nine years. The prediction was verified and the wager won. This anecdote is confidently cited by Moslem doctors as a proof that the Koran came down from heaven, and that Mohammed possessed the gift of prophecy. The whole, if true, was no doubt a shrewd guess into futurity, suggested by a knowledge of the actual state of the warring powers.

Not long after his return to Mecca, Mohammed was summoned to close the eyes of his uncle Abu Taleb, then more than fourscore years of age and venerable in character as in person. As the hour of death drew nigh, Mohammed exhorted his uncle to make the profession of faith necessary, according to the Islam creed, to secure a blissful resurrection.

A spark of earthly pride lingered in the breast of the dying patriarch. "O son of my brother!" he replied, "should I repeat those words, the Koreishites would say I did so through fear of death."

Abulfeda, the historian, insists that Abu Taleb actually died in the faith. Al Abbas, he says, hung over the bed of his expiring brother and, perceiving his lips to move, approached his ear to catch his dying words. They were the wished-for confession. Others affirm that his last words were, "I die in the faith of Abd al Motâlleb." Commentators have sought to reconcile the two accounts by asserting that Abd al Motâlleb in his latter days renounced the worship of idols, and believed in the unity of God.

Scarcely three days had elapsed from the death of the venerable Abu Taleb when Cadijah, the faithful and devoted wife of Mohammed, likewise sank into the grave. She was sixty-five years of age. Mohammed wept bitterly at her tomb and clothed himself in mourning for her, and for Abu Taleb, so that this year was called the year of mourning. He was comforted in his affliction, says the Arabian author Abu Horaira, by an assurance from the angel Gabriel that a silver palace was allotted to Cadijah in Paradise, as a reward for her great faith and her early services to the cause.

Though Cadijah had been much older than Mohammed at the time of their marriage, and past the bloom of years when women are desirable in the East, and though the prophet was noted for an amorous temperament, yet he is said to have remained true to her to the last, and never availed himself of the Arabian law, permitting a plurality of wives, to give her a rival in his house. When, however, she was laid in the grave, and the first transport of his grief had subsided, he sought to console himself for her loss by entering anew into wedlock, and henceforth indulged in a plurality of wives. He permitted, by his law, four wives to each of his followers, but did not limit himself to that number; for he observed that a prophet, being peculiarly gifted and privileged, was not bound to restrict himself to the same laws as ordinary mortals.

His first choice was made within a month after the death of Cadijah, and fell upon a beautiful child named Ayesha, the daughter of his faithful adherent, Abu Beker. Perhaps be sought, by this alliance, to grapple Abu Beker still more strongly to his side, he being one of the bravest and most popular of his tribe. Ayesha, however, was but seven years of age, and, though females soon bloom and ripen in those eastern climes, she was yet too young to enter into the married state. He was merely betrothed to her, therefore, and postponed their nuptials for two years, during which time he caused her to be carefully instructed in the accomplishments proper to an Arabian maiden of distinguished rank.

Upon this wife, thus chosen in the very blossom of her years, the prophet doted more passionately than upon any of those whom he subsequently married. All these had been previously experienced in wedlock; Ayesha, he said, was the only one who came a pure unspotted virgin to his arms.

Still, that he might not be without due solace while Ayesha was attaining the marriageable age, he took as a wife Sawda, the widow of Sokran, one of his followers. She had been nurse to his daughter Fatima, and was one of the faithful who fled into Abyssinia from the early persecutions of the people of Mecca. It is pretended that, while in exile, she had a mysterious intimation of the future honor which awaited her; for she dreamt that Mohammed laid his head upon her bosom. She recounted the dream to her husband Sokran, who interpreted it as a prediction of his speedy death, and of her marriage with the prophet.

The marriage, whether predicted or not, was one of mere expediency. Mohammed never loved Sawda with the affection he manifested for his other wives. He would even have put her away in after years, but she implored to be allowed the honor of still calling herself his wife, proffering that, whenever it should come to her turn to share the marriage bed, she would relinquish her right to Ayesha. Mohammed consented to an arrangement which favored his love for the latter, and Sawda continued as long as she lived to be nominally his wife.

Mohammed soon became sensible of the loss he had sustained in the death of Abu Taleb, who had been not merely an affectionate relative, but a steadfast and powerful protector, from his great influence in Mecca. At his death there was no one to check and counteract the hostilities of Abu Sofian and Abu Jahl, who soon raised up such a spirit of persecution among the Koreishites that Mohammed found it unsafe to continue in his native place. He set out, therefore, accompanied by his freedman Zeid, to seek a refuge at Taif, a small walled town about seventy miles from Mecca, inhabited by the Thakifites, or Arabs of the tribe of Thakeef. It was one of the favored places of Arabia, situated among vineyards and gardens. Here grew peaches and plums, melons and pomegranates, figs, blue and green, the nebeck tree producing the lotus, and palm trees with their clusters of green and golden fruit. So fresh were its pastures and fruitful its fields, contrasted with the sterility of the neighboring deserts, that the Arabs fabled it to have orignally been a part of Syria, broken off and floated hither at the time of the deluge.

Mohammed entered the gates of Taif with some degree of confidence, trusting for protection to the influence of his uncle Al Abbas, who had possessions there. He could not have chosen a worse place of refuge. Taif was one of the strongholds of idolatry. Here was maintained in all its force the worship of El Lat, one of the female idols already mentioned. Her image of stone was covered with jewels and precious stones, the offerings of her votaries. It was believed to be inspired with life, and the intercession of El Lat was implored as one of the daughters of God.

Mohammed remained about a month in Taif, seeking in vain to make proselytes among its inhabitants. When he attempted to preach his doctrines, his voice was drowned by clamors. More than once he was wounded by stones thrown at him, and which the faithful Zeid endeavored in vain to ward off. So violent did the popular fury become at last that he was driven from the city, and even pursued for some distance beyond the walls by an insulting rabble of slaves and children.

Thus driven ignominiously from his hoped-for place of refuge, and not daring to return openly to his native city, he remained in the desert until Zeid should procure a secret asylum for him among his friends in Mecca. In this extremity, he had one of those visions or supernatural visitations which appear always to have occurred in lonely or agitated moments, when we may suppose him to have been in a state of mental excitement. It was after the evening prayer, he says, in a solitary place in the Valley of Naklah, between Mecca and Taif. He was reading the Koran, when he was overheard by a passing company of Gins or Genii. These are spiritual beings, some good, others bad, and liable like man to future rewards and punishments. "Hark! give ear!" said the Genii one to the other. They paused and listened as Mohammed continued to read. "Verily," said they at the end, "we have heard an admirable discourse, which directeth unto the right institution; wherefore we believe therein."

This spiritual visitation consoled Mohammed for his expulsion from Taif, showing that though he and his doctrines might be rejected by men, they were held in reverence by spiritual intelligences. At least so we may infer from the mention he makes of it in the forty-sixth and seventy-second chapters of the Koran. Thenceforward, he declared himself sent for the conversion of these genii as well as of the human race.[1]

12

Night journey of the Prophet from Mecca to Jerusalem, and thence to the seventh heaven

An asylum being provided for Mohammed in the house of Mutem Ibn Adi, one of his disciples, he ventured to return to Mecca. The supernatural visitation of genii in the Valley of Naklah was soon followed by a vision or revelation far more extraordinary, and which has ever since remained a theme of comment and conjecture among devout Mohammedans. We allude to the famous night journey to Jerusalem, and thence to the seventh heaven. The particulars of it, though given as if in the very words of Mohammed, rest merely on tradition; some, however, cite texts corroborative of it, scattered here and there in the Koran.

We do not pretend to give this vision or revelation in its amplitude and wild extravagance, but will endeavor to seize upon its most essential features.

The night on which it occurred is described as one of the darkest and most awfully silent that had ever been known. There was no crowing of cocks nor barking of dogs, no howling of wild beasts nor hooting of owls. The very waters ceased to murmur, and the winds to whistle; all nature seemed motionless and dead. In the mid watches of the night, Mohammed was roused by a voice crying, "Awake, thou sleeper!" The angel Gabriel stood before him. His forehead was clear and serene, his complexion white as snow, his hair floated on his shoulders. He had wings of many dazzling hues, and his robes were sown with pearls and embroidered with gold.

He brought Mohammed a white steed of wonderful form and qualities, unlike any animal he had ever seen; and in truth, it differs from any animal ever before described. It had a human face, but the cheeks of a horse: its eyes were as jacinths and radiant as stars. It had eagle's wings all glittering with rays of light, and its whole form was resplendent with gems and precious stones. It was a female, and from its dazzling splendor and incredible velocity was called Al Borak, or Lightning.

Mohammed prepared to mount this supernatural steed, but as he extended his hand it drew back and reared.

"Be still, O Borak!" said Gabriel; "respect the prophet of God. Never wert thou mounted by mortal man more honored of Allah."

"O Gabriel!" replied Al Borak, who at this time was miraculously endowed with speech, "did not Abrabam of old, the friend of God, bestride me when he visited his son Ishmael? O Gabriel! is not this the mediator, the intercessor, the author of the profession of faith?"

"Even so, O Borak, this is Mohammed Ibn Abdallah, of one of the tribes of Arabia the Happy, and of the true faith. He is chief of the sons of Adam, the greatest of the divine legates, the seal of the prophets. All creatures must have his intercession before they can enter paradise. Heaven is on his right hand, to be the reward of those who believe in him; the fire of Jehennam is on his left hand, into which all shall be thrust who oppose his doctrines."

"O Gabriel!" entreated Al Borak, "by the faith existing between thee and him, prevail on him to intercede for me at the day of the resurrection."

"Be assured, O Borak !" exclaimed Mohammed, "that through my intercession thou shalt enter paradise."

No sooner had he uttered these words than the animal approached and submitted to be mounted; then rising with Mohammed on its back, it soared aloft far above the mountains of Mecca.

As they passed like lightning between heaven and earth, Gabriel cried aloud, "Stop, O Mohammed! descend to the earth, and make the prayer with two inflections of the body."

They alighted on the earth, and having made the prayer—

"O friend and well beloved of my soul !" said Mohammed, "why dost thou command me to pray in this place?"

"Because it is Mount Sinai, on which God communed with Moses."

Mounting aloft, they again passed rapidly between heaven and earth, until Gabriel called out a second time, "Stop, O

Mohammed! descend, and make the prayer with two inflections."

They descended, Mohammed prayed, and again demanded, "Why didst thou command me to pray in this place?"

"Because it is Bethlehem, where Jesus the Son of Mary was born."

They resumed their course through the air, until a voice was heard on the right, exclaiming, "O Mohammed, tarry a moment, that I may speak to thee; of all created beings I am most devoted to thee."

But Borak pressed forward, and Mohammed forbore to tarry, for he felt that it was not with him to stay his course, but with God the all-powerful and glorious.

Another voice was now heard on the left, calling on Mohammed in like words to tarry; but Borak still pressed forward, and Mohammed tarried not. He now beheld before him a damsel of ravishing beauty, adorned with all the luxury and riches of the earth. She beckoned him with alluring smiles: "Tarry a moment, O Mohammed, that I may talk with thee. I, who, of all beings, am the most devoted to thee." But still Borak pressed on, and Mohammed tarried not, considering that it was not with him to stay his course, but with God the all-powerful and glorious.

Addressing himself, however, to Gabriel, "What voices are those I have heard? " said he, "and what damsel in this who has beckoned to me?"

"The first, O Mohammed, was the voice of a Jew; hadst thou listened to him, all thy nation would have been won to Judaism.

"The second was the voice of a Christian; hadst thou listened to him, thy people would have inclined to Christianity.

"The damsel was the world, with all its riches, its vanities, and allurements; hadst thou listened to her, thy nation would have chosen the pleasures of this life, rather than the bliss of eternity, and all would have been doomed to perdition."

Continuing their aerial course, they arrived at the gate of the holy temple at Jerusalem, where, alighting from Al Borak, Mohammed fastened her to the rings where the prophets before him had fastened her. Then, entering the temple, he found there Abraham, and Moses, and Isa (Jesus), and many more of the prophets. After he had prayed in company with them for a time, a ladder of light was let down from heaven, until the lower end rested on the Shakra, or foundation-stone of the sacred house, being the stone of Jacob. Aided by the angel Gabriel, Mohammed ascended this ladder with the rapidity of lightning.

Being arrived at the first heaven, Gabriel knocked at the gate. "Who is there?" was demanded from within. "Gabriel." "Who is with thee?" "Mohammed." "Has he received his mission?" "He has." "Then he is welcome!" and the gate was opened.

The first heaven was of pure silver, and in its resplendent vault the stars are suspended by chains of gold. In each star an angel is placed sentinel, to prevent the demons from scaling the sacred abodes. As Mohammed entered, an ancient man approached him, and Gabriel said, "Here is thy father Adam, pay him reverence." Mohammed did so, and Adam embraced him, calling him the greatest among his children, and the first among the prophets.

In this heaven were innumerable animals of all kinds, which Gabriel said were angels, who, under these forms, interceded with Allah for the various races of animals upon earth. Among these was a cock of dazzling whiteness, and of such marvelous height that his crest touched the second heaven, though five hundred years' journey above the first. This wonderful bird saluted the ear of Allah each morning with his melodious chant. All creatures on earth, save man, are awakened by his voice, and all the fowls of his kind chant hallelujahs in emulation of his note.[1]

They now ascended to the second heaven. Gabriel, as before, knocked at the gate; the same questions and replies were exchanged; the door opened and they entered.

This heaven was all of polished steel, and dazzling splendor. Here they found Noah, who, embracing Mohammed, hailed him as the greatest among the prophets.

Arrived at the third heaven, they entered with the same ceremonies. It was all studded with precious stones, and too brilliant for mortal eyes. Here was seated an angel of immeasurable height, whose eyes were seventy thousand days' journey apart. He had at his command a hundred thousand battalions of armed men. Before him was spread a vast book, in which he was continually writing and blotting out.

"This, O Mohammed," said Gabriel, "is Asrael, the angel of death, who is in the confidence of Allah. In the book before him he is continually writing the names of those who are to be born, and blotting out the names of those who have lived their allotted time, and who, therefore, instantly die."

They now mounted to the fourth heaven, formed of the finest silver. Among the angels who inhabited it was one five hundred days' journey in height. His countenance was troubled, and rivers of tears ran from his eyes. "This," said Gabriel, "is the angel of tears, appointed to weep over the children of men, and to predict the evils which await them."

The fifth heaven was of the finest gold. Here Mohammed was received by Aaron with embraces and congratulations. The avenging angel dwells in this heaven, and presides over the element of fire. Of all the angels seen by Mohammed, he was the most hideous and terrific. His visage seemed of copper, and was covered with wens and warts. His eyes flashed lightning, and he grasped a flaming lance. He sat on a throne surrounded by flames, and before him was a heap of red-hot chains. Were he to alight upon earth in his true form, the mountains would be consumed, the seas dried up, and all the inhabitants would die with terror. To him, and the angels his ministers, is intrusted the execution of divine vengeance on infidels and sinners.

Leaving this awful abode, they mounted to the sixth heaven, composed of a transparent stone, called Hasala, which may be rendered carbuncle. Here was a great angel, composed half of snow and half of fire; yet the snow melted not, nor was the fire extinguished. Around him a choir of lesser angels continually exclaimed, "O Allah! who hast united snow and fire, unite all thy faithful servants in obedience to thy law."

"This," said Gabriel,"is the guardian angel of heaven and earth. It is he who dispatches angels unto individuals of thy nation, to incline them in favor of thy mission, and call them to the service of God; and he will continue to do so until the day of resurrection."

Here was the prophet Musa (Moses), who, however, instead of welcoming Mohammed with joy, as the other prophets had done, shed tears at sight of him.

"Wherefore dost thou weep?" inquired Mohammed.

"Because I behold a successor, who is destined to conduct more of his nation into paradise than ever I could of the backsliding children of Israel."

Mounting hence to the seventh heaven, Mohammed was received by the patriarch Abraham. This blissful abode is formed of divine light, and of such transcendent glory that the tongue of man cannot describe it. One of its celestial inhabitants will suffice to give an idea of the rest. He surpassed the whole earth in magnitude, and had seventy thousand heads; each head seventy thousand mouths; each mouth seventy thousand tongues; each tongue spoke seventy thousand different languages, and all these were incessantly employed in chanting the praises of the Most High.

While contemplatiug this wonderful being, Mohammed was suddenly transported aloft to the lotus tree, called Sedrat, which flourishes on the right hand of the invisible throne of Allah. The branches of this tree extend wider than the distance between the sun and the earth. Angels more numerous than the sands of the seashore, or of the beds of all the streams and rivers, rejoice beneath its shade. The leaves resemble the ears of an elephant; thousands of immortal birds sport among its branches, repeating the sublime verses of the Koran. Its fruits are milder than milk and sweeter than honey. If all the creatures of God were assembled, one of these fruits would be sufficient for their sustenance. Each seed incloses an houri, or celestial virgin, provided for the felicity of true believers. From this tree issue four rivers; two flow into the interior of paradise, two issue beyond it, and become the Nile and Euphrates.

Mohammed and his celestial guide now proceeded to Al Mamour, or the House of Adoration, formed of red jacinths or rubies, and surrounded by innumerable lamps, perpetually burning. As Mohammed entered the portal, three vases were offered him, one containing wine, another milk, and the third, honey. He took and drank of the vase containing milk.

"Well hast thou done; auspicious is thy choice," exclaimed Gabriel. "Hadst thou drunk of the wine, thy people had all gone astray."

The sacred house resembles in form the Caaba at Mecca, and is perpendicularly above it in the seventh heaven. It is visited every day by seventy thousand angels of the highest order. They were at this very time making their holy circuit, and Mohammed, joining with them, walked round it seven times.

Gabriel could go no further. Mohammed now traversed, quicker than thought, an immense space, passing through two regions of dazzling light, and one of profound darkness. Emerging from this utter gloom, he was filled with awe and terror at finding himself in the presence of Allah, and but two

bow-shots from his throne. The face of the Deity was covered
with twenty thousand veils, for it would have annihilated man
to look upon its glory. He put forth his hands, and placed one
upon the breast and the other upon the shoulder of Mohammed,
who felt a freezing chill penetrate to his heart and to the very
marrow of his bones. It was followed by a feeling of ecstatic
bliss, while a sweetness and fragrance prevailed around, which
none can understand but those who have been in the divine
presence.

Mohammed now received from the Deity himself many of
the doctrines contained in the Koran, and fifty prayers were
prescribed as the daily duty of all true believers.

When he descended from the divine presence and again met
with Moses, the latter demanded what Allah had required.
"That I should make fifty prayers every day."

"And thinkest thou to accomplish such a task? I have made
the experiment before thee. I tried it with the children of Israel,
but in vain; return, then, and beg a diminution of the task."

Mohammed returned accordingly, and obtained a
diminution of ten prayers; but when he related his success to
Moses, the latter made the same objection to the daily amount of
forty. By his advice Mohammed returned repeatedly, until the
number was reduced to five.

Moses still objected. "Thinkest thou to exact five prayers
daily from thy people? By Allah! I have had experience with the
children of Israel, and such a demand is vain; return,
therefore, and entreat still further mitigation of the task."

"No," replied Mohammed, "I have already asked
indulgence until I am ashamed." With these words he saluted
Moses and departed.

By the ladder of light he descended to the temple of
Jerusalem, where he found Borak fastened as he had left her,
and mounting, was borne back in an instant to the place whence
he had first been taken.

This account of the vision, or nocturnal journey, is chiefly
according to the words of the historians Abulfeda, Al Bokhari,
and Abu Horaira, and is given more at large in the *Life of
Mahomet* by Jean Gagnier. The journey itself has given rise to
endless commentaries and disputes among the doctors. Some
affirm that it was no more than a dream or vision of the night,
and support their assertion by a tradition derived from Ayesha,
the wife of Mohammed, who declared that, on the night in

question, his body remained perfectly still, and it was only in spirit that he made his nocturnal journey. In giving this tradition, however, they did not consider that at the time the journey was said to have taken place, Ayesha was still a child, and, though espoused, had not become the wife of Mohammed.

Others insist that he made the celestial journey bodily, and that the whole was miraculously effected in so short a space of time, that, on his return, he was able to prevent the complete overturn of a vase of water which the angel Gabriel had struck with his wing on his departure.

Others say that Mohammed only pretended to have made the nocturnal journey to the temple of Jerusalem, and that the subsequent ascent to heaven was a vision. According to Ahmed ben Joseph, the nocturnal visit to the temple was testified to by the patriarch of Jerusalem himself. "At the time," says he, "that Mohammed sent an envoy to the Emperor Heraclius, at Constantinople, inviting him to embrace Islamism, the patriarch was in the presence of the emperor. The envoy having related the nocturnal journey of the prophet, the patriarch was seized with astonishment, and informed the emperor of a circumstance coinciding with the narrative of the envoy. 'It is my custom,' said he, 'never to retire to rest at night until I have fastened every door of the temple. On the night here mentioned, I closed them according to my custom, but there was one which it was impossible to move. Upon this, I sent for the carpenters, who, having inspected the door, declared that the lintel over the portal, and the edifice itself, had settled to such a degree that it was out of their power to close the door. I was obliged, therefore, to leave it open. Early in the morning, at the break of day, I repaired thither, and behold, the stone placed at the corner of the temple was perforated, and there were vestiges of the place where Al Borak had been fastened. Then, said I, to those present, this portal would not have remained fixed unless some prophet had been here to pray."

Traditions go on to say that when Mohammed narrated his nocturnal journey to a large assembly in Mecca, many marveled yet believed, some were perplexed with doubt, but the Koreishites laughed it to scorn. "Thou sayest that thou hast been to the temple of Jerusalem," said Abu Jahl; "prove the truth of thy words, by giving a description of it."

For a moment Mohammed was embarrassed by the demand, for he had visited the temple in the night, when its form was not discernible. Suddenly, however, the angel Gabriel stood by his side, and placed before his eyes an exact type of the sacred edifice, so that he was enabled instantly to answer the most minute questions.

The story still transcended the belief even of some of his disciples, until Abu Beker, seeing them wavering in their faith, and in danger of backsliding, roundly vouched for the truth of it, in reward for which support Mohammed gave him the title of Al Seddek, or the Testifier to the Truth, by which he was thenceforth distinguished.

As we have already observed, this nocturnal journey rests almost entirely upon tradition, though some of its circumstances are vaguely alluded to in the Koran. The whole may be a fanciful superstructure of Moslem fanatics on one of these visions or ecstasies to which Mohammed was prone, and the relations of which caused him to be stigmatized by the Koreishites as a madman.

13

*Mohammed makes converts of pilgrims from Medina -
Determines to fly to that city - A plot to slay him - His
miraculous escape - His hegira, or flight - His reception
at Medina*

The fortunes of Mohammed were becoming darker and darker
in his native place. Cadijah, his original benefactress, the
devoted companion of his solitude and seclusion, the zealous
believer in his doctrines, was in her grave: so also was Abu
Taleb, once his faithful and efficient protector. Deprived of the
sheltering influence of the latter, Mohammed had become, in a
manner, an outlaw in Mecca, obliged to conceal himself and
remain a burden on the hospitality of those whom his own
doctrines had involved in persecution. If worldly advantage
had been his object, how had it been attained? More than ten
years had elapsed since he first announced his prophetic
mission—ten long years of enmity, trouble, and misfortune.
Still he persevered, and now, at a period of life when men seek to
enjoy in repose the fruition of the past, rather than risk all in
new schemes for the future, we find him, after having sacrificed
ease, fortune, and friends, prepared to give up home and country
also, rather than his religious creed.

As soon as the privileged time of pilgrimage arrived, he
emerged once more from his concealment, and mingled with
the multitude assembled from all parts of Arabia. His earnest
desire was to find some powerful tribe, or the inhabitants of
some important city, capable and willing to receive him as a
guest, and protect him in the enjoyment and propagation of his
faith.

His quest was for a time unsuccessful. Those who had come
to worship at the Caaba drew back from a man stigmatized as an

apostate, and the worldly-minded were unwilling to befriend one proscribed by the powerful of his native place.

At length, as he was one day preaching on the hill Al Akaba, a little to the north of Mecca, he drew the attention of certain pilgrims from the city of Yathreb. This city, since called Medina, was about two hundred and seventy miles north of Mecca. Many of its inhabitants were Jews and heretical Christians. The pilgrims in question were pure Arabs of the ancient and powerful tribe of Khazradites, and in habits of friendly intercourse with the Keneedites and Naderites, two Jewish tribes inhabiting Mecca, who claimed to be of the sacerdotal line of Aaron. The pilgrims had often heard their Jewish friends explain the mysteries of their faith, and talk of an expected Messiah. They were moved by the eloquence of Mohammed, and struck with the resemblance of his doctrines to those of the Jewish law, so that when they heard him proclaim himself a prophet, sent by Heaven to restore the ancient faith, they said to one another, "Surely this must be the promised Messiah of which we have been told." The more they listened, the stronger became their persuasion of the fact, until in the end they avowed their conviction, and made a final profession of the faith.

As the Khazradites belonged to one of the most powerful tribes of Yathreb, Mohammed sought to secure their protection, and proposed to accompany them on their return. But they informed him that they were at deadly feud with the Awsites, another powerful tribe of that city, and advised him to defer his coming until they should be at peace. He consented; but on the return home of the pilgrims, he sent with them Musab Ibn Omeir, one of the most learned and able of his disciples, with instructions to strengthen them in the faith, and to preach it to their townsmen. Thus were the seeds of Islam first sown in the city of Medina. For a time they thrived but slowly. Musab was opposed by the idolaters, and his life threatened. But he persisted in his exertions, and gradually made converts among the principal inhabitants. Among these were Saad Ibn Maadi, a prince or chief of the Awsites, and Osaid Ibn Hodheir, a man of great authority in the city. Numbers of the Moslems of Mecca, also, driven away by persecution, took refuge in Medina, and aided in propagating the new faith among its inhabitants, until it found its way into almost every household.

Feeling now assured of being able to give Mohammed an asylum in the city, more than seventy of the converts of Medina, led by Musab Ibn Omeir, repaired to Mecca with the pilgrims in the holy month of the thirteenth year of "the mission," to invite him to take up his abode in their city. Mohammed gave them a midnight meeting on the hill Al Akaba. His uncle Al Abbas, who, like the deceased Abu Taleb, took an affectionate interest in his welfare, though no convert to his doctrines, accompanied him to this secret conference, which he feared might lead him into danger. He entreated the pilgrims from Medina not to entice his nephew to their city until more able to protect him, warning them that their open adoption of the new faith would bring all Arabia in arms against them. His warnings and entreaties were in vain: a solemn compact was made between the parties. Mohammed demanded that they should abjure idolatry, and worship the one true God openly and fearlessly. For himself he exacted obedience in weal and woe; and for the disciples who might accompany him, protection, even such as they would render to their own wives and children. On these terms he offered to bind himself to remain among them, to be the friend of their friends, the enemy of their enemies. "But, should we perish in your cause," they asked, "what will be our reward?" "Paradise!" replied the prophet.

The terms were accepted; the emissaries from Medina placed their hands in the hands of Mohammed, and swore to abide by the compact. The latter then singled out twelve from among them, whom he designated as his apostles, in imitation, it is supposed, of the example of our Saviour. Just then a voice was heard from the summit of the hill, denouncing them as apostates, and menacing them with punishment. The sound of this voice, heard in the darkness of the night, inspired temporary dismay. "It is the voice of the fiend Iblis," said Mohammed, scornfully. "He is the foe of God: fear him not." It was probably the voice of some spy or eavesdropper of the Koreishites, for the very next morning they manifested a knowledge of what had taken place in the night, and treated the new confederates with great harshness as they were departing from the city.

It was this early accession to the faith, and this timely aid proffered and subsequently afforded to Mohammed and his disciples, which procured for the Moslems of Medina the appellation of Ansarians, or auxiliaries, by which they were afterwards distinguished.

After the departure of the Ansarians, and the expiration of the holy month, the persecutions of the Moslems were resumed with increased virulence. Mohammed, seeing that a crisis was at hand and resolving to leave the city, advised his adherents generally to provide for their safety. For himself, he still lingered in Mecca with a few devoted followers.

Abu Sofian, his implacable foe, was at this time governor of the city. He was both incensed and alarmed at the spreading growth of the new faith, and held a meeting of the chief of the Koreishites to devise some means of effectually putting a stop to it. Some advised that Mohammed should be banished from the city, but it was objected that he might gain other tribes to his interest, or perhaps the people of Medina, and return at their head to take his revenge. Others proposed to wall him up in a dungeon, and supply him with food until he died, but it was surmised that his friends might effect his escape. All these objections were raised by a violent and pragmatical old man, a stranger from the province of Nedja, who, say the Moslem writers, was no other than the devil in disguise, breathing his malignant spirit into those present. At length it was declared by Abu Jahl that the only effectual check on the growing evil was to put Mohammed to death. To this all agreed, and as a means of sharing the odium of the deed, and withstanding the vengeance it might awaken among the relatives of the victim, it was arranged that a member of each family should plunge his sword into the body of Mohammed.

It is to this conspiracy that allusion is made in the eighth chapter of the Koran. "And call to mind how the unbelievers plotted against thee, that they might either detain thee in bonds, or put thee to death, or expel thee the city; but God laid a plot against them; and God is the best layer of plots."

In fact, by the time the murderers arrived before the dwelling of Mohammed, he was apprised of the impending danger. As usual, the warning is attributed to the angel Gabriel, but it is probable it was given by some Koreishite, less bloody-minded than his confederates. It came just in time to save Mohammed from the hands of his enemies. They paused at his door, but hesitated to enter. Looking through a crevice they beheld, so they thought, Mohammed wrapped in his green mantle, and lying asleep on his couch. They waited for a while, consulting whether to fall on him while he was sleeping, or wait until he should go forth. At length they burst open the door and rushed toward the couch. The sleeper started up; but, instead of Mohammed, Ali stood before them. Amazed and confounded, they demanded, "Where is Mohammed?" "I know not," replied Ali, sternly, and walked forth; nor did any one venture to molest him. Enraged at the escape of their victim, however, the Koreishites proclaimed a reward of a hundred camels to any one who should bring them Mohammed alive or dead.

Divers accounts are given of the mode in which Mohammed made his escape from the house after the faithful Ali had wrapped himself in his mantle and taken his place upon the couch. The most miraculous account is that he opened the door silently, as the Koreishites stood before it, and, scattering a handful of dust in the air, cast such blindness upon them that he walked through the midst of them without being perceived. This, it is added, is confirmed by the verse of the thirtieth chapter of the Koran: "We have thrown blindness upon them, that they shall not see."

The most probable account is that he clambered over the wall in the rear of the house, by the help of a servant, who bent his back for him to step upon it.

He repaired immediately to the house of Abu Beker, and they arranged for instant flight. It was agreed that they should take refuge in a cave in Mount Thor, about an hour's distance from Mecca, and wait there until they could proceed safely to Medina; and in the meantime the children of Abu Beker should secretly bring them food. They left Mecca while it was still dark, making their way on foot by the light of the stars, and the day dawned as they found themselves at the foot of Mount Thor. Scarcely were they within the cave, when they heard the sound of pursuit. Abu Beker, though a brave man, quaked with fear. "Our pursuers," he said, "are many, and we are but two." "Nay," replied Mohammed, "there is a third; God is with us!" And here the Moslem writers relate a miracle, dear to the minds of all true believers. By the time, they say, that the Koreishites reached the mouth of the cavern, an acacia tree had sprung up before it, in the spreading branches of which a pigeon had made its nest, and laid its eggs, and over the whole a spider had woven its web. When the Koreishites beheld these signs of undisturbed quiet, they concluded that no one could recently have entered the cavern. So they turned away, and pursued their search in another direction.

Whether protected by miracle or not, the fugitives remained for three days undiscovered in the cave, and Asama, the daughter of Abu Beker, brought them food in the dusk of the evenings.

On the fourth day, when they presumed the ardor of pursuit had abated, the fugitives ventured forth, and set out for Medina on camels which a servant of Abu Beker had brought in the night for them. Avoiding the main road usually taken by the caravans, they bent their course nearer to the coast of the Red Sea. They had not proceeded far, however, before they were overtaken by a troop of horse, headed by Soraka Ibn Malec. Abu Beker was again dismayed by the number of their pursuers; but Mohammed repeated the assurance, "Be not troubled; Allah is with us." Soraka was a grim warrior, with shaggy iron-gray locks, and naked sinewy arms rough with hair. As he overtook Mohammed, his horse reared and fell with him. His superstitious mind was struck with it as an evil sign. Mohammed perceived the state of his feelings, and by an eloquent appeal wrought upon him to such a degree that Soraka, filled with awe, entreated his forgiveness and, turning back with his troop, suffered him to proceed on his way unmolested.

The fugitives continued their journey without further interruption until they arrived at Koba, a hill about two miles from Medina. It was a favorite resort of the inhabitants of the city, and a place to which they sent their sick and infirm, for the air was pure and salubrious. Hence, too, the city was supplied with fruit, the hill and its environs being covered with vineyards, and with groves of the date and lotus, with gardens producing citrons, oranges, pomegranates, figs, peaches, and apricots, and being irrigated with limpid streams.

On arriving at this fruitful spot, Al Kaswa, the camel of Mohammed, crouched on her knees and would go no further. The prophet interpreted it as a favorable sign, and determined to remain at Koba and prepare for entering the city. The place where his camel knelt is still pointed out by pious Moslems, a mosque named Al Takwa having been built there to commemorate the circumstance. Some affirm that it was actually founded by the prophet. A deep well is also shown in the vicinity, beside which Mohammed reposed under the shade of the trees, and into which he dropped his seal ring. It is believed still to remain there, and has given sanctity to the well, the waters of which are conducted by subterraneous conduits to Medina. At Koba he remained four days, residing in the house of an Awsite named Colthum Ibn Hadem. While at this village he was joined by a distinguished chief, Boreida Ibn Hoseib, with seventy followers, all of the tribe of Saham. These made profession of faith between the hands of Mohammed.

Another renowned proselyte who repaired to the prophet at this village was Salman al Parsi (or the Persian). He is said to have been a native of a small place near Ispahan, who, on passing one day by a Christian church, was so much struck by the devotion of the people and the solemnity of the worship that he became disgusted with the idolatrous faith in which he had been brought up. He afterwards wandered about the East, from city to city, and convent to convent, in quest of a religion, until an ancient monk, full of years and infirmities, told him of a prophet who had arisen in Arabia to restore the pure faith of Abraham.

This Salman rose to power in after years, and was reputed by the unbelievers of Mecca to have assisted Mohammed in compiling his doctrine. This is alluded to in the sixteenth chapter of the Koran: "Verily, the idolaters say, that a certain man assisted to compose the Koran; but the language of this man is Ajami (or Persian), and the Koran is indited in the pure Arabian tongue."[1]

The Moslems of Mecca, who had taken refuge some time before in Medina, hearing that Mohammed was at hand, came forth to meet him at Koba. Among these were the early convert Talha, and Zobeir, the nephew of Cadijah. These, seeing the travel-stained garments of Mohammed and Abu Beker, gave them white mantles with which to make their entrance into Medina. Numbers of the Ansarians, or auxiliaries, of Medina, who had made their compact with Mohammed in the preceding year, now hastened to renew their vow of fidelity.

Learning from them that the number of proselytes in the city was rapidly augmenting, and that there was a general disposition to receive him favorably, Mohammed appointed Friday, the Moslem sabbath, the sixteenth day of the month Rabi, for his public entrance.

Accordingly, on the morning of that day he assembled all his followers to prayer; and, after a sermon in which he expounded the main principles of his faith, he mounted his camel Al Kaswa and set forth for that city which was to become renowned in after ages as his city of refuge.

Boreida Ibn al Hoseib, with his seventy horsemen of the tribe of Saham, accompanied him as a guard. Some of the disciples took turns to hold a canopy of palm leaves over his head, and by his side rode Abu Beker. "O apostle of God!" cried Boreida, "thou shalt not enter Medina without a standard." So saying, he unfolded his turban, and tying one end of it to the point of his lance, bore it aloft before the prophet.

The city of Medina was fair to approach, being extolled for beauty of situation, salubrity of climate, and fertility of soil, for the luxuriance of its palm trees, and the fragrance of its shrubs and flowers. At a short distance from the city a crowd of new proselytes to the faith came forth in sun and dust to meet the cavalcade. Most of them had never seen Mohammed, and paid reverence to Abu Beker through mistake. But the latter put aside the screen of palm leaves,and pointed out the real object of homage, who was greeted with loud acclamations.

In this way did Mohammed, so recently a fugitive from his native city, with a price upon his head, enter Medina, more as a conqueror in triumph than an exile seeking an asylum. He alighted at the house of a Khazradite, named Abu Ayub, a devout Moslem, to whom moreover he was distantly related. Here he was hospitably received, and took up his abode in the basement story.

Shortly after his arrival he was joined by the faithful Ali, who had fled from Mecca and journeyed on foot, hiding himself in the day and travelling only at night, lest he should fall into the hands of the Koreishites. He arrived weary and wayworn, his feet bleeding with the roughness of the journey.

Within a few days more came Ayesha, and the rest of Abu Beker's household, together with the family of Mohammed, conducted by his faithful freedman Zeid, and by Abu Beker's servant Abdallah.

Such is the story of the memorable Hegira, or "Flight of the Prophet"—the era of the Arabian calendar from which time is calculated by all true Moslems. It corresponds to the 622d year of the Christian era.

14

*Moslems in Medina, Mohadjerins and Ansarians - The
party of Abdallah Ibn Obba and the Hypocrites -
Mohammed builds a mosque; preaches; makes converts
among the Christians - The Jews slow to believe -
Brotherhood established between fugitives and allies*

Mohammed soon found himself at the head of a numerous and
powerful sect in Medina, partly made up of those of his disciples
who had fled from Mecca, and were thence called Mohadjerins
or Fugitives, and partly of inhabitants of the place, who on
joining the faith were called Ansarians or Auxiliaries. Most of
these latter were of the powerful tribes of the Awsites and
Khazradites, which, though descended from two brothers, Al
Aws and Al Khazraj, had for a hundred and twenty years
distracted Medina by their inveterate and mortal feuds, but had
now become united in the bonds of faith. With such of these
tribes as did not immediately adopt his doctrines he made a
covenant.

The Khazradites were very much under the sway of a prince
or chief named Abdallah Ibn Obba, who, it is said, was on the
point of being made king, when the arrival of Mohammed and
the excitement caused by his doctrines gave the popular feeling a
new direction. Abdallah was stately in person, of a graceful
demeanor, and ready and eloquent tongue. He professed great
friendship for Mohammed and, with several companions of his
own type and character, used to attend the meetings of the
Moslems. Mohammed was captivated at first by their personal
appearance, their plausible conversation, and their apparent
deference. But he found in the end that Abdallah was jealous of
his popularity and cherished secret animosity against him, and
that his companions were equally false in their pretended

friendship; hence, he stamped them with the name of "The Hypocrites." Abdallah Ibn Obba long continued to be his political rival in Medina.

Being now enabled publicly to exercise his faith and preach his doctrines, Mohammed proceeded to erect a mosque. The place chosen was a graveyard or burying ground, shaded by date trees. He is said to have been guided in his choice by what he considered a favorable omen, his camel having knelt opposite to this place on his public entry into the city. The dead were removed, and the trees cut down to make way for the intended edifice. It was simple in form and structure, suited to the unostentatious religion which he professed and to the scanty and precarious means of its votaries. The walls were of earth and brick; the trunks of the palm trees recently felled served as pillars to support the roof, which was framed of their branches and thatched with their leaves. It was about a hundred ells square, and had three doors: one to the south, where the Kebla was afterwards established, another called the gate of Gabriel, and the third the gate of Mercy. A part of the edifice, called Soffat, was assigned as a habitation to such of the believers as were without a home.

Mohammed assisted with his own hands in the construction of this mosque. With all his foreknowledge, he little thought that he was building his own tomb and monument; for in that edifice his remains are deposited. It has in after times been repeatedly enlarged and beautified, but still bears the name Mesjed al Nebi (the Mosque of the Prophet), from having been founded by his hands. He was for some time at a loss in what manner his followers should be summoned to their devotions, whether with the sound of trumpets, as among the Jews, or by lighting fires on high places, or by the striking of timbrels. While he was in this perplexity, a form of words to be cried aloud was suggested by Abdallah, the son of Zeid, who declared that it was revealed to him in a vision. It was instantly adopted by Mohammed, and such is given as the origin of the following summons, which is to this day heard from the lofty minarets throughout the East, calling the Moslems to the place of worship: "God is great! God is great! There is no God but God. Mohammed is the apostle of God. Come to prayers! come to prayers! God is great! God is great! There is no God but God." To which at dawn of day is added the exhortation, "Prayer is better than sleep! Prayer is better than sleep!"

Everything in this humble mosque was at first conducted with great simplicity. At night it was lighted up by splinters of the date tree: and it was some time before lamps and oil were introduced. The prophet stood on the ground and preached, leaning with his back against the trunk of one of the date trees which served as pillars. He afterwards had a pulpit or tribune erected, to which he ascended by three steps, so as to be elevated above the congregation. Tradition asserts that when he first ascended this pulpit, the deserted date tree uttered a groan; whereupon, as a consolation, he gave it the choice either to be transplanted to a garden again to flourish, or to be transferred to paradise, there to yield fruit, in after life, to true believers. The date tree wisely chose the latter, and was subsequently buried beneath the pulpit, there to await its blissful resurrection.

Mohammed preached and prayed in the pulpit, sometimes sitting, sometimes standing and leaning on a staff. His precepts as yet were all peaceful and benignant, inculcating devotion to God and humanity to man. He seems to have emulated for a time the benignity of the Christian faith. "He who is not affectionate to God's creatures, and to his own children," he would say, "God will not be affectionate to him. Every Moslem who clothes the naked of his faith will be clothed by Allah in the green robes of paradise."

In one of his traditional sermons transmitted by his disciples is the following apologue on the subject of charity: "When God created the earth it shook and trembled, until he put mountains upon it, to make it firm. Then the angels asked, 'O God, is there anything of thy creation stronger than these mountains?' And God replied, 'Iron is stronger than the mountains, for it breaks them.' 'And is there anything of thy creation stronger than iron?' 'Yes; fire is stronger than iron, for it melts it.' 'Is there anything of thy creation stronger than fire?' 'Yes; water, for it quenches fire.' 'O Lord, is there anything of thy creation stronger than water?' 'Yes, wind; for it overcomes water and puts it in motion.' 'O, our Sustainer! is there anything of thy creation stronger than wind?' 'Yes, a good man giving alms; if he give with his right hand and conceal it from his left, he overcomes all things.'"

His definition of charity embraced the wide circle of kindness. Every good act, he would say, is charity. Your smiling in your brother's face is charity; an exhortation of your fellow man to virtuous deeds is equal to alms-giving; your putting a wanderer in the right road is charity; your assisting the blind is charity; your removing stones and thorns and other obstructions from the road is charity; your giving water to the thirsty is charity.

"A man's true wealth hereafter is the good he does in this world to his fellow man. When he dies, people will say, 'What property has he left behind him?' But the angels, who examine him in the grave, will ask, 'What good deeds hast thou sent before thee?'"

"O prophet!" said one of his disciples, "my mother Omm-Sad,is dead; what is the best alms I can send for the good of her soul?" "Water!" replied Mohammed, bethinking himself of the panting heats of the desert. "Dig a well for her, and give water to the thirsty." The man dug a well in his mother's name, and said "This well is for my mother, that its rewards may reach her soul."

Charity of the tongue, also, that most important and least cultivated of charities, was likewise earnestly inculcated by Mohammed. Abu Jaraiya, an inhabitant of Basrah, coming to Medina, and being persuaded of the apostolical office of Mohammed, entreated of him some great rule of conduct. "Speak evil of no one," answered the prophet. "From that time," says Abu Jaraiya, "I never did abuse any one, whether freeman or slave."

The rules of Islam extended to the courtesies of life. Make a salam (or salutation) to a house on entering and leaving it. Return the salute of friends and acquaintances, and wayfarers on the road. He who rides must be the first to make the salute to him who walks; he who walks to him who is sitting; a small party to a large party, and the young to the old.

On the arrival of Mohammed at Medina, some of the Christians of the city promptly enrolled themselves among his followers. They were probably of those sectarians who held to the human nature of Christ, and found nothing repugnant in Islam, which venerated Christ as the greatest among the prophets. The rest of the Christians resident there showed but little hostility to the new faith, considering it far better than the old idolatry. Indeed, the schisms and bitter dissensions among the Christians of the East had impaired their orthodoxy, weakened their zeal, and disposed them easily to be led away by new doctrines.

The Jews, of which there were rich and powerful families in Medina and its vicinity, showed a less favorable disposition. With some of them Mohammed made covenants of peace, and trusted to gain them in time to accept him as their promised Messiah or prophet. Biased, perhaps unconsciously, by such views, he had modeled many of his doctrines on the dogmas of their religion, and observed certain of their fasts and ordinances. He allowed such as embraced Islamism to continue in the observance of their Sabbath, and of several of the Mosaic laws and ceremonies. It was the custom of the different religions of the East to have each a Kebla or sacred point towards which they turned their faces in the act of adoration: the Sabeans toward the North Star; the Persian fire-worshippers towards the east, the place of the rising sun; the Jews toward their holy city of Jerusalem. Hitherto Mohammed had prescribed nothing of the kind; but now, out of deference to the Jews, he made Jerusalem the Kebla toward which all Moslems were to turn their faces when in prayer.

While new converts were daily made among the inhabitants of Medina, sickness and discontent began to prevail among the fugitives from Mecca. They were not accustomed to the climate; many suffered from fevers, and in their sickness and debility languished after the home whence they were exiled.

To give them a new home, and link them closely with their new friends and allies, Mohammed established a brotherhood between fifty-four of them and as many of the inhabitants of Medina. Two persons thus linked together were pledged to stand by each other in weal and woe. It was a tie which knit their interests more closely even than that of kindred, for they were to be heirs to each other in preference to blood relations.

This institution was one of expediency, and lasted only until the newcomers had taken firm root in Medina; extended merely to those of the people of Mecca who had fled from persecution; and is alluded to in the following verse of the eighth chapter of the Koran: "They who have believed and have fled their country, and employed their substance and their persons in fighting for the faith, and they who have given the prophet a refuge among them, and have assisted him, these shall be deemed the one nearest of kin to the other."

15

Marriage of Mohammed with Ayesha - Of his daughter
Fatima with Ali - Their household arrangements

The family relations of Mohammed had been much broken up
by the hostility brought upon him by his religious zeal. His
daughter Rokaia was still an exile with her husband, Othman
Ibn Aman, in Abyssinia; his daughter Zeinab had remained in
Mecca with her husband, Abul Aass, who was a stubborn opposer
of the new faith. The family with Mohammed in Medina
consisted of his recently wedded wife Sawda, and Fatima and
Um Colthum, daughters of his late wife Cadijah. He had a heart
prone to affection, and subject to female influence, but he had
never entertained much love for Sawda; and though he always
treated her with kindness, he felt the want of some one to supply
the place of his deceased wife Cadijah.

"O Omar," said he one day, "the best of man's treasures is a
virtuous woman, who acts by God's orders, and is obedient and
pleasing to her husband: he regards her personal and mental
beauties with delight; when he orders her to do anything she
obeys him; and when he is absent she guards his right in
property and honor."

He now turned his eyes upon his betrothed spouse Ayesha, the
beautiful daughter of Abu Beker. Two years had elapsed since
they were betrothed, and she had now attained her ninth year;
an infantine age it would seem, though the female form is
wonderfully precocious in the quickening climates of the East.
Their nuptials took place a few mouths after their arrival in
Medina, and were celebrated with great simplicity; the wedding
supper was of milk, and the dowry of the bride was twelve okes of
silver.

The betrothing of Fatima, his youngest daughter, with his loyal disciple Ali followed shortly after, and their marriage at a somewhat later period. Fatima was between fifteen and sixteen years of age, of great beauty, and extolled by Arabian writers as one of the four perfect women with whom Allah has deigned to bless the earth. The age of Ali was about twenty-two.

Heaven and earth, say the Moslem writers, joined in paying honor to these happy espousals. Medina resounded with festivity, and blazed with illuminations, and the atmosphere was laden with aromatic odors. As Mohammed, on the nuptial night, conducted his daughter to her bride room, heaven sent down a celestial pomp to attend her. On her right hand was the archangel Gabriel; on her left was Michael, and she was followed by a train of seventy thousand angels, who all night kept watch round the mansion of the youthful pair.

Such are the vaunting exaggerations with which Moslem writers are prone to overlay every event in the history of the prophet, and destroy the real grandeur of his career, which consists in its simplicity. A more reliable account states that the wedding feast was of dates and olives; that the nuptial couch was a sheepskin; that the portion of the bride consisted of two skirts, one headdress, two silver armlets, one leathern pillow stuffed with palm leaves, one beaker or drinking cup, one handmill, two large jars for water, and one pitcher. All this was in unison with the simplicity of Arab housekeeping, and with the circumstances of the married couple; and to raise the dowry required of him, Ali, it is said, had to sell several camels and some shirts of mail.

The style of living of the prophet himself was not superior to that of his disciple. Ayesha, speaking of it in after years, observed: "For a whole month together we did not light a fire to dress victuals; our food was nothing but dates and water, unless anyone sent us meat. The people of the prophet's household never got wheatbread two successive days."

His food, in general, was dates and barley bread, with milk and honey. He swept his chamber, lit his fire, mended his clothes, and was in fact his own servant. For each of his two wives he provided a separate house adjoining the mosque. He resided with them by turns, but Ayesha ever remained his favorite.

Mohammed has been extolled by Moslem writers for the chastity of his early life; and it is remarkable that, with all the plurality of wives indulged in by the Arabs, and which he permitted himself in subsequent years, and with all that constitutional fondness which he evinced for the sex, he remained single in his devotion to Cadijah to her dying day, never giving her a rival in his house, nor in his heart. Even the fresh and budding charms of Ayesha, which soon assumed such empire over him, could not obliterate the deep and mingled feeling of tenderness and gratitude for his early benefactress. Ayesha was piqued one day at hearing him indulge in these fond recollections: "O, apostle of God," demanded the youthful beauty, "was not Cadijah stricken in years? Has not Allah given thee a better wife in her stead?"

"Never!" exclaimed Mohammed, with an honest burst of feeling— "never did God give me a better! When I was poor, she enriched me; when I was pronounced a liar, she believed in me; when I was opposed by all the world, she remained true to me!"

16

The sword announced as the instrument of faith - First foray against the Koreishites - Surprisal of a caravan

We come now to an important era in the career of Mohammed. Hitherto he had relied on argument and persuasion to make proselytes, enjoining the same on his disciples. His exhortations to them to bear with patience and long suffering the violence of their enemies almost emulated the meek precept of our Saviour: "If they smite thee on the one cheek, turn to them the other also." He now arrived at a point where he completely diverged from the celestial spirit of the Christian doctrines, and stamped his religion with the alloy of fallible mortality. His human nature was not capable of maintaining the sublime forbearance he had hitherto inculcated. Thirteen years of meek endurance had been rewarded by nothing but aggravated injury and insult. His greatest persecutors had been those of his own tribe, the Koreishites, especially those of the rival line of Abd Schems, whose vindictive chief, Abu Sofian, had now the sway at Mecca. By their virulent hostility his fortunes had been blasted, his family degraded, impoverished and dispersed, and he himself driven into exile. All this he might have continued to bear with involuntary meekness, had not the means of retaliation unexpectedly sprung up within his reach. He had come to Medina a fugitive seeking an asylum, and craving merely a quiet home. In a little while, and probably to his own surprise, he found an army at his command: for among the many converts daily made in Medina, the fugitives flocking to him from Mecca, and proselytes from the tribes of the desert, were men of resolute spirit, skilled in the use of arms, and fond of partisan warfare. Human passions and mortal resentments were awakened by this sudden accession of power. They mingled with that zeal for religious reform, which was still his predominant motive. In the exaltations of his enthusiastic spirit he endeavored to persuade himself, and perhaps did so effectually, that the power thus placed within his reach was intended as a means of effecting his great purpose, and that he was called upon by divine command to use it. Such, at least, is the purport of the memorable manifesto which he issued at this epoch, and which changed the whole tone and fortunes of his faith.

"Different prophets," said he, "have been sent by God to illustrate his different attributes: Moses his clemency and providence; Solomon his wisdom, majesty, and glory; Jesus Christ his righteousness, omniscience, and power—his righteousness by purity of conduct, his omniscience by the knowledge he displayed of the secrets of all hearts, his power by the miracles he wrought. None of these attributes, however, have been sufficient to enforce conviction, and even the miracles of Moses and Jesus have been treated with unbelief. I, therefore, the last of the prophets, am sent with the sword! Let those who promulgate my faith enter into no argument nor discussion; but slay all who refuse obedience to the law. Whoever fights for the true faith, whether he fall or conquer, will assuredly receive a glorious reward."

"The sword," he added, "is the key of heaven and hell; all who draw it in the cause of the faith will be rewarded with temporal advantages; every drop shed of their blood, every peril and hardship endured by them, will be registered on high as more meritorious than even fasting and praying. If they fall in battle, their sins will at once be blotted out, and they will be transported to paradise, there to revel in eternal pleasures in the arms of black-eyed houris."

Predestination was brought to aid these belligerent doctrines. Every event, according to the Koran, was predestined from eternity, and could not be avoided. No man could die sooner or later than his allotted hour, and when it arrived, it would be the same, whether the angel of death should find him in the quiet of his bed, or amid the storm of battle.

Such were the doctrines and revelations which converted Islam of a sudden from a religion of meekness and philanthropy to one of violence and the sword. They were peculiarly acceptable to the Arabs, harmonizing with their habits and encouraging their predatory propensities. As they were virtually pirates of the desert, it is not to be wondered at that, after this open promulgation of the Religion of the Sword, they should flock in crowds to the standard of the prophet. Still no violence was authorized by Mohammed against those who should persist in unbelief provided they should readily submit to his temporal sway, and agree to pay tribute; and here we see the first indication of worldly ambition and a desire for temporal dominion dawning upon his mind. Still it will be found that the tribute thus exacted was subsidiary to his ruling passion, and mainly expended by him in the extension of the faith.

The first warlike enterprises of Mohammed betray the lurking resentment we have noted. They were directed against the caravans of Mecca belonging to his implacable enemies the Koreishites. The three first were headed by Mohammed in person, but without any material result. The fourth was confided to a Moslem named Abdallah Ibn Jasch, who was sent out with eight or ten resolute followers on the road toward South Arabia. As it was now the holy month of Radjab, sacred from violence and rapine, Abdallah had sealed orders, not to be opened until the third day. These orders were vaguely yet significantly worded. Abdallah was to repair to the valley of Naklah, between Mecca and Tayef (the same in which Mohammed had the revelation of the Genii), where he was to watch for an expected caravan of the Koreishites. "Perhaps," added the letter of instructions shrewdly,— "perhaps thou mayest be able to bring us some tidings of it."

Abdallah understood the true meaning of the letter, and acted up to it. Arriving in the valley of Naklah, he descried the caravan, consisting of several camels laden with merchandise, and conducted by four men. Following it at a distance, he sent one of his men, disguised as a pilgrim, to overtake it. From the words of the latter the Koreishites supposed his companions to be like himself, pilgrims bound to Mecca. Besides, it was the month of Radjab, when the desert might be travelled in security. Scarce had they come to a halt, however, when Abdallah and his comrades fell on them. They killed one and took two prisoners; the fourth escaped. The victors then returned to Medina with their prisoners and booty.

All Medina was scandalized at this breach of the holy month. Mohammed, finding that he had ventured too far, pretended to be angry with Abdallah, and refused to take the share of the booty offered to him. Confiding in the vagueness of his instructions, he insisted that he had not commanded Abdallah to shed blood, or commit any violence during the holy month.

The clamor still continuing, and being echoed by the Koreishites of Mecca, produced the following passage of the Koran:

"They will ask thee concerning the sacred month, whether they may make war therein. Answer: To war therein is grievous; but to deny God, to bar the path of God against his people, to drive true believers from his holy temple, and to worship idols, are sins far more grievous than to kill in the holy months."

Having thus proclaimed divine sanction for the deed, Mohammed no longer hesitated to take his share of the booty. He delivered one of the prisoners on ransom; the other embraced Islam.

The above passage of the Koran, however satisfactory it may have been to devout Moslems, will scarcely serve to exculpate their prophet in the eyes of the profane. The expedition of Abdallah Ibn Jasch was a sad practical illustration of the new religion of the sword. It contemplated not merely an act of plunder and revenge, a venial act in the eyes of Arabs, and justified by the new doctrines by being exercised against the enemies of the faith, but an outrage also on the holy month, that period sacred from time immemorial against violence and bloodshed, and which Mohammed himself professed to hold in reverence. The craft and secrecy also with which the whole was devised and conducted, the sealed letter of instructions to Abdallah, to be opened only at the end of three days, at the scene of projected outrage, and couched in language vague, equivocal, yet sufficiently significant to the agent—all were in direct opposition to the conduct of Mohammed in the earlier part of his career, when he dared openly to pursue the path of duty, "though the sun should be arrayed against him on the right hand, and the moon on the left;" all showed that he was conscious of the turpitude of the act he was authorizing. His disavowal of the violence committed by Abdallah, yet his bringing the Koran to his aid to enable him to profit by it with impunity, give still darker shades to this transaction, which altogether shows how immediately and widely he went wrong the moment he departed from the benevolent spirit of Christianity, which he at first endeavored to emulate. Worldly passions and worldly interests

were fast getting the ascendency over that religious enthusiasm
which first inspired him. As has well been observed, the "first
drop of blood shed in his name in the Holy Week displayed him
a man in whom the slime of earth had quenched the holy flame
of prophecy."

17

The Battle of Beder

In the second year of the Hegira, Mohammed received intelligence that his arch foe, Abu Sofian, with a troop of thirty horsemen, was conducting back to Mecca a caravan of a thousand camels, laden with the merchandise of Syria. Their route lay through the country of Medina, between the range of mountains and the sea. Mohammed determined to intercept them. About the middle of the month Ramadhan, therefore, he sallied forth with three hundred and fourteen men, of whom eighty-three were Mohadjerins, or exiles from Mecca, sixty-one Awsites, and a hundred and seventy Khazradites. Each troop had its own banner. There were but two horses in this little army,[1] but there were seventy fleet camels, which the troop mounted by turns, so as to make a rapid march without much fatigue.

Othman Ibn Affan, the son-in-law of Mohammed, was now returned with his wife Rokaia from their exile in Abyssinia, and would have joined the enterprise, but his wife was ill almost unto death, so that he was obliged reluctantly to remain in Medina.

Mohammed for a while took the main road to Mecca, then leaving it to the left, turned toward the Red Sea and entered a fertile valley, watered by the brook Beder. Here he lay in wait near a ford, over which the caravans were accustomed to pass. He caused his men to dig a deep trench, and to divert the water therein, so that they might resort thither to slake their thirst, out of reach of the enemy.

In the meantime Abu Sofian, having received early intelligence that Mohammed had sallied forth to waylay him with a superior force, despatched a messenger named Omair, on a fleet dromedary, to summon instant relief from Mecca.

The messenger arrived at the Caaba haggard and breathless. Abu Jahl mounted the roof and sounded the alarm. All Mecca was in confusion and consternation. Henda, the wife of Abu Sofian, a woman of a fierce and intrepid nature, called upon her father Otha, her brother Al Walid, her uncle Shaiba, and all the warriors of her kindred, to arm and hasten to the relief of her husband. The brothers, too, of the Koreishite slain by Abdallah Ibn Jasch, in the valley of Naklah, seized their weapons to avenge his death. Motives of interest were mingled with eagerness for vengeance, for most of the Koreishites had property embarked in the caravan. In a little while a force of one hundred horse and seven hundred camels hurried forward on the road toward Syria. It was led by Abu Jahl, now threescore and ten years of age, a veteran warrior of the desert, who still retained the fire, and almost the vigor and activity of youth, combined with the rancor of old age.

While Abu Jahl, with his forces, was hurrying on in one direction, Abu Sofian was approaching in another. On arriving at the region of danger, he preceded his caravan a considerable distance, carefully regarding every track and footprint. At length he came upon the track of the little army of Mohammed. He knew it from the size of the kernels of the dates, which the troops had thrown by the wayside as they marched—those of Medina being remarkable for their smallness. On such minute signs do the Arabs depend in tracking their foes through the deserts.

Observing the course Mohammed had taken, Abu Sofian changed his route, and passed along the coast of the Red Sea until he considered himself out of danger. He then sent another messenger to meet any Koreishites that might have sallied forth, and to let them know that the caravan was safe, and they might return to Mecca.

The messenger met the Koreishites when in full march. On hearing that the caravan was safe, they came to a halt and held council. Some were for pushing forward and inflicting a signal punishment on Mohammed and his followers; others were for turning back. In this dilemma, they sent a scout to reconnoiter the enemy. He brought back word that they were about three hundred strong; this increased the desire of those who were for battle. Others remonstrated. "Consider," they said, "these are men who have nothing to lose; they have nothing but their swords; not one of them will fall without slaying his man. Beside, we have relatives among them; if we conquer, we will not be able to look each other in the face, having slain each other's relatives." These words were producing their effect, but the brothers of the Koreishite who had been slain in the valley of Naklah, were instigated by Abu Jahl to cry for revenge. That fiery old Arab seconded their appeal. "Forward!" he cried; "let us get water from the brook Beder for the feast with which we shall make merry over the escape of our caravan." The main body of the troops, therefore, elevated their standards and resumed their march, though a considerable number turned back to Mecca.

The scouts of Mohammed brought him notice of the approach of this force. The hearts of some of his followers failed them; they had come forth in the expectation of little fighting and much plunder, and were dismayed at the thoughts of such an overwhelming host. But Mohammed bade them be of good cheer, for Allah had promised him an easy victory.

The Moslems posted themselves on a rising ground, with water at the foot of it. A hut, or shelter of the branches of trees, had been hastily erected on the summit for Mohammed, and a dromedary stood before it, on which he might fly to Medina in case of defeat.

The vanguard of the enemy entered the valley panting with thirst, and hastened to the stream to drink; but Hamza, the uncle of Mohammed, set upon them with a number of his men, and slew the leader with his own hand. Only one of the vanguard escaped, who was afterwards converted to the faith.

The main body of the enemy now approached with sound of trumpet. Three Koreishite warriors advancing in front defied the bravest of the Moslems to equal combat. Two of these challengers were Otha, the father-in-law of Abu Sofian, and Al Walid, his brother-in-law. The third challenger was Shaiba, the brother of Otha. These it will be recollected had been instigated to sally forth from Mecca by Henda, the wife of Abu Sofian. They were all men of rank in their tribe.

Three warriors of Medina stepped forward and accepted their challenge; but they cried, "No! Let the renegades of our own city of Mecca advance, if they dare." Upon this Hamza and Ali, the uncle and cousin of Mohammed, and Obeidah Ibn al Hareth undertook the fight. After a fierce and obstinate contest, Hamza and Ali each slew his antagonist. They then went to the aid of Obeidah, who was severely wounded and nearly overcome by Otha. They slew the Koreishite and bore away their associate, but he presently died of his wounds.

The battle now became general. The Moslems, aware of the inferiority of their number, at first merely stood on the defensive, maintaining their position on the rising ground, and galling the enemy with flights of arrows whenever they sought to slake their intolerable thirst at the stream below. Mohammed remained in his hut on the hill, accompanied by Abu Beker, and earnestly engaged in prayer. In the course of the battle he had a paroxysm, or fell into a kind of trance. Coming to himself, he declared that God in a vision had promised him the victory. Rushing out of the hut, he caught up a handful of dust and cast it into the air toward the Koreishites, exclaiming, "May confusion light upon their faces." Then ordering his followers to charge down upon the enemy: "Fight, and fear not," he cried; "the gates of paradise are under the shade of swords. He will assuredly find instant admission, who falls fighting for the faith."

In the shock of battle which ensued, Abu Jahl, who was urging his horse into the thickest of the conflict, received a blow of a scimitar in the thigh, which brought him to the ground. Abdallah Ibn Masoud put his foot upon his breast, and while the fiery veteran was still uttering imprecations and curses on Mohammed, severed his head from his body.

The Koreishites now gave way and fled. Seventy remained dead on the field, and nearly the same number were taken prisoners. Fourteen Moslems were slain, whose names remain on record as martyrs to the faith.

This signal victory was easily to be accounted for on natural principles, the Moslems being fresh and unwearied, and having the advantage of a rising ground and a supply of water, while the Koreishites were fatigued by a hasty march, parched with thirst, and diminished in force by the loss of numbers who had turned back to Mecca. Moslem writers, however, attribute this early triumph of the faith to supernatural agency. When Mohammed scattered dust in the air, they say, three thousand angelic warriors in white and yellow turbans, and long dazzling robes, and mounted on black and white steeds, came rushing like a blast, and swept the Koreishites before them. Nor is this affirmed on Moslem testimony alone, but given on the word of an idolater, a peasant who was attending sheep on an adjacent hill. "I was with a companion, my cousin," said the peasant, "upon the fold of the mountain watching the conflict, and waiting to join with the conquerors and share the spoil. Suddenly, we beheld a great cloud sailing toward us, and within it were the neighing of steeds and the braying of trumpets. As it approached, squadrons of angels sallied forth, and we heard the terrific voice of the archangel as he urged his mare Haizum, 'Speed! speed! O Haizum!' At which awful sound the heart of my companion burst with terror, and he died on the spot; and I had well nigh shared his fate."[2]

When the conflict was over, Abdallah Ibn Masoud brought the head of Abu Jahl to Mohammed, who eyed the grisly trophy with exultation, exclaiming, " This man was the Pharaoh of our nation." The true name of this veteran warrior was Amru Ibn Hasham. The Koreishites had given him the surname of Abu 'lhoem, or Father of Wisdom, on account of his sagacity. The Moslems had changed it to Abu Jahl, Father of Folly. The latter appellation has adhered to him in history, and he is never mentioned by true believers without the ejaculation, "May he be accursed of God."

The Moslems who had fallen in battle were honorably interred. As to the bodies of the Koreishites, they were contemptuously thrown into a pit which had been dug for them. The question was how to dispose of the prisoners. Omar was for striking off their heads, but Abu Beker advised that they should be given up on ransom. Mohammed observed that Omar was like Noah, who prayed for the destruction of the guilty by the deluge; but Abu Beker was like Abraham, who interceded for the guilty. He decided on the side of mercy. But two of the prisoners were put to death: one, named Nadhar, for having ridiculed the Koran as a collection of Persian tales and fables; the other, named Okba, for the attempt upon the life of Mohammed when he first preached in the Caaba, and when he was rescued by Abu Beker. Several of the prisoners who were poor were liberated on merely taking an oath never again to take up arms against Mohammed or his followers. The rest were detained until ransoms should be sent by their friends.

Among the most important of the prisoners, was Al Abbas, the uncle of Mohammed. He had been captured by Abu Yaser, a man of small stature. As the bystanders scoffed at the disparity of size, Al Abbas pretended that he really had surrendered to a horseman of gigantic size, mounted on a steed the like of which he had never seen before. Abu Yaser would have steadily maintained the truth of his capture, but Mohammed, willing to spare the humiliation of his uncle, intimated that the captor had been aided by the angel Gabriel.

Al Abbas would have excused himself from paying ransom, alleging that he was a Moslem in heart, and had only taken part in the battle on compulsion; but his excuse did not avail. It is thought by many that he really had a secret understanding with his nephew, and was employed by him as a spy in Mecca, both before and after the battle of Beder.

Another prisoner of great importance to Mohammed was Abul Aass, the husband of his daughter Zeinab. The prophet would fain have drawn his son-in-law to him and enrolled him among his disciples, but Abul Aass remained stubborn in unbelief. Mohammed then offered to set him at liberty on condition of his returning to him his daughter. To this the infidel agreed, and Zeid, the faithful freedman of the prophet, was sent with several companions to Mecca, to bring Zeinab to Medina. In the meantime, her husband Abul Aass, remained a hostage for the fulfillment of the compact.

Before the army returned to Medina there was a division of the spoils; for, though the caravan of Abu Sofian had escaped, yet considerable booty of weapons and camels had been taken in the battle, and a large sum of money would accrue from the ransom of the prisoners. On this occasion Mohammed ordered that the whole should be equally divided among all the Moslems engaged in the enterprise, and though it was a long-established custom among the Arabs to give a fourth part of the booty to the chief, yet he contented himself with the same share as the rest. Among the spoils which fell to his lot was a famous sword of admirable temper, called Dhul Fakar, or the Piercer. He ever afterwards bore it when in battle, and his son-in-law Ali inherited it at his death.

This equal distribution of the booty caused great murmurs among the troops. Those who had borne the brunt of the fight, and had been most active in taking the spoils, complained that they had to share alike with those who had stood aloof from the affray, and with the old men who had remained to guard the camp. The dispute, observes Sale,[3] resembles that of the soldiers of David in relation to spoils taken from the Amalekites, those who had been in the action insisting that they who tarried by the stuff should have no share of the spoil. The decision was the same—that they should share alike (1 Samuel, xxx, 21-25).

Mohammed, from his knowledge of Bible history, may have been guided by this decision. The division of the spoils was an important point to settle for a leader about to enter on a career of predatory warfare. Fortunately, he had a timely revelation shortly after his return to Mecca, regulating for the future the division of all booty gained in fighting for the faith.

Such are the particulars of the famous battle of Beder, the first victory of the Saracens under the standard of Mohammed; inconsiderable, perhaps, in itself, but stupendous in its results, being the commencement of a career of victories which changed the destinies of the world.

18

*Death of the prophet's daughter Rokaia - Restoration of
his daughter Zeinab - Effect of the prophet's malediction
on Abu Lahab and his family - Frantic rage of Henda,
the wife of Abu Sofian - Mohammed narrowly escapes
assassination - Embassy of the Koreishites - The king of
Abyssinia*

Mohammed returned in triumph to Medina with the spoils and
prisoners taken in his first battle. His exultation, however, was
checked by domestic grief. Rokaia, his beloved daughter, so
recently restored from exile, was no more. The messenger who
preceded Mohammed with tidings of his victory met the funeral
train at the gate of the city, bearing her body to the tomb.

The affliction of the prophet was soothed shortly afterward
by the arrival from Mecca of his daughter Zeinab, conducted by
the faithful Zeid. The mission of Zeid had been attended with
difficulties. The people of Mecca were exasperated by the late
defeat, and the necessity of ransoming the prisoners. Zeid
remained, therefore, without the walls, and sent in a message to
Kenanah, the brother of Abul Aass, informing him of the
compact, and appointing a place where Zeinab should be
delivered into his hands. Kenanah set out to conduct her there
in a litter. On the way he was beset by a throng of Koreishites,
determined to prevent the daughter of Mohammed from being
restored to him. In the confusion one Habbar Ibn Aswad made a
thrust at the litter with a lance, which, had not Kenanah parried
it with his bow, might have proved fatal to Zeinab. Abu Sofian
was attracted to the place by the noise and tumult, and rebuked
Kenanah for restoring Mohammed's daughter thus publicly, as
it might be construed into a weak concession. Zeinab was taken

back, therefore, to her home, and Kenanah delivered her up secretly to Zeid in the course of the following night.

Mohammed was so exasperated at hearing of the attack on his daughter that he ordered whoever should take Habbar to burn him alive. When his rage had subsided he modified this command. "It is for God alone," said he, " to punish man with fire. If taken, let Habbar be put to death with the sword."

The recent triumph of the Moslems at Beder struck the Koreishites of Mecca with astonishment and mortification. The man so recently driven a fugitive from their walls had suddenly started up a powerful foe. Several of their bravest and most important men had fallen beneath his sword; others were his captives, and awaited a humiliating ransom. Abu Lahab, the uncle of Mohammed, and always his vehement opposer, had been unable, from illness, to take the field. He died a few days after hearing of the victory, his death being hastened by the exasperation of his spirits. Pious Moslems, however, attribute it to the curse pronounced previously by Mohammed on him and his family, when he raised his hand to hurl a stone at the prophet on the hill of Safa. That curse, they say, fell heavily also on his son Otho, who had repudiated the prophet's daughter Rokaia; he was torn to pieces by a lion, in the presence of a whole caravan, when on a journey to Syria.

By no one was the recent defeat at Beder felt so severely as by Abu Sofian. He reached Mecca in safety with his caravan, it is true; but it was to hear of the triumph of the man he detested, and to find his home desolate. His wife Henda met him with frantic lamentations for the death of her father, her uncle, and her brother. Rage mingled with her grief, and she cried night and day for vengeance on Hamza and Ali, by whose hands they had fallen.[1]

Abu Sofian summoned two hundred fleet horsemen, each with a sack of meal at his saddle-bow, the scanty provisions of an Arab for a foray; as he sallied forth he vowed neither to anoint his head, perfume his beard, nor approach a female, until he had met Mohammed face to face. Scouring the country to within three miles of the gates of Medina, he slew two of the prophet's followers, ravaged the fields, and burned the date trees.

Mohammed sallied forth to meet him at the head of a superior force. Abu Sofian, regardless of his vow, did not wait his approach, but turned bridle and fled. His troop clattered after him, throwing off their sacks of meal in the hurry of their flight; whence this scampering affair was derisively called "the war of the meal sacks."

Moslem writers record an imminent risk of the prophet, while yet in the field on this occasion. He was one day sleeping alone at the foot of a tree, at a distance from his camp, when he was awakened by a noise, and beheld Durthur, a hostile warrior, standing over him with a drawn sword. "O Mohammed," he cried, "who is there now to save thee?" "God!" replied the prophet. Struck with conviction, Durthur let fall his sword, which was instantly seized upon by Mohammed. Brandishing the weapon, he exclaimed in turn, "Who is there now to save thee, O Durthur?" "Alas, no one!" replied the soldier. "Then learn from me to be merciful." So saying, he returned the sword. The heart of the warrior was overcome; he acknowledged Mohammed as the prophet of God, and embraced the faith.

As if the anecdote were not sufficiently marvelous, other devout Moslems affirm that the deliverance of Mohammed was through the intervention of the angel Gabriel, who, at the moment Durthur was about to strike, gave him a blow on the breast with his invisible hand, which caused him to let fall his sword.

About this time the Koreishites of Mecca bethought themselves of the relatives and disciples of Mohammed who had taken refuge from their persecutions in Abyssinia, most of whom still remained there under the protection of the Najashee or Abyssinian king. To this potentate the Koreishites sent an embassy to obtain the persons of the fugitives. One of the ambassadors was Abdallah Ibn Rabia; another was Amru Ibn Al Aass, the distinguished poet who had assailed Mohammed at the outset of his mission with lampoons and madrigals. He was now more matured in years, and as remarkable for his acute sagacity as for his poetic talents. He was still a redoubtable opponent of the faith of Islam, of which in after years he was to prove one of the bravest and most distinguished champions.

Amru and Abdallah opened their embassy in the oriental style by the parade of rich presents, and then requested, in the name of the Koreish authorities of Mecca, that the fugitives might be delivered up to them. The king was a just man, and summoned the Moslems before him to explain this new and dangerous heresy of which they were accused. Among their number was Giafar, or Jaafar, the son of Abu Taleb and brother of Ali, consequently the cousin of Mohammed. He was a man of persuasive eloquence and a most prepossessing appearance. He stood forth on this occasion, and expounded the doctrines of Islam with zeal and power. The king, who, as has been observed, was a Nestorian Christian, found these doctrines so similar in many respects to those of his sect, and so opposed to the gross idolatry of the Koreishites, that, so far from giving up the fugitives, he took them more especially into favor and protection and, returning to Amru and Abdallah the presents they had brought, dismissed them from his court.

19

Growing power of Mohammed - His resentment against the Jews - Insult to an Arab damsel by the Jewish tribes of Kainoka - A tumult - The Beni Kainoka take refuge in their castle - Subdued and punished by confiscation and banishment - Marriage of Othman to the prophet's daughter Omm Kolthum, and of the prophet to Hafza

The battle of Beder had completely changed the position of Mohammed; he was now a triumphant chief of a growing power. The idolatrous tribes of Arabia were easily converted to a faith which flattered their predatory inclinations with the hope of spoil, and which, after all, professed but to bring them back to the primitive religion of their ancestors. The first cavalcade, therefore, which entered the gates of Medina with the plunder of a camp made converts of almost all its heathen inhabitants, and gave Mohammed the control of the city. His own tone now became altered, and he spoke as a lawgiver and a sovereign. The first evidence of this change of feeling was in his treatment of the Jews, of whom there were three principal and powerful families in Medina.

All the concessions made by him to that stiff-necked race had proved fruitless; they not only remained stubborn in unbelief, but treated him and his doctrines with ridicule. Assma, the daughter of Merwân, a Jewish poetess, wrote satires against him. She was put to death by one of his fanatic disciples. Abu Afak, an Israelite, one hundred and twenty years of age, was likewise slain for indulging in satire against the prophet. Kaab Ibn Aschraf, another Jewish poet, repaired to Mecca after the battle of Beder, and endeavored to stir up the Koreishites to vengeance, reciting verses in which he extolled the virtues and bewailed the death of those of their tribe who had fallen in the battle. Such was his infatuation, that he recited these verses in public, on his return to Medina, and in the presence of some of the prophet's adherents who were related to the slain. Stung by this invidious hostility, Mohammed one day exclaimed in his anger, "Who will rid me of this son of Aschraf?" Within a few days afterwards, Kaab paid for his poetry with his life, being slain by a zealous Ansarian of the Awsite tribe.

An event at length occurred which caused the anger of Mohammed against the Jews to break out in open hostility. A damsel of one of the pastoral tribes of Arabs who brought milk to the city was one day in the quarter inhabited by the Beni Kainoka, or children of Kainoka, one of the three principal Jewish families. Here she was accosted by a number of young Israelites who, having heard her beauty extolled, besought her to uncover her face. The damsel refused an act contrary to the laws of propriety among her people. A young goldsmith, whose shop was hard by, secretly fastened the end of her veil to the bench on which she was sitting, so that when she rose to depart the garment remained, and her face was exposed to view. Upon this there was laughter and scoffing among the young Israelites, and the damsel stood in the midst confounded and abashed. A Moslem who was present, resenting the shame put upon her, drew his sword and thrust it through the body of the goldsmith; he in his turn was instantly slain by the Israelites. The Moslems from a neighboring quarter flew to arms; the Beni Kainoka did the same, but being inferior in numbers, took refuge in a stronghold. Mohammed interfered to quell the tumult; but, being generally exasperated against the Israelites, insisted that the offending tribe should forthwith embrace the faith. They pleaded the treaty which he had made with them on his coming to Medina, by which they were allowed the enjoyment of their religion; but he was not to be moved. For some time the Beni Kainoka refused to yield, and remained obstinately shut up in their stronghold; but famine compelled them to surrender. Abdallah Ibn Obba Solul, the leader of the Khazradites, who was a protector of this Jewish tribe, interfered in their favor, and prevented their being put to the sword; but their wealth and effects were confiscated, and they were banished to Syria, to the number of seven hundred men.

The arms and riches accruing to the prophet and his followers from this confiscation were of great avail in the ensuing wars of the faith. Among the weapons which fell to the share of Mohammed are enumerated three swords: Medham, the Keen; al Battar, the Trenchant; and Hatef, the Deadly. Two lances: al Monthari, the Disperser; and al Monthawi, the Destroyer. A cuirass of silver, named al Fadha; and another named al Saadia, said to have been given by Saul to David, when he was about to encounter Goliath. There was a bow, too, called al Catûm, or the Strong; but it did not answer to its name for, in the first battle in which the prophet used it, he drew it with such force that he broke it in pieces. In general, he used the Arabian kind of bow, with appropriate arrows and lances, and forbade his followers to use those of Persia.

Mohammed now sought no longer to conciliate the Jews; on the contrary, they became objects of his religious hostility. He revoked the regulation by which he had made Jerusalem the Kebla or point of prayer, and established Mecca in its place— towards which, ever since, the Moslems turn their faces when performing their devotions.

The death of the prophet's daughter Rokaia had been properly deplored by her husband Othman. To console the latter for his loss, Omar, his brother in arms, offered him, in the course of the year, his daughter Hafza for wife. She was the widow of Hobash, a Suhamite, eighteen years of age, and of tempting beauty, yet Othman declined the match. Omar was indignant at what he conceived a slight to his daughter and to himself, and complained of it to Mohammed. "Be not grieved, Omar," replied the prophet, "a better wife is destined for Othman, and a better husband for thy daughter." He in effect gave his own daughter Omm Kolthum to Othman; and took the fair Hafza to wife himself. By these politic alliances he grappled both Othman and Omar more strongly to his side, while he gratified his own inclinations for female beauty. Hafza, next to Ayesha, was the most favored of his wives, and was entrusted with the coffer containing the chapters and verses of the Koran as they were revealed.

20

Henda incites Abu Sofian and the Koreishites to revenge the death of her relations slain in the battle of Beder - The Koreishites sally forth, followed by Henda and her female companions - Battle of Ohod - Ferocious triumph of Henda - Mohammed consoles himself by marrying Hend, daughter of Omeya

As the power of Mohammed increased in Medina, the hostility of the Koreishites in Mecca augmented in virulence. Abu Sofian held command in the sacred city, and was incessantly urged to warfare by his wife Henda, whose fierce spirit could take no rest until "blood revenge" had been wreaked on those by whom her father and brother had been slain. Akrema, also, a son of Abu Jahl who inherited his father's hatred of the prophet, clamored for vengeance. In the third year of the Hegira, therefore, the year after the battle of Beder, Abu Sofian took the field at the head of three thousand men, most of them Koreishites, though there were also Arabs of the tribes of Kanana and Tehama. Seven hundred were armed with corselets and two hundred were horsemen. Akrema was one of the captains, as was also Khaled Ibn al Waled, a warrior of indomitable valor, who afterwards rose to great renown. The banners were borne in front by the race of Abd al Dar, a branch of the tribe of Koreish, who had a hereditary right to the foremost place in council, the foremost rank in battle, and to bear the standard in the advance of the army.

In the rear of the host followed the vindictive Henda, with fifteen principal women of Mecca, relatives of those slain in the battle of Beder, sometimes filling the air with wailings and lamentations for the dead, at other times animating the troops with the sound of timbrels and warlike chants. As they passed through the village of Abwa, where Amina the mother of Mohammed was interred, Henda was with difficulty prevented from tearing the mouldering bones out of the grave.

Al Abbas, the uncle of Mohammed, who still resided in Mecca and was considered hostile to the new faith, seeing that destruction threatened his nephew should that army come upon him by surprise, sent secretly a swift messenger to inform him of his danger. Mohammed was at the village of Koba when the message reached him. He immediately hastened back to Medina and called a council of his principal adherents. Representing the insufficiency of their force to take to the field, he gave it as his opinion that they should await an attack on Medina, where the very women and children could aid them by hurling stones from the housetops. The elder among his followers joined in his opinion; but the young men, of heady valor at all times, and elated by the late victory at Beder, cried out for a fair fight in the open field.

Mohammed yielded to their clamors, but his forces, when mustered, were scarce a thousand men; one hundred only had cuirasses, and but two were horsemen. The hearts of those recently so clamorous to sally forth now misgave them, and they would fain await the encounter within the walls. "No," replied Mohammed," it becomes not a prophet when once he has drawn the sword to sheathe it; nor when once he has advanced, to turn back, until God has decided between him and the foe." So saying, he led forth his army. Part of it was composed of Jews and Khazradites, led by Abdallah Ibn Obba Solûl. Mohammed declined the assistance of the Jews, unless they embraced the faith of Islam, and as they refused, he ordered them back to Medina; upon which their protector, Abdallah, turned back also with his Khazradites, thus reducing the army to about seven hundred men.

With this small force Mohammed posted himself upon the hill of Ohod, about six miles from Medina. His position was partly defended by rocks and the asperities of the hill, and archers were stationed to protect him in flank and rear from the attacks of cavalry. He was armed with a helmet and two shirts of mail. On his sword was engraved, "Fear brings disgrace; forward lies honor. Cowardice saves no man from his fate." As he was not prone to take an active part in battle, he confided his sword to a brave warrior, Abu Dudjana, who swore to wield it as long as it had edge and temper. For himself, Mohammed, as usual, took a commanding stand whence he might overlook the field.

The Koreishites, confident in their numbers, came marching to the foot of the hill with banners flying. Abu Sofian led the centre; there were a hundred horsemen on each wing; the left commanded by Akrema, the son of Abu Jahl, the right by Khaled Ibn al Waled. As they advanced, Henda and her companions struck their timbrels and chanted their war song, shrieking out at intervals the names of those who had been slain in the battle of Beder. "Courage, sons of Abd al Dar!" they cried to the standard-bearers, "forward to the fight! close with the foe! strike home and spare not. Sharp be your swords and pitiless your hearts!"

Mohammed restrained the impatience of his troops, ordering them not to commence the fight, but to stand firm and maintain their advantage of the rising ground. Above all, the archers were to keep their post, let the battle go as it might, lest the cavalry should fall upon his rear.

The horsemen of the left wing, led by Akrema, now attempted to take the Moslems in flank, but were repulsed by the archers, and retreated in confusion. Upon this Hamza set up the Moslem war cry, "Amit! amit!" ("Death! death!") and rushed down with his forces upon the centre. Abu Dudjana was at his right hand, armed with the sword of Mohammed, and having a red band round his head, on which was written, "Help comes from God! victory is ours!"

The enemy were staggered by the shock. Abu Dudjana dashed into the midst of them, dealing deadly blows on every side, and exclaiming, "The sword of God and his prophet!" Seven standard-bearers, of the race of Abd al Dar, were, one after the other, struck down, and the centre began to yield. The Moslem archers, thinking the victory secure, forgot the commands of Mohammed and, leaving their post, dispersed in quest of spoil, crying "Booty! booty!" Upon this Khaled, rallying the horse, got possession of the ground abandoned by the archers, attacked the Moslems in rear, put some to flight, and threw the rest in confusion. In the midst of the confusion a horseman, Obbij Ibn Chalaf by name, pressed through the throng, crying, "Where is Mohammed? There is no safety while he lives." But Mohammed, seizing a lance from an attendant, thrust it through the throat of the idolater, who fell dead from his horse. "Thus," says the pious Al Jannabi, "died this enemy of God, who, some years before, had menaced the prophet, saying, 'I shall find a day to slay thee.' 'Have care,' was the reply; 'if it please Allah, thou thyself shall fall beneath my hand.'"

In the midst of the mêlée a stone from a sling struck Mohammed on the mouth, cutting his lip and knocking out one of his front teeth. He was wounded in the face also by an arrow, the iron head of which remained in the wound. Hamza, too, while slaying a Koreishite, was transfixed by the lance of Waksa, an Ethiopian slave, who had been promised his freedom if he should revenge the death of his master, slain by Hamza in the battle of Beder. Mosaab Ibn Omair, also, who bore the standard of Mohammed, was laid low, but Ali seized the sacred banner and bore it aloft amidst the storm of battle.

As Mosaab resembled the prophet in person, a shout was put up by the enemy that Mohammed was slain. The Koreishites were inspired with redoubled ardor at the sound; the Moslems fled in despair, bearing with them Abu Beker and Omar, who were wounded. Raab, the son of Malek, however, beheld Mohammed lying among the wounded in a ditch, and knew him by his armor. "Oh believers!" cried he, "the prophet of God yet lives. To the rescue! to the rescue!" Mohammed was drawn forth and borne up the hill to the summit of a rock, where the Moslems prepared for a desperate defense. The Koreishites, however, thinking Mohammed slain, forbore to pursue them, contenting themselves with plundering and mutilating the dead. Henda and her female companions were foremost in the savage work of vengeance, and the ferocious heroine sought to tear out and devour the heart of Hamza. Abu Sofian bore a part of the mangled body upon his lance and, descending the hill in triumph, exclaimed exultingly, "War has its vicissitudes. The battle of Ohod succeeds to the battle of Beder."

The Koreishites having withdrawn, Mohammed descended from the rock and visited the field of battle. At sight of the body of his uncle Hamza so brutally mangled and mutilated, he vowed to inflict a like outrage on seventy of the enemy when they came within his power. His grief, we are told, was soothed by the angel Gabriel, who assured him that Hamza was enregistered as an inhabitant of the seventh heaven, by the title of "The lion of God and of his prophet."

The bodies of the slain were interred two and two, and three and three, in the places where they had fallen. Mohammed forbade his followers to mourn for the dead by cutting off their hair, rending their garments, and the other modes of lamentation usual among the Arabs; but he consented that they should weep for the dead, as tears relieve the overladen heart.

The night succeeding the battle was one of great disquietude, lest the Koreishites should make another attack or should surprise Medina. On the following day Mohammed marched in the direction of that city, hovering near the enemy, and on the return of night lighting numerous watch fires. Abu Sofian, however, had received intelligence that Mohammed was still alive. He felt himself too weak to attack the city, therefore, while Mohammed was in the field, and might come to its assistance; and he feared that the latter might be reinforced by its inhabitants, and seek him with superior numbers. Contenting himself, therefore, with the recent victory, he made a truce with the Moslems for a year, and returned in triumph to Mecca.

Mohammed sought consolation for this mortifying defeat by taking to himself another wife, Hend, the daughter of Omeya, a man of great influence. She was a widow, and had, with her husband, been among the number of the fugitives in Abyssinia. She was now twenty-eight years of age, and had a son named Salma, whence she was commonly called Omm Salma, or the Mother of Salma. Being distinguished for grace and beauty, she had been sought by Abu Beker and Omar, but without success. Even Mohammed at first met with difficulty. "Alas !" said she, "what happiness can the prophet of God expect with me? I am no longer young; I have a son, and I am of a jealous disposition." "As to thy age," replied Mohammed, "thou art much younger than I. As to thy son, I will be a father to him; as to thy jealous disposition, I will pray Allah to root it from thy heart."

A separate dwelling was prepared for the bride, adjacent to the mosque. The household goods, as stated by a Moslem writer, consisted of a sack of barley, a handmill, a pan, and a pot of lard or butter. Such were as yet the narrow means of the prophet; or rather, such the frugality of his habits and the simplicity of Arab life.

21

Treachery of certain Jewish tribes; their punishment -
Devotion of the prophet's freedman Zeid; divorces his
beautiful wife Zeinab, that she may become the wife of the
prophet

The defeat of Mohammed at the battle of Ohod acted for a time
unfavorably to his cause among some of the Arab and Jewish
tribes, as was evinced by certain acts of perfidy. The
inhabitants of two towns, Adhal and Kara, sent a deputation to
him, professing an inclination to embrace the faith, and
requesting missionaries to teach them its doctrines. He
accordingly sent six disciples to accompany the deputation; but
on the journey, while reposing by the brook Radje within the
boundaries of the Hodseitites, the deputies fell upon the
unsuspecting Moslems, slew four of them, and carried the other
two to Mecca, where they gave them up to the Koreishites, who put
them to death.

A similar act of treachery was practiced by the people of the
province of Nadjed. Pretending to be Moslems, they sought
succor from Mohammed against their enemies. He sent a
number of his followers to their aid, who were attacked by the
Beni Suleim or Suleimites, near the brook Manna, about four
days' journey from Medina, and slain almost to a man. One of
the Moslems, Amru Ibn Omeya, escaped the carnage and made
for Medina. On the way he met two unarmed Jews of the Beni
Amir; either mistaking these for enemies, or provoked to
wanton rage by the death of his comrades, he fell upon them and
slew them. The tribe, who were at peace with Mohammed, called
upon him for redress. He referred the matter to the mediation of
another Jewish tribe, the Beni Nadher, who had rich possessions
and a castle, called Zohra, within three miles of Medina. This

tribe had engaged by a treaty, when Mohammed came a fugitive from Mecca, to maintain a neutrality between him and his opponents. The chief of this tribe, being now applied to as a mediator, invited Mohammed to an interview. He went, accompanied by Abu Beker, Omar, Ali, and a few others. A repast was spread in the open air before the mansion of the chief. Mohammed, however, received private information that he had been treacherously decoyed hither, and was to be slain as he sat at the repast: it is said that he was to be crushed by a millstone, flung from the terraced roof of the house. Without intimating his knowledge of the treason, he left the company abruptly, and hastened back to Medina.

His rage was now kindled against the whole race of Nadher, and he ordered them to leave the country within ten days on pain of death. They would have departed, but Abdallah the Khazradite secretly persuaded them to stay by promising them aid. He failed in his promise. The Beni Nadher, thus disappointed by the "Chief of the Hypocrites," shut themselves up in their castle of Zohra, where they were besieged by Mohammed, who cut down and burned the date trees on which they depended for supplies. At the end of six days they capitulated, and were permitted to depart, each with a camel load of effects, arms excepted. Some were banished to Syria, others to Khaïbar, a strong Jewish city and fortress, distant several days' journey from Medina. As the tribe was wealthy, there were great spoils, which Mohammed took entirely to himself. His followers demurred that this was contrary to the law of partition revealed in the Koran; but he let them know that according to another revelation, all booty gained, like the present, without striking a blow, was not won by man, but was a gift from God, and must be delivered over to the prophet to be expended by him in good works, and the relief of orphans, of the poor, and the traveller. Mohammed, in effect, did not appropriate it to his own benefit, but shared it among the Mohadjerins, or exiles from Mecca; two Nadherite Jews who had embraced Islam; and two or three Ansarians or Auxiliaries of Medina, who had proved themselves worthy, and were poor.

We forbear to enter into details of various petty expeditions of Mohammed about this time, one of which extended to the neighborhood of Tabuk, on the Syrian frontier, to punish a horde which had plundered the caravans of Medina. These expeditions were checkered in their results, though mostly productive of booty, which now began to occupy the minds of the

Moslems almost as much as the propagation of the faith. The spoils thus suddenly gained may have led to riot and debauchery, as we find a revelation of the passage of the Koran forbidding wine and games of hazard, those fruitful causes of strife and insubordination in predatory camps.

During this period of his career, Mohammed in more than one instance narrowly escaped falling by the hand of an assassin. He himself is charged with the use of insidious means to rid himself of an enemy; for it is said that he sent Amru Ibn Omeya on a secret errand to Mecca to assassinate Abu Sofian, but that the plot was discovered and the assassin only escaped by rapid flight. The charge, however, is not well substantiated, and is contrary to his general character and conduct.

If Mohammed had relentless enemies, he had devoted friends, an instance of which we have in the case of his freedman and adopted son Zeid Ibn Horath. He had been one of the first converts to the faith, and one of its most valiant champions. Mohammed consulted him on all occasions, and employed him in his domestic concerns. One day he entered his house with the freedom with which a father enters the dwelling of a son. Zeid was absent, but Zeinab his wife, whom he had recently married, was at home. She was the daughter of Djasch, of the country of Kaiba, and considered the fairest of her tribe. In the privacy of home she had laid aside her veil and part of her attire, so that her beauty stood revealed to the gaze of Mohammed on his sudden entrance. He could not refrain from expressions of wonder and admiration, to which she made no reply, but repeated them all to her husband on his return. Zeid knew the amorous susceptibility of Mohammed, and saw that he had been captivated by the beauty of Zeinab. Hastening after him, he offered to repudiate his wife; but the prophet forbade it as contrary to the law. The zeal of Zeid was not to be checked; he loved his beautiful wife, but he venerated the prophet, and he divorced himself without delay. When the requisite term of separation had elapsed, Mohammed accepted with gratitude his pious sacrifice. His nuptials with Zeinab surpassed in splendor all his other marriages. His doors were open to all comers; they were feasted with the flesh of sheep and lambs, with cakes of barley, with honey, and fruits, and favorite beverages; so they ate and drank their fill and then departed—railing against the divorce as shameful, and the marriage as incestuous.

At this critical juncture was revealed that part of the thirty-third chapter of the Koran, distinguishing relatives by adoption from relatives by blood, according to which there was no sin in marrying one who had been the wife of an adopted son. This timely revelation pacified the faithful; but, to destroy all shadow of a scruple, Mohammed revoked his adoption, and directed Zeid to resume his original appellation of Ibn Hareth, after his natural father. The beautiful Zeinab, however, boasted thenceforth a superiority over the other wives of the prophet on the score of the revelation, alleging that her marriage was ordained by heaven.[1]

22

Expedition of Mohammed against the Beni Mostalek - He espouses Barra, a captive - Treachery of Abdallah Ibn Obba - Ayesha slandered - Her vindication - Her innocence proved by a revelation

Among the Arab tribes which ventured to take up arms against Mohammed after his defeat at Ohod, were the Beni Mostalek, a powerful race of Koreishite origin. Mohammed received intelligence of their being assembled in warlike guise under their prince Al Hareth, near the wells of Moraïsi, in the territory of Kedaid, and within five miles of the Red Sea. He immediately took the field at the head of a chosen band of the faithful, accompanied by numbers of the Khazradites, led by their chief Abdallah Ibn Obba. By a rapid movement he surprised the enemy; Al Hareth was killed at the onset by the flight shot of an arrow; his troops fled in confusion after a brief resistance, in which a few were slain. Two hundred prisoners, five thousand sheep, and one thousand camels were the fruits of this easy victory. Among the captives was Barra, the daughter of Al Hareth, and wife to a young Arab of her kin. In the division of the spoils she fell to the lot of Thabet Ibn Reis, who demanded a high ransom. The captive appealed to Mohammed against this extortion, and prayed that the ransom might be mitigated. The prophet regarded her with eyes of desire, for she was fair to look upon. "I can serve thee better," said he, "than by abating thy ransom: be my wife." The beautiful Barra gave ready consent; her ransom was paid by the prophet to Thabet; her kindred were liberated by the Moslems, to whose lot they had fallen; most of them embraced the faith, and Barra became the wife of Mohammed after his return to Medina.

After the battle, the troops crowded round the wells of Moraïsi to assuage their thirst. In the press a quarrel rose between some of the Mohadjerins, or exiles of Mecca, and the Khazradites, in which one of the latter received a blow. His comrades rushed to revenge the insult, and blood would have been shed but for the interference of Mohammed. The Khazradites remained incensed, and other of the people of Medina made common cause with them. Abdallah Ibn Obba, eager to take advantage of every circumstance adverse to the rising power of Mohammed, drew his kindred and townsfolk apart. "Behold," said he, "the insults you have brought upon yourselves by harboring these fugitive Koreishites. You have taken them to your houses, and given them your goods, and now they turn upon and maltreat you. They would make themselves your masters even in your own house; but by Allah, when we return to Medina, we will see which of us is strongest."

Secret word was brought to Mohammed of this seditious speech. Omar counselled him at once to make way with Abdallah; but the prophet feared to excite the vengeance of the kindred and adherents of the powerful Khazradite. To leave no time for mutiny, he set off immediately on the homeward march, although it was in the heat of the day, and continued on throughout the night, nor halted until the following noon, when the wearied soldiery cared for nothing but repose.

On arriving at Medina, he called Abdallah to account for his seditious expressions. He flatly denied them, pronouncing the one who had accused him a liar. A revelation from heaven, however, established the charge against him and his adherents. "These are the men," says the Koran, "who say to the inhabitants of Medina, do not bestow anything on the refugees who are with the apostle of God, that they may be compelled to separate from him. They say, verily, if we return to Medina, the worthier will expel thence the meaner. God curse them! how are they turned aside from the truth."

Some of the friends of Abdallah, convinced by this revelation, advised him to ask pardon of the prophet; but he spurned their counsel. "You have already," said he, "persuaded me to give this man my countenance and friendship, and now you would have me put myself beneath his very feet."

Nothing could persuade him that Mohammed was not an idolater at heart, and his revelations all imposture and deceit. He considered him, however, a formidable rival, and sought in every way to injure and annoy him. To this implacable hostility is attributed a scandalous story which he propagated about Ayesha, the favorite wife of the prophet.

It was the custom with Mohammed always to have one of his wives with him on his military expeditions, as companion and solace; she was taken by lot, and on the recent occasion the lot had fallen on Ayesha. She travelled in a litter, inclosed by curtains, and borne on the back of a camel, which was led by an attendant. On one occasion, when the army halted on its return homeward, the attendants of Ayesha were astonished to find the litter empty. Before they had recovered from their surprise, she arrived on a camel, led by a youthful Arab named Safwan Ibn al Moattel. This circumstance having come to the knowledge of Abdallah, he proclaimed it to the world after his return to Medina, affirming that Ayesha had been guilty of wantonness with the youthful Safwan.

The story was eagerly caught up and circulated by Hamna, the sister of the beautiful Zeinab, whom Mohammed had recently espoused, and who hoped to benefit her sister by the downfall of her deadly rival Ayesha. It was echoed also by Mistah, a kinsman of Abu Beker, and was celebrated in satirical verses by a poet named Hasan.

It was some time before Ayesha knew of the scandal thus circulating at her expense. Sickness had confined her to the house on her return to Medina, and no one ventured to tell her of what she was accused. She remarked, however, that the prophet was stern and silent, and no longer treated her with his usual tenderness. On her recovery, she heard with consternation the crime alleged against her, and protested her innocence. The following is her version of the story.

The army, on its homeward march, had encamped not far from Medina, when orders were given in the night to march. The attendants, as usual, brought a camel before the tent of Ayesha and, placing the litter on the ground, retired until she could take her seat within it. As she was about to enter, she missed her necklace, and returned into the tent to seek it. In the meantime the attendants lifted the litter upon the camel and strapped it fast, not perceiving that it was empty, she being slender and of light weight. When she returned from seeking the necklace, the camel was gone, and the army was on the march; whereupon she wrapped herself in her mantle and sat down, trusting that, when her absence should be discovered, some persons would be sent back in quest of her.

While she was thus seated, Safwan Ibn al Moattel, the young Arab, being one of the rear guard, came up, and, recognizing her, accosted her with the usual Moslem salutation. "To God we belong, and to God we must return! Wife of the prophet, why dost thou remain behind?"

Ayesha made no reply, but drew her veil closer over her face. Safwan then alighted, aided her to mount the camel, and, taking the bridle, hastened to rejoin the army. The sun had risen, however, before he overtook it, just without the walls of Medina.

This account, given by Ayesha, and attested by Safwan Ibn al Moattel, was satisfactory to her parents and particular friends, but was scoffed at by Abdallah and his adherents, "the Hypocrites." Two parties thus arose on the subject, and great strife ensued. As to Ayesha, she shut herself up within her dwelling, refusing all food, and weeping day and night in the bitterness of her soul.

Mohammed was sorely troubled in mind, and asked counsel of Ali in his perplexity. The latter made light of the affair, observing that his misfortune was the frequent lot of man. The prophet was but little consoled by this suggestion. He remained separated from Ayesha for a mouth; but his heart yearned toward her, not merely on account of her beauty, but because he loved her company. In a paroxysm of grief, he fell into one of those trances which unbelievers have attributed to epilepsy, in the course of which be received a seasonable revelation, which will be found in a chapter of the Koran. It was to this effect :

They who accuse a reputable female of adultery, and produce not four witnesses of the fact, shall be scourged with fourscore stripes, and their testimony rejected. As to those who have made the charge against Ayesha, have they produced four witnesses thereof? If they have not, they are liars in the sight of God. Let them receive, therefore, the punishment of their crime.

The innocence of the beautiful Ayesha being thus miraculously made manifest, the prophet took her to his bosom with augmented affection. Nor was he slow in dealing the prescribed castigation. It is true that Abdallah Ibn Obba was too powerful a personage to be subjected to the scourge, but it fell the heavier on the shoulders of his fellow calumniators. The poet

Hasan was cured for some time of his propensity to make satirical verses, nor could Hamna, though a female, and of great personal charms, escape the infliction of stripes; for Mohammed observed that such beauty should have been accompanied by a gentler nature.

The revelation at once convinced the pious Ali of the purity of Ayesha, but she never forgot nor forgave that he had doubted; and the hatred thus implanted in her bosom was manifested to his great detriment in many of the most important concerns of his after life.

23

The battle of the moat - Bravery of Saad Ibn Moad - Defeat of the Koreishites - Capture of the Jewish castle of Koraida - Saad decides as to the punishment of the Jews - Mohammed espouses Rihana, a Jewish captive - His life endangered by sorcery; saved by a revelation of the angel Gabriel

During the year of truce which succeeded the battle of Ohod, Abu Sofian, the restless chief of the Koreishites, formed a confederacy with the Arab tribe of Ghatafan and other tribes of the desert, as well as with many of the Jews of the race of Nadher, whom Mohammed had driven from their homes. The truce being ended, he prepared to march upon Medina with these confederates, their combined forces amounting to ten thousand men.

Mohammed had early intelligence of the meditated attack, but his late reverse at Ohod made him wary of taking the field against such numbers, especially as he feared the enemy might have secret allies in Medina, where he distrusted the Jewish inhabitants and the Hypocrites, the partisans of Abdallah Ibn Obba, who were numerous and powerful.

Great exertions were now made to put the city in a state of defense. Salmân the Persian, who had embraced the faith, advised that a deep moat should be dug at some distance beyond the wall, on the side on which the enemy would approach. This mode of defense, hitherto unused in Arabia, was eagerly adopted by Mohammed, who set a great number of men to dig the moat, and even assisted personally in the labor. Many miracles are recorded of him during the progress of this work. At one time, it is said, he fed a great multitude from a single basket of dates, which remained full after all were satisfied. At another time he feasted a thousand men upon a roasted lamb and a loaf of barley bread, yet enough remained for all his fellow-laborers in the moat. Nor must we omit to note the wonderful blows which be gave to a rock with an iron mallet, striking off sparks which in one direction lighted up all Yemen, or Arabia the Happy; in another, revealed the imperial palace of Constantinople; and in a third, illumined the towers of the royal residents of Persia— all signs and portents of the future conquests of Islam.

Scarcely was the moat completed when the enemy appeared in great force on the neighboring hills. Leaving Ibn Omm Mactum, a trusty officer, to command in the city, and keep a vigilant eye on the disaffected, Mohammed sallied forth with three thousand men, whom he formed in battle array, having the deep moat in front. Abu Sofian advanced confidently with his combined force of Koreishites and Ghatafanites, but was unexpectedly checked by the moat, and by a galling fire from the Moslems drawn up beyond it. The enemy now encamped—the Koreishites in the lower part of the valley, the Ghatafanites in the upper—and for some days the armies remained on each side of the moat, keeping up a distant combat with slings and stones, and flights of arrows.

In the meantime, spies brought word to Mohammed that a Jewish tribe, the Beni Koraida, who had a strong castle near the city, and had made a covenant of peace with him, were in secret league with the enemy. He now saw the difficulty, with his scanty forces, to man the whole extent of the moat; to guard against a perfidious attack from the Koraidites; and to maintain quiet in the city, where the Jews must have secret confederates. Summoning a council of war, he consulted with his captains on the policy of bribing the Ghatafanites to a separate peace, by offering them a third of the date harvest of Medina. Upon this, Saad Ibn Moad, a stout leader of the Awsites of Medina, demanded: "Do you propose this by the command of Allah, or is it an idea of your own?" "If it had been a command of Allah," replied Mohammed, "I should never have asked your advice. I see you pressed by enemies on every side, and I seek to break their confederacy." "O prophet of God!" rejoined Saad, "when we were fellow-idolaters with these people of Ghatafan, they got none of our dates without paying for them; and shall we give them up gratuitously now that we are of the true faith, and led by thee? No, by Allah! if they want our dates they must win them with their swords."

The stout Saad had his courage soon put to the proof. A prowling party of Koreishite horsemen, among whom was Akrema, the son of Abu Jahl, and Amru, uncle of Mohammed's first wife Cadijah, discovered a place where the moat was narrow and, putting spurs to their steeds succeeded in leaping over, followed by some of their comrades. They then challenged the bravest of the Moslems to equal combat. The challenge was accepted by Saad Ibn Moad, by Ali, and several of their companions. Ali had a close combat with Amru; they fought on horseback and on foot until, grappling with each other, they rolled in the dust. In the end, Ali was victorious and slew his foe. The general conflict was maintained with great obstinacy; several were slain on both sides, and Saad Ibn Moad was severely wounded. At length the Koreishites gave way, and spurred their horses to recross the moat. The steed of one of them, Nawfal Ibn Abdallah, leaped short; his rider was assailed with stones while in the moat, and defied the Moslems to attack him with nobler weapons. In an instant Ali sprang down into the moat, and Nawfal soon fell beneath his sword. Ali then joined his companions in pursuit of the retreating foe, and wounded Akrema with a javelin. The skirmish was dignified with the name of the Battle of the Moat.

Mohammed, still unwilling to venture a pitched battle, sent Rueim, a secretly converted Arab of the tribe of Ghatafan, to visit the camps of the confederates, and artfully to sow dissensions among them. Rueim first repaired to the Koraidites, with whom he was in old habits of friendship. "What folly is this," said he, "to suffer yourselves to be drawn by the Koreishites of Mecca into their quarrel! Bethink you how different is your situation from theirs! If defeated, they have only to retreat to Mecca, and be secure. Their allies from the desert will also retire to their distant homes, and you will be left to bear the whole brunt of the vengeance of Mohammed and the people of Medina. Before you make common cause with them, therefore, let them pledge themselves and give hostages, never to draw back until they have broken the power of Mohammed."

He then went to the Koreishites and the tribe of Ghatafan, and warned them against confiding in the Jews of Koraida, who intended to get hostages from them, and deliver them up into the hands of Mohammed.

The distrust thus artfully sown among the confederates soon produced its effects. Abu Sofian sent word on Friday evening to the Koraidites to be ready to join next morning in a general assault. The Jews replied, that the following day was their Sabbath, on which they could not engage in battle; at the same time they declined to join in any hostile act, unless their allies should give hostages to stand by them to the end.

The Koreishites and Ghatafanites were now convinced of the perfidy of the Koraidites, and dared not venture upon the meditated attack, lest these should fall upon them in the rear. While they lay idly in their camp a cold storm came on, with drenching rain, and sweeping blasts from the desert. Their tents were blown down; their campfires were extinguished; in the midst of the uproar the alarm was given that Mohammed had raised the storm by enchantment, and was coming upon them with his forces. All now was panic and confusion. Abu Sofian, finding all efforts vain to produce order, mounted his camel in despair, and gave the word to retreat. The confederates hurried off from the scene of tumult and terror, the Koreishites towards Mecca, the others to their homes in the desert.

Abu Sofian, in rage and mortification, wrote a letter to Mohammed, upbraiding him with his cowardice in lurking behind a ditch—a thing unknown in Arabian warfare—and threatening to take his revenge on some future day, when they might meet in open fight, as in the field of Ohod. Mohammed hurled back a defiance, and predicted that the day was approaching when he would break in pieces the idols of the Koreishites.

The invaders having disappeared, Mohammed turned to take vengeance on the Beni Koraida, who shut themselves up in their castle and withstood a siege of many days. At length, pinched by famine, they implored the intercession of their ancient friends and protectors, the Awsites. The latter entreated the prophet to grant these Hebrews the same terms he had formerly granted to the Beni Kainoka, at the prayer of Abdallah the Khazradite. Mohammed reflected a moment, and offered to leave their fate to the decision of Saad Ibn Moad, the Awsite chief. The Koraidites gladly agreed, knowing him to have been formerly their friend. They accordingly surrendered themselves, to the number of seven hundred, and were conducted in chains to Medina. Unfortunately for them, Saad considered their perfidious league with the enemy as one cause of the recent hostility. He was still smarting with the wound received in the battle of the Moat, and in his moments of pain and anger had repeatedly prayed that his life might be spared to see vengeance wreaked on the Koraidites. Such was the state of his feelings when summoned to decide upon their fate.

Being a gross, full-blooded man, he was with difficulty helped upon an ass, propped up by a leather cushion, and supported in his seat until he arrived at the tribunal of justice. Before ascending it, he exacted an oath from all present to abide by his decision. The Jews readily took it, anticipating a favorable sentence. No sooner was he helped into the tribunal, than, extending his hand, he condemned the men to death, the women and children to slavery, and their effects to be shared among the victors.

The wretched Jews looked aghast, but there was no appeal. They were conducted to a public place since called the Market of the Koraidites, where great graves had been dug. Into these they were compelled to descend, one by one, their prince Hoya Ibn Ahktab among the number, and were successively put to death. Thus the prayer of Saad Ibn Moad for vengeance on the Koraidites was fully gratified. He witnessed the execution of the men he had condemned, but such was his excitement that his wound broke out afresh, and he died shortly afterwards.

In the castle of Koraida was found a great quantity of pikes, lances, cuirasses, and other armor; and its lands were covered with flocks and herds and camels. In dividing the spoils each foot soldier had one lot, each horseman three—two for his horse, and one for himself. A fifth part of the whole was set apart for the prophet.

The most precious prize in the eyes of Mohammed was Rihana, daughter of Simeon, a wealthy and powerful Jew, and the most beautiful female of her tribe. He took her to himself and, having converted her to the faith, added her to the number of his wives.

But, though thus susceptible of the charms of the Israelite women, Mohammed became more and more vindictive in his hatred of the men, no longer putting faith in their covenants, and suspecting them of the most insidious attempts upon his life. Moslem writers attribute to the spells of Jewish sorcerers a long and languishing illness, with which he was afflicted about this time, and which seemed to defy all remedy. They describe the very charm by which it was produced. It was prepared, say they, by a Jewish necromancer from the mountains, aided by his daughters, who were equally skilled in the diabolic art. They formed a small waxen effigy of Mohammed, wound round it some of his hair, and thrust through it eleven needles. They then made eleven knots in a bowstring, blowing with their breaths on each, and, winding the string round the effigy, threw the whole into a well.

Under the influence of this potent spell Mohammed wasted away, until his friend, the angel Gabriel, revealed the secret to him in a vision. On awaking, he sent Ali to the well, where the image was discovered. When it was brought to Mohammed, continues the legend, he repeated over it the two last chapters of the Koran, which had been communicated to him in the recent vision. They consist of eleven verses, and are to the following purport:

In the name of the all merciful God! I will fly for refuge to the Lord of the light of day.

That he may deliver me from the danger of beings and things created by himself.

From the dangers of the darksome night, and of the moon when in eclipse.

From the danger of sorcerers, who tie knots and blow on them with their breath.

From the danger of the envious, who devise deadly harm.

I will fly for refuge to Allah, the Lord of men.

To Allah, the King of men.

To Allah, the God of men.

That he may deliver me from the evil spirit who flies at the mention of his holy name.

Who suggests evil thoughts into the hearts of the children of men.

And from the evil Genii, and men who deal in magic.

At the repetition of each one of those verses, says the legend, a knot of the bowstring came loose, a needle fell from the effigy, and Mohammed gained strength. At the end of the eleventh verse he rose, renovated in health and vigor, as one restored to freedom after having been bound with cords.

The two final chapters of the Koran, which comprise these verses, are entitled the amulets, and are considered by the superstitious Moslems effectual talismans against sorcery and magic charms.

The conduct of Mohammed in the affair narrated in this chapter has been censured as weak and vacillating, and deficient in military decision, and his measures as wanting in true greatness of mind, and the following circumstances are adduced to support these charges. When threatened with violence from without, and perfidy from within, he is for bribing a part of his confederate foes to a separate peace, but suffers himself to be, in a manner, hectored out of this crafty policy by Saad Ibn Moad; yet, subsequently, he resorts to a scheme still more subtle and crafty, by which he sows dissension among his enemies. Above all, his conduct towards the Jews has been strongly reprobated. His referring the appeal of the Beni Koraida for mercy to the decision of one whom he knew to be bent on their destruction has been stigmatized as cruel mockery; and the massacre of those unfortunate men in the marketplace of Medina is pronounced one of the darkest pages of his history. In fact, his conduct towards this race from the time that he had power in his hands forms an exception to the general tenor of his disposition, which was forgiving and humane. He may have been especially provoked against them by proofs of treachery and deadly rancor on their part; but we see in this, as in other parts of his policy in this part of his career, instances of that worldly alloy which at times was debasing his spirit, now that he had become the Apostle of the Sword.

24

Mohammed undertakes a pilgrimage to Mecca - Evades Khaled and a troop of horse set against him - Encamps near Mecca - Negotiates with the Koreishites for permission to enter and complete his pilgrimage - Treaty for ten years, by which he is permitted to make a yearly visit of three days - He returns to Medina

Six years had now elapsed since the flight of Mohammed from Mecca. As that city was sacred in the eyes of the Arabs and their great point of pilgrimage, his long exile from it, and his open warfare with the Koreishites, who had charge of the Caaba, prejudiced him in the opinion of many of the tribes, and retarded the spread of his doctrines. His followers, too, who had accompanied him in his flight, languished once more to see their native home, and there was danger of their faith becoming enfeebled under a protracted exile.

Mohammed felt more and more the importance of linking the sacred city with his religion, and maintaining the ancient usages of his race. Besides, he claimed but to be a reformer, anxious to restore the simplicity and purity of the patriarchal faith. The month Doul Kaada was at hand, the month of pilgrimage, when there was a truce to warfare, and enemies might meet in peace within the holy boundaries. A timely vision assured Mohammed that he and his followers might safely avail themselves of the protection of this venerable custom to revisit the ancient shrines of Arabian worship. The revelation was joyfully received by his followers, and in the holy month he set forth from Medina on his pilgrimage, at the head of fourteen hundred men— partly Mohadjerins or Fugitives, and partly Ansarians or Auxiliaries. They took with them seventy camels to be slain in sacrifice at the Caaba. To manifest publicly that they came in peace and not in war, they halted at Dsu Huleifa, a village about a day's journey from Medina, where they laid aside all their weapons, excepting their sheathed swords, and thence continued on in pilgrim garb.

In the meantime a confused rumor of this movement had reached Mecca. The Koreishites, suspecting hostilities, sent forth Khaled Ibn Waled with a powerful troop of horse, to take post in a valley about two days' journey from Mecca, and check the advance of the Moslems.

Mohammed, hearing that the main road was thus barred against him, took a rugged and difficult route through the defiles of the mountains and, avoiding Khaled and his forces, decended into the plain near Mecca, where he encamped at Hodeïba, within the sacred boundaries. Hence he sent assurances to the Koreishites of his peaceable intentions, and claimed the immunities and rights of pilgrimage.

Envoys from the Koreishites visited his camp to make observations. They were struck with the reverence with which he was regarded by his followers. The water with which he performed his ablutions became sanctified; a hair falling from his head, or the paring of a nail, was caught up as a precious relic. One of the envoys, in the course of conversation, unconsciously touched the flowing beard of the prophet; he was thrust back by the disciples, and warned of the impiety of the act. In making his report to the Koreishites on his return, "I have seen the king of Persia, and the emperor of Constantinople, surrounded by their courts," said he, "but never did I behold a sovereign so revered by his subjects as is Mohammed by his followers."

The Koreishites were the more loath to admit into their city an adversary to their sect, so formidable in his influence over the minds and affections of his fellow men. Mohammed sent repeated missions to treat for a safe access to the sacred shrines, but in vain. Othman Ibn Affan, his son-in-law, was his last envoy. Several days elapsed without his return, and it was rumored that he was slain. Mohammed determined to revenge his fall. Standing under a tree, and summoning his people around him, he exacted an oath to defend him even to the death, and never to desert the standard of the faith. This ceremony is known among Moslems by the name of the Spontaneous Inauguration.

The reappearance of Othman in the camp restored tranquillity. He was accompanied by Solhail, an ambassador from the Koreishites, to arrange a treaty of peace. They perceived the impolicy of warring with a man whose power was incessantly increasing, and who was obeyed with such fanatic devotion. The treaty proposed was for ten years, during which time Mohammed and his adherents were to have free access to Mecca as pilgrims, there to remain, three days at a time, in the exercise of their religious rites. The terms were readily accepted, and Ali was employed to draw up the treaty. Mohammed dictated the words. "Write," said he, "these are the conditions of peace made by Mohammed the apostle of God." "Hold!" cried Solhail, the ambassador, "had I believed thee to be the apostle of God, I should never have taken up arms against thee. Write, therefore, simply thy name, and the name of thy father." Mohammed was fain to comply, for he felt he was not sufficiently in force at this moment to contend about forms; so he merely denominated himself in the treaty Mohammed Ibn Abdallah (Mohammed the son of Abdallah), an abnegation which gave some little scandal to his followers. Their discontent was increased when he ordered them to shave their heads, and to sacrifice on the spot the camels brought to be offered up at the Caaba, as it showed he had not the intention of entering Mecca (these rites being properly done at the conclusion of the ceremonials of pilgrimage). They reminded him of his vision which promised a safe entrance of the sacred city; he replied that the present treaty was an earnest of its fulfillment, which would assuredly take place in the following year. With this explanation they had to content themselves; and when they had performed the ceremony, and made the sacrifice prescribed, the camp was broken up, and the pilgrim host returned, somewhat disappointed and dejected, to Medina.

25

*Expedition against the city of Khaïbar; siege - Exploits of
Mohammed's captains - Battle of Ali and Marhab -
Storming of the citadel - Ali makes a buckler of the gate -
Capture of the place - Mohammed poisoned; he marries
Safiya, a captive; also Omm Habiba, a widow*

To console his followers for the check their religious devotion
had experienced at Mecca, Mohammed now set on foot an
expedition calculated to gratify that love of plunder which began
to rival fanaticism in attaching them to his standard.

About five days' journey to the northeast of Medina was
situated the city of Khaïbar, and its dependent territory. It was
inhabited by Jews who had grown wealthy by commerce as well
as agriculture. Their rich domain was partly cultivated with
grain, and planted with groves of palm trees; partly devoted to
pasturage and covered with flocks and herds; and it was
fortified by several castles. So venerable was its antiquity that
Abulfeda, the Arabian historian, assures us that Moses, after the
passage of the Red Sea, sent an army against the Amalekites,
inhabiting Yathreb (Medina), and the strong city of Khaïbar.

This region had become a place of refuge for the hostile Jews
driven by Mohammed from Medina and its environs, and for
all those who had made themselves obnoxious to his vengeance.
These circumstances, together with its teeming wealth, pointed
it out as a fit and ripe object for that warfare which he had
declared against all enemies of the faith.

In the beginning of the seventh year of the Hegira,
Mohammed departed on an expedition against Khaïbar, at the
head of twelve hundred foot and two hundred horse,
accompanied by Abu Beker, by Ali, by Omar, and other of his
principal officers. He had two standards: one representing the

sun, the other a black eagle, which last became famous in after years as the standard of Khaled.

Entering the fertile territory of Khaïbar, he began his warfare by assailing the inferior castles with which it was studded. Some of these capitulated without making resistance; in which cases, being considered "gifts from God," the spoils went to the prophet, to be disposed of by him the way before mentioned. Others of more strength, and garrisoned by stouter hearts, had to be taken by storm.

After the capture of these minor fortresses, Mohammed advanced against the city of Khaïbar. It was strongly defended by outworks, and its citadel, Al Kamus, built on a steep rock, was deemed impregnable, insomuch that Kenana Ibn al Rabi, the chief or king of the nation, had made it the depository of all his treasures.

The siege of this city was the most important enterprise the Moslems had yet undertaken. When Mohammed first came in sight of its strong and frowning walls, and its rock-built citadel, he is said to have put up the following prayer:

"O Allah! Lord of the seven heavens, and of all things which they cover! Lord of the seven earths, and all which they sustain! Lord of the evil spirits, and of all whom they lead astray! Lord of the winds, and of all whom they scatter and disperse! We supplicate thee to deliver into our hands this city, and all that it contains, and the riches of all its lands. To thee we look for aid against this people, and against all the perils by which we are environed."

To give more solemnity to his prayers, he chose as his place of worship a great rock, in a stony place called Mansela, and, during all the time that he remained encamped before Khaïbar, made daily seven circuits round it, as are made round the Caaba. A mosque was erected on this rock in after times in memorial of this devout ceremonial, and it became an object of veneration to all pious Moslems.

The siege of the citadel lasted for some time, and tasked the skill and patience of Mohammed and his troops, as yet but little practiced in the attack of fortified places. They suffered too from want of provisions, for the Arabs in their hasty expeditions seldom burden themselves with supplies, and the Jews on their approach had laid waste the level country, and destroyed the palm trees round their capital.

Mohammed directed the attacks in person; the besiegers protected themselves by trenches, and brought battering-rams to play upon the walls; a breach was at length effected, but for several days every attempt to enter was vigorously repelled. Abu Beker at one time led the assault, bearing the standard of the prophet; but, after fighting with great bravery, he was compelled to retreat. The next attack was headed by Omar Ibn Khattâb, who fought until the close of day with no better success. A third attack was led by Ali, whom Mohammed armed with his own scimitar, called Dhu'l Fakar, or the Trenchant. On confiding to his hands the sacred banner, he pronounced him "a man who loved God and his prophet, and whom God and his prophet loved. A man who knew not fear, nor ever turned his back upon a foe."

And here it may be well to give a traditional account of the person and character of Ali. He was of the middle height, but robust and square, and of prodigious strength. He had a smiling countenance, exceedingly florid, with a bushy beard. He was distinguished for an amiable disposition, sagacious intellect, and religious zeal, and, from his undaunted courage, was surnamed the Lion of God.

Arabian writers dwell with fond exaggeration on the exploits, at Khaïbar, of this their favorite hero. He was clad, they say, in a scarlet vest, over which was buckled a cuirass of steel. Scrambling with his followers up the great heap of stones and rubbish in front of the breach, he planted his standard on the top, determined never to recede until the citadel was taken. The Jews sallied forth to drive down the assailants. In the conflict which ensued, Ali fought hand to hand with the Jewish commander, Al Hareth, whom he slew. The brother of the slain advanced to revenge his death. He was of gigantic stature, with a double cuirass, a double turban, wound round a helmet of proof, in front of which sparkled an immense diamond. He had a sword girt to each side, and brandished a three-pronged spear, like a trident. The warriors measured each other with the eye, and accosted each other in boasting oriental style.

"I," said the Jew, "am Marhab; armed at all points, and terrible in battle."

"And I am Ali, whom his mother, at his birth, surnamed Al Haïdara (the rugged lion)."

The Moslem writers make short work of the Jewish champion. He made a thrust at Ali with his three-pronged lance, but it was dexterously parried; and before he could recover

himself, a blow from the scimitar Dhu'l Fakar divided his
buckler, passed through the helmet of proof, through doubled
turban and stubborn skull, cleaving his head even to his teeth.
His gigantic form fell lifeless to the earth.

The Jews now retreated into the citadel, and a general
assault took place. In the heat of the action the shield of Ali was
severed from his arm, leaving his body exposed. Wrenching a
gate, however, from its hinges, he used it as a buckler through
the remainder of the fight. Abu Rafe, a servant of Mohammed,
testifies to the fact. "I afterwards," says he, "examined this gate
in company with seven men and all eight of us attempted in
vain to wield it."[1]

The citadel being captured, every vault and dungeon was
ransacked for the wealth said to be deposited there by Kenana,
the Jewish prince. None being discovered, Mohammed
demanded of him where he had concealed his treasure. He
declared that it had all been expended in the subsistence of his
troops, and in preparations for defense. One of his faithless
subjects, however, revealed the place where a great amount had
been hidden. It did not equal the expectations of the victors, and
Kenana was put to the torture to reveal the rest of his supposed
wealth. He either could not or would not make further
discoveries, so he was delivered up to the vengeance of a
Moslem, whose brother he had crushed to death by a piece of
millstone hurled from the wall, and who struck off his head with
a single blow of his sabre.[2]

While in the citadel of Khaïbar, Mohammed came near
falling a victim to Jewish vengeance. When he demanded
something to eat, a shoulder of lamb was set before him. At the
first mouthful he perceived something unusual in the taste, and
spat it forth, but instantly felt acute internal pain. One of his
followers, named Baschar, who had eaten more freely, fell
down and expired in convulsions. All now was confusion and
consternation; on diligent inquiry, it was found that the lamb
had been cooked by Zaïnab, a female captive, niece to Marhab,
the gigantic warrior slain by Ali. Being brought before
Mohammed, and charged with having infused poison into the
viand, she boldly avowed it, vindicating it as a justifiable
revenge for the ills he had brought upon her tribe and her
family. "I thought," said she, "if thou wert indeed a prophet, thou
wouldst discover thy danger; if but a chieftain, thou wouldst fall,
and we should be delivered from a tyrant."

Arabian writers are divided as to the fate of this heroine. According to some, she was delivered up to the vengeance of the relatives of Baschar, who had died of the poison. According to others, her beauty pleaded in her behalf, and Mohammed restored her unharmed to her family.

The same writers seldom permit any remarkable event of Mohammed's life to pass without a miracle. In the present instance, they assure us that the poisoned shoulder of lamb became miraculously gifted with speech, and warned Mohammed of his danger. If so, it was rather slow of speech, for he had imbibed sufficient poison to injure his constitution throughout the remainder of his life, affecting him often with paroxysms of pain; and in his last moments he complained that the veins of his heart throbbed with the poison of Khaïbar. He experienced kinder treatment at the hands of Safiya (or Sophia), another female captive, who had still greater motives for vengeance than Zaïnab; for she was the recently espoused wife of Kenana, who had just been sacrificed for his wealth, and she was the daughter of Hoya Ibn Akhtab, prince of the Beni Koraida, who, with seven hundred of his people, had been put to death in the square of Medina, as has been related.

This Safiya was of great beauty; it is not surprising, therefore, that she should find instant favor in the eyes of Mohammed, and that he should seek, as usual, to add her to his harem; but it may occasion surprise that she should contemplate such a lot with complacency. Moslem writers, however, explain this by assuring us that she was supernaturally prepared for the event.

While Mohammed was yet encamped before the city, and carrying on the siege, she had a vision of the night, in which the sun descended from the firmament and nestled in her bosom. When she recounted her dream to her husband Kenana in the morning, he smote her on the face, exclaiming, "Woman, you speak in parables of this Arab chief who has come against us."

The vision of Safiya was made true; for, having converted her with all decent haste to the faith of Islam, Mohammed took her to wife before he left Khaïbar. Their nuptials took place on the homeward march, at Al Sahba, where the army halted for three days. Abu Ayub, one of the prophet's most ardent disciples and marshal of his household, patrolled around the nuptial tent throughout the night, sword in hand. Safiya was one of the most favored wives of Mohammed, whom she survived for forty years of widowhood.

Besides the marriages of affection which we have recorded, the prophet, about this time, made another of policy. Shortly after his return to Medina, he was gladdened by the arrival, from Abyssinia, of the residue of the fugitives. Among these was a comely widow, thirty years of age, whose husband, Abdallah, had died while in exile. She was generally known by the name of Omm Habiba, the mother of Habiba, from a daughter to whom she had given birth. This widow was the daughter of Mahomet's arch enemy, Abu Sofian; and the prophet conceived that a marriage with the daughter might soften the hostility of the father, a politic consideration which is said to have been either suggested or sanctioned by a revelation of a chapter of the Koran.

When Abu Sofian heard of the espousals, "By heaven," exclaimed he, "this camel is so rampant that no muzzle can restrain him."

26

Mission to various princes: to Heraclius; to Khosru II; to the Prefect of Egypt - Their result

During the residue of the year Mohammed remained at Medina, sending forth his trusty disciples, by this time experienced captains, on various military expeditions, by which refractory tribes were rapidly brought into subjection. His views as a statesman widened as his territories increased. Though he professed, in cases of necessity, to propagate his religion by the sword, he was not neglectful of the peaceful measures of diplomacy, and sent envoys to various princes and potentates whose dominions bordered on his political horizon, urging them to embrace the faith of Islam—which was, in effect, to acknowledge him, through his apostolic office, their superior.

Two of the most noted of these missions were to Khosru II, King of Persia, and Heraclius, the Roman Emperor, at Constantinople. The wars between the Romans and the Persians for the dominion of the East, which had prevailed from time to time through several centuries, had been revived by these two potentates with varying fortunes, and for several years past had distracted the eastern world. Countries had been overrun by either power; states and kingdoms had changed hands under alternate invasions, and according to the conquests and defeats of the warring parties. At one time, Khosru with three armies, one vauntingly called the Fifty Thousand Golden Spears, had wrested Palestine, Cappadocia, Armenia and several other great and wealthy provinces from the Roman emperor; had made himself master of Jerusalem, and carried off the Holy Cross to Persia; had invaded Africa, conquered Libya and Egypt, and extended his victories even to Carthage.

In the midst of his triumphant career, a Moslem envoy arrived bearing him a letter from Mohammed. Khosru sent for his secretary or interpreter, and ordered him to read it. The letter began as follows:

"In the name of the most merciful God! Mohammed, son of Abdallah, and apostle of God, to Khosru, King of Persia."

"What!" cried Khosru, starting up in haughty indignation, "does one who is my slave dare to put his name first in writing to me?" So saying, he seized the letter and tore it in pieces, without seeking to know its contents. He then wrote to his viceroy in Yemen, saying, "I am told there is in Medina a madman, of the tribe of Koreish, who pretends to be a prophet. Restore him to his senses; or if you cannot, send me his head."

When Mohammed was told how Khosru had torn his letter, "Even so," said he, "shall Allah rend his empire in pieces."

The letter from the prophet to Heraclius was more favorably received, reaching him probably during his reverses. It was signed in characters of silver, Mohammed Azzarel, Mohammed the messenger of God, and invited the emperor to renounce Christianity and embrace the faith of Islam. Heraclius, we are told, deposited the epistle respectfully upon his pillow, treated the envoy with distinction, and dismissed him with magnificent presents. Engrossed, however, by his Persian wars, he paid no further attention to this mission, from one whom he probably considered a mere Arab fanatic; nor attached sufficient importance to his military operations, which may have appeared mere predatory forays of the wild tribes of the desert.

Another mission of Mohammed was to the Mukowkis, or governor of Egypt, who had originally been sent there by Heraclius to collect tribute; but who, availing himself of the confusion produced by the wars between the Romans and Persians, had assumed sovereign power, and nearly thrown off all allegiance to the emperor. He received the envoy with signal honor, but evaded a direct reply to the invitation to embrace the faith, observing that it was a grave matter requiring much consideration. In the meantime, he sent presents to Mohammed of precious jewels; garments of Egyptian linen; exquisite honey and butter; a white she-ass, called Yafur; a white mule, called Daldal; and a fleet horse called Lazlos, or the Prancer. The most acceptable of his presents, however, were two Coptic damsels, sisters, called Mariyah (or Mary), and Shiren.

The beauty of Mariyah caused great perturbation in the mind of the prophet. He would fain have made her his concubine, but was impeded by his own law in the seventeenth chapter of the Koran, ordaining that fornication should be punished with stripes.

He was relieved from his dilemma by another revelation, revoking the law in regard to himself alone, allowing him intercourse with his handmaid. It remained in full force, however, against all other Moslems. Still, to avoid scandal, and above all, not to excite the jealousy of his wives, he carried on his intercourse with the beautiful Mariyah in secret— which may be one reason why she remained long a favorite.

27

Mohammed's pilgrimage to Mecca - His marriage with Maimuna - Khaled Ibn Al Waled and Amru Ibn Al Aass become proselytes

The time had now arrived when, by treaty with the Koreishites, Mohammed and his followers were permitted to make a pilgrimage to Mecca, and pass three days unmolested at the sacred shrines. He departed accordingly with a numerous and well-armed host, and seventy camels for sacrifices. His old adversaries would fain have impeded his progress, but they were overawed, and on his approach withdrew silently to the neighboring hills. On entering the bounds of Mecca, the pilgrims, according to compact and usage, laid aside all their warlike accoutrements excepting their swords, which they carried sheathed.

Great was their joy on beholding once more the walls and towers of the sacred city. They entered the gates in pilgrim garb, with devout and thankful hearts, and Mohammed performed all the ancient and customary rites with a zeal and devotion which gratified beholders and drew to him many converts. When be had complied with all the ceremonials, he threw aside the Iram or pilgrim's garb, and withdrew to Sarif, a hamlet two leagues distant, and without the sacred boundaries. Here he had a ceremonial of a different kind to perform, but one in which he was prone to act with unfeigned devotion. It was to complete his marriage with Maimuna, the daughter of Al Hareth, the Helalite. He had become betrothed to her on his arrival at Mecca, but had postponed the nuptials until after he had concluded the rites of pilgrimage. This was doubtless another marriage of policy, for Maimuna was fifty-one years of age, and a widow, but the connection gained him two powerful proselytes.[1]   One was Khaled Ibn al Waled, a nephew of the widow, an intrepid warrior who had come near destroying Mohammed at the battle of Ohod. He now became one of the most victorious champions of Islamism, and by his prowess obtained the appellation of "The Sword of God."

The other proselyte was Khaled's friend, Amru Ibn al Aass, the same who had assailed Mohammed with poetry and satire at the commencement of his prophetic career; who had been an ambassador from the Koreishites to the king of Abyssinia, to obtain the surrender of the fugitive Moslems, and who was henceforth destined with his sword to carry victoriously into foreign lands the faith he had once so strenuously opposed.

28

A Moslem envoy slain in Syria - Expedition to avenge his death - Battle of Muta - Its results

Among the different missions which had been sent by Mohammed beyond the bounds of Arabia to invite neighboring princes to embrace his religion, was one to the governor of Bosra, the great mart on the confines of Syria, to which he had made his first caravan journey in the days of his youth. Syria had been alternately under Roman and Persian domination, but was at that time subject to the emperor, though probably in a great state of confusion. The envoy of Mohammed was slain at Muta, a town about three days' journey eastward from Jerusalem. The one who slew him was an Arab of the Christian tribe of Gassan, and son to Shorhail, an emir, who governed Muta in the name of Heraclius.

To revenge the death of his legate, and to insure respect to his envoys in future, Mohammed prepared to send an army of three thousand men against the offending city. It was a momentous expedition, as it might, for the first time, bring the arms of Islam in collision with those of the Roman Empire; but Mohammed presumed upon his growing power, the energy of his troops, and the disordered state of Syrian affairs. The command was entrusted to his freedman Zeid, who had given such signal proof of devotion in surrendering to him his beautiful wife Zeinab. Several chosen officers were associated with him. One was Mahomet's cousin Jaafar, son of Abu Taleb, and brother of Ali; the same who, by his eloquence, had vindicated the doctrines of Islam before the king of Abyssinia, and defeated the Koreishite embassy. He was now in the prime of life, and noted for great courage and manly beauty. Another of the associate officers was Abdallah Ibn Kawaha, the poet, but who had signalized himself in arms as well as poetry. A third was the new proselyte Khaled, who joined the expedition as a volunteer, being eager to prove by his sword the sincerity of his conversion.

The orders to Zeid were to march rapidly, so as to come upon Muta by surprise, to summon the inhabitants to embrace the faith, and to treat them with lenity. Women, children, monks, and the blind, were to be spared at all events; nor were any houses to be destroyed, nor trees cut down.

The little army sallied from Medina in the full confidence of coming upon the enemy unawares. On their march, however, they learned that a greatly superior force of Romans, or rather Greeks and Arabs, was advancing to meet them. A council of war was called. Some were for pausing, and awaiting further orders from Mohammed; but Abdallah, the poet, was for pushing fearlessly forward without regard to numbers. "We fight for the faith!" cried he; "if we fall, paradise is our reward. On, then, to victory or martyrdom!"

All caught a spark of the poet's fire, or rather, fanaticism. They met the enemy near Muta, and encountered them with fury rather than valor. In the heat of the conflict Zeid received a mortal wound. The sacred banner was falling from his grasp, but was seized and borne aloft by Jaafar. The battle thickened round him, for the banner was the object of fierce contention. He defended it with desperate valor. The hand by which he held it was struck off; he grasped it with the other. That, too, was severed; he embraced it with his bleeding arms. A blow from a scimitar cleft his skull; he sank dead upon the field, still clinging to the standard of the faith. Abdallah the poet next reared the banner, but he too fell beneath the sword. Khaled, the new convert, seeing the three Moslem leaders slain, now grasped the fatal standard, but in his hand it remained aloft. His voice rallied the wavering Moslems; his powerful arm cut its way through the thickest of the enemy. If his own account may be credited, and he was one whose deeds needed no exaggeration, nine scimitars were broken in his hand by the fury of the blows given by him in this deadly conflict.

Night separated the combatants. In the morning Khaled, whom the army acknowledged as their commander, proved himself as wary as he was valiant. By dint of marches and countermarches, he presented his forces in so many points of view, that the enemy were deceived as to his number, and supposed he had received a strong reinforcement. At his first charge, therefore, they retreated. Their retreat soon became a flight, in which they were pursued with great slaughter. Khaled then plundered their camp, in which was found great booty. Among the slain in the field of battle was found the body of Jaafar, covered with wounds, but all in front. Out of respect to his valor, and to his relationship with the prophet, Khaled ordered that his corpse should not be buried on the spot, but borne back for honorable interment at Medina.

The army, on its return, though laden with spoil, entered the city more like a funeral train than a triumphant pageant, and was received with mingled shouts and lamentations. While the people rejoiced in the success of their arms, they mourned the loss of three of their favorite generals. All bewailed the fate of Jaafar, brought home a ghastly corpse to that city whence they had so recently seen him sally forth in all the pride of valiant manhood, the admiration of every beholder. He had left behind him a beautiful wife and infant son. The heart of Mohammed was touched by her affliction. He took the orphan child in his arms and bathed it with his tears. But most he was affected when he beheld the young daughter of his faithful Zeid approaching him. He fell on her neck and wept in speechless emotion. A bystander expressed surprise that he should give way to tears for a death which, according to Moslem doctrine, was but a passport to paradise. "Alas!" replied the prophet, "these are the tears of friendship for the loss of a friend!"

The obsequies of Jaafar were performed on the third day after the arrival of the army. By that time Mohammed had recovered his self-possession, and was again the prophet. He gently rebuked the passionate lamentations of the multitude, taking occasion to inculcate one of the most politic and consolatory doctrines of his creed. "Weep no more," said he, "over the death of this my brother. In place of the two hands lost in defending the standard of the faith, two wings have been given him to bear him to paradise, there to enjoy the endless delights insured to all believers who fall in battle."

It was in consequence of the prowess and generalship displayed by Khaled in this perilous fight that he was honored by Mohammed with the appellation of "The Sword of God," by which he was afterwards renowned.

29

Designs upon Mecca - Mission of Abu Sofian; its result

Mohammed, by force either of arms or eloquence, had now acquired dominion over a great number of the Arabian tribes. He had many thousand warriors under his command—sons of the desert inured to hunger, thirst, and the scorching rays of the sun, and to whom war was a sport rather than a toil. He had corrected their intemperance, disciplined their valor, and subjected them to rule. Repeated victories had given them confidence in themselves and in their leader, whose standard they followed with the implicit obedience of soldiers, and the blind fanaticism of disciples.

The views of Mohammed expanded with his means, and a grand enterprise now opened upon his mind. Mecca, his native city, the abode of his family for generations, the scene of his happiest years, was still in the hands of his implacable foes. The Caaba, the object of devotion and pilgrimage to all the children of Ishmael, the shrine of his earliest worship, was still profaned by the emblems and rites of idolatry. To plant the standard of the faith on the walls of his native city; to rescue the holy house from profanation; to restore it to the spiritual worship of the one true God, and make it the rallying point of Islam, formed now the leading object of his ambition.

The treaty of peace existing with the Koreishites was an impediment to any military enterprise, but some casual feuds and skirmishings soon gave a pretext for charging them with having violated the treaty stipulations. The Koreishites had by this time learned to appreciate and dread the rapidly increasing power of the Moslems, and were eager to explain away, or atone for, the quarrels and misdeeds of a few heedless individuals. They even prevailed on their leader, Abu Sofian, to repair to

Medina as ambassador of peace, trusting that he might have some influence with the prophet through his daughter, Omm Habiba.

It was a sore trial to this haughty chief to come almost a suppliant to the man whom he had scoffed at as an impostor, and treated with inveterate hostility; and his proud spirit was doomed to still further mortification, for Mohammed, judging from his errand of the weakness of his party, and being secretly bent on war, vouchsafed him no reply.

Repressing his rage, Abu Sofian sought the intermediation of Abu Beker, of Omar, and Ali; but they all rebuked and repulsed him, for they knew the secret wishes of Mohammed. He next endeavored to secure the favor of Fatima, the daughter of Mohammed and wife of Ali, by flattering a mother's pride, entreating her to let her son Hasan, a child but six years old, be his protector; but Fatima answered haughtily, "My son is too young to be a protector; and no protection can avail against the will of the prophet of God." Even his daughter, Omm Habiba, the wife of Mohammed, on whom Abu Sofian had calculated for influence, added to his mortification, for on his offering to seat himself on a mat in her dwelling, she hastily folded it up, exclaiming, "It is the bed of the prophet of God, and too sacred to be made the resting place of an idolater."

The cup of humiliation was full to overflowing, and in the bitterness of his heart Abu Sofian cursed his daughter. He now turned again to Ali, beseeching his advice in the desperate state of his embassy.

"I can advise nothing better," replied Ali, "than for thee to promise, as the head of the Koreishites, a continuance of thy protection; and then to return to thy home."

"But thinkest thou that promise will be of any avail?"

"I think not," replied Ali, dryly; "but I know not to the contrary."

In pursuance of this advice, Abu Sofian repaired to the mosque and made public declaration, in behalf of the Koreishites, that on their part the treaty of peace should be faithfully maintained, after which he returned to Mecca, deeply humiliated by the imperfect result of his mission. He was received with scoffs by the Koreishites, who observed that his declaration of peace availed nothing without the concurrence of Mohammed.

30

Surprise and capture of Mecca

Mohammed now prepared for a secret expedition to take Mecca by surprise. His allies were summoned from all quarters to Medina, but no intimation was given of the object he had in view. All the roads leading to Mecca were barred to prevent any intelligence of his movements being carried to the Koreishites. With all his precautions the secret came near being discovered. Among his followers, fugitives from Mecca, was one named Hateb, whose family had remained behind, and were without connections or friends to take an interest in their welfare. Hateb now thought to gain favor for them among the Koreishites by betraying the plans of Mohammed. He accordingly wrote a letter revealing the intended enterprise, and gave it in charge to a singing woman named Sara, a Haschemite slave, who undertook to carry it to Mecca.

She was already on the road when Mohammed was apprised of the treachery. Ali and five others, well mounted, were sent in pursuit of the messenger. They soon overtook her, but searched her person in vain. Most of them would have given up the search and turned back, but Ali was confident that the prophet of God could not be mistaken nor misinformed. Drawing his scimitar he swore to strike off the head of the messenger unless the letter were produced. The threat was effectual. She drew forth the letter from among her hair.

Hateb, on being taxed with his perfidy, acknowledged it, but pleaded his anxiety to secure favor for his destitute family, and his certainty that the letter would be harmless, and of no avail against the purposes of the apostle of God. Omar spurned at his excuses and would have struck off his head; but Mohammed, calling to mind that Hateb had fought bravely in support of the faith in the battle of Beder, admitted his excuses and forgave him.

The prophet departed with ten thousand men on this momentous enterprise. Omar, who had charge of regulating the march and appointing the encampments, led the army by lonely passes of the mountains, prohibiting the sound of attabal or trumpet, or anything else that could betray their movements. While on the march, Mohammed was joined by his uncle Al Abbas, who had come forth with his family from Mecca to rally under the standard of the faith. Mohammed received him graciously, yet with a hint at his tardiness. "Thou art the last of the emigrants," said he, "as I am the last of the prophets." Al Abbas sent his family forward to Medina, while he turned and accompanied the expedition. The army reached the valley of Marr Azzahran, near to the sacred city, without being discovered. It was nightfall when they silently pitched their tents, and now Omar for the first time permitted them to light their watch fires.

In the meantime, though Al Abbas had joined the standard of the faith in all sincerity, yet he was sorely disquieted at seeing his nephew advancing against Mecca, with such a powerful force and such hostile intent, and feared the entire destruction of the Koreishites unless they could be persuaded in time to capitulate. In the dead of the night, he mounted Mohammed's white mule Fadda, and rode forth to reconnoitre. In skirting the camp, he heard the tramp of men and sound of voices. A scouting party were bringing in two prisoners captured near the city. Al Abbas approached, and found the captives to be Abu Sofian and one of his captains. They were conducted to the watch fire of Omar, who recognized Abu Sofian by the light. "God be praised," cried he, "that I have such an enemy in my hands, and without conditions." His ready scimitar might have given fatal significance to his words, had not Al Abbas stepped forward and taken Abu Sofian under his protection, until the will of the prophet should be known. Omar rushed forth to ascertain that will, or rather to demand the life of the prisoner; but Al Abbas, taking the latter up behind him, put spurs to his mule, and was the first to reach the tent of the prophet, followed hard by Omar, clamoring for the head of Abu Sofian.

Mohammed thus beheld in his power his inveterate enemy who had driven him from his home and country, and persecuted his family and friends; but he beheld in him the father of his wife Omm Habiba, and felt inclined to clemency. He postponed all decision in the matter until morning, giving Abu Sofian in charge of Al Abbas.

When the captive was brought before him on the following day: "Well, Abu Sofian," cried he, "is it not at length time to know that there is no other God but God?"

"That I already knew," replied Abu Sofian.

"Good! and is it not time for thee to acknowledge me as the apostle of God?"

"Dearer art thou to me than my father and my mother," replied Abu Sofian, using an oriental phrase of compliment; "but I am not yet prepared to acknowledge thee a prophet."

"Out upon thee !" cried Omar, "testify instantly to the truth, or thy head shall be severed from thy body."

To these threats were added the counsels and entreaties of Al Abbas, who showed himself a real friend in need. The rancor of Abu Sofian had already been partly subdued by the unexpected mildness of Mohammed; so, making a merit of necessity, he acknowledged the divinity of his mission, furnishing an illustration of the Moslem maxim, "To convince stubborn unbelievers, there is no argument like the sword."

Having now embraced the faith, Abu Sofian obtained favorable terms for the people of Mecca, in case of their submission. None were to be harmed who should remain quietly in their houses; or should take refuge in the houses of Abu Sofian and Hakim; or under the banner of Abu Rawaiha.

That Abu Sofian might take back to the city a proper idea of the force brought against it, he was stationed with Al Abbas at a narrow defile where the whole army passed in review. As the various Arab tribes marched by with their different arms and ensigns, Al Abbas explained the name and country of each. Abu Sofian was surprised at the number, discipline, and equipment of the troops, for the Moslems had been rapidly improving in the means and art of war. But when Mohammed approached, in the midst of a chosen guard, armed at all points and glittering with steel, his astonishment passed all bounds. "There is no withstanding this!" he cried to Al Abbas, with an oath—"truly thy nephew wields a mighty power."

"Even so," replied the other; "return then to thy people; provide for their safety, and warn them not to oppose the apostle of God."

Abu Sofian hastened back to Mecca and, assembling the inhabitants, told them of the mighty host at hand, led on by Mohammed; of the favorable terms offered in case of their submission; and of the vanity of all resistance. As Abu Sofian had been the soul of the opposition to Mohammed and his doctrines, his words had instant effect in producing acquiescence in an event which seemed to leave no alternative. The greater part of the inhabitants, therefore, prepared to witness, without resistance, the entry of the prophet.

Mohammed, in the meantime, who knew not what resistance he might meet with, made a careful distribution of his forces as he approached the city. While the main body marched directly forward, strong detachments advanced over the hills on each side. To Ali, who commanded a large body of cavalry, was confided the sacred banner, which he was to plant on Mount Hadjun, and maintain it there until joined by the prophet. Express orders were given to all the generals to practice forbearance, and in no instance to make the first attack; for it was the earnest desire of Mohammed to win Mecca by moderation and clemency, rather than subdue it by violence. It is true, all who offered armed resistance were to be cut down, but none were to be harmed who submitted quietly. Overhearing one of his captains exclaim, in the heat of his zeal, that "no place was sacred on the day of battle," he instantly appointed a cooler-headed commander in his place.

The main body of the army advanced without molestation. Mohammed brought up the rear guard, clad in a scarlet vest, and mounted on his favorite camel Al Kaswa. He proceeded but slowly, however, his movements being impeded by the immense multitude which thronged around him. When he arrived on Mount Hadjun, where Ali had planted the standard of the faith, a tent was pitched for him. Here he alighted, put off his scarlet garment, and assumed the black turban and the pilgrim garb. Casting a look down into the plain, however, he beheld, with grief and indignation, the gleam of swords and lances, and Khaled, who commanded the left wing, in a full career of carnage. His troops, composed of Arab tribes converted to the faith, had been galled by a flight of arrows from a body of Koreishites; whereupon the fiery warrior charged into the thickest of them with sword and lance; his troops pressed after him, put the enemy to flight, entered the gates of Mecca pell-mell with them, and nothing but the swift commands of Mohammed preserved the city from a general massacre.

The carnage being stopped, and no further opposition manifested, the prophet descended from the mount and approached the gates, seated on his camel, accompanied by Abu Beker on his right hand, and followed by Osama, the son of Zeid. The sun was just rising as he entered the gates of his native city, with the glory of a conqueror but the garb and humility of a pilgrim. He entered, repeating verses of the Koran, which he said had been revealed to him at Medina, and were prophetic of the event. He triumphed in the spirit of a religious zealot, not of a warrior. "Unto God," said he, "belong the hosts of heaven and earth, and God is mighty and wise. Now hath God verified unto his apostle the vision, wherein he said, ye shall surely enter the holy temple of Mecca in full security."

Without dismounting, Mohammed repaired directly to the Caaba, the scene of his early devotions, the sacred shrine of worship since the days of the patriarchs, and which he regarded as the primitive temple of the one true God. Here he made the seven circuits round the sacred edifice, a reverential rite from the days of religious purity; with the same devout feeling he each time touched the black stone with his staff, regarding it as a holy relic. He would have entered the Caaba, but Othman Ibn Talha, the ancient custodian, locked the door. Ali snatched the keys, but Mohammed caused them to be returned to the venerable officer, and so won him by his kindness that he not merely threw open the doors but subsequently embraced the faith of Islam; whereupon he was continued in his office.

Mohammed now proceeded to execute the great object of his religious aspirations, the purifying of the sacred edifice from the symbols of idolatry, with which it was crowded. All the idols in and about it, to the number of three hundred and sixty, were thrown down and destroyed. Among these, the most renowned was Hobal, an idol brought from Balka, in Syria, and fabled to have the power of granting rain. It was, of course, a great object of worship among the inhabitants of the thirsty desert. There were statues of Abraham and Ishmael also, represented with divining arrows in their hands—"an outrage on their memories," said Mohammed, "being symbols of a diabolical art which they had never practiced." In reverence of their memories, therefore, these statues were demolished. There were paintings, also, depicting angels in the guise of beautiful women. "The angels," said Mohammed indignantly, "are no such beings. There are celestial houris provided in paradise for the solace of true believers; but angels are ministering spirits of the Most High, and of too pure a nature to admit of sex." The paintings were accordingly obliterated.

Even a dove, curiously carved of wood, he broke with his own hands, and cast upon the ground, as savoring of idolatry.

From the Caaba he proceeded to the well of Zem Zem. It was sacred in his eyes, from his belief that it was the identical well revealed by the angel to Hagar and Ishmael, in their extremity. He considered the rite connected with it as pure and holy, and continued it in his faith. As he approached the well, his uncle Al Abbas presented him a cruse of the water, that he might drink, and make the customary ablution. In commemoration of this pious act, he appointed his uncle guardian of the cup of the well, an office of sacred dignity which his descendants retain to this day.

At noon one of his followers, at his command, summoned the people to prayer from the top of the Caaba, a custom continued ever since throughout Moslem countries, from minarets or towers provided in every mosque. He also established the Kebla, toward which the faithful in every part of the world should turn their faces in prayer.

He afterwards addressed the people in a kind of sermon, setting forth his principal doctrines, and announcing the triumph of the faith as a fulfillment of prophetic promise. Shouts burst from the multitude in reply, "Allah Achbar, God is great!" they cried. "There is no God but God, and Mohammed is his prophet."

The religious ceremonials being ended, Mohammed took his station on the hill Al Safa, and the people of Mecca, male and female, passed before him, taking the oath of fidelity to him as the prophet of God, and renouncing idolatry. This was in compliance with a revelation in the Koran: "God hath sent his apostle with the direction and the religion of truth, that he may exalt the same over every religion. Verily, they who swear fealty to him, swear fealty unto God; the hand of God is over their hands." In the midst of his triumph, however, he rejected all homage paid exclusively to himself, and all regal authority. "Why dost thou tremble?" said he, to a man who approached with timid and faltering steps. "Of what dost thou stand in awe? I am no king, but the son of a Koreishite woman, who ate flesh dried in the sun."

His lenity was equally conspicuous. The once haughty chiefs of the Koreishites appeared with abject countenances before the man they had persecuted, for their lives were in his power.

"What can you expect at my hands?" he demanded sternly.

"Mercy, O generous brother! Mercy, O son of a generous line!"

"Be it so!" he cried, with a mixture of scorn and pity. "Away! begone! ye are free!"

Some of his followers who had shared his persecutions were disappointed in their anticipations of a bloody revenge and murmured at his clemency; but he persisted in it, and established Mecca as an inviolable sanctuary, or place of refuge, so to continue until the final resurrection. He reserved to himself, however, the right on the present occasion, and during that special day, to punish a few of the people of the city who had grievously offended, and been expressly proscribed; yet even these, for the most part, were ultimately forgiven.

Among the Koreishite women who advanced to take the oath, he descried Henda, the wife of Abu Sofian, the savage woman who had animated the infidels at the battle of Ohod, and had gnawed the heart of Hamza, in revenge for the death of her father. On the present occasion she had disguised herself to escape detection; but seeing the eyes of the prophet fixed on her, she threw herself at his feet, exclaiming, "I am Henda: pardon! pardon!" Mohammed pardoned her—and was requited for his clemency by her making his doctrines the subject of contemptuous sarcasms.

Among those destined to punishment was Wacksa, the Ethiopian who had slain Hamza; but he had fled from Mecca on the entrance of the army. At a subsequent period he presented himself before the prophet, and made the profession of faith before he was recognized. He was forgiven, and made to relate the particulars of the death of Hamza; after which Mohammed dismissed him with an injunction never again to come into his presence. He survived until the time of the Caliphat of Omar, during whose reign he was repeatedly scourged for drunkenness.

Another of the proscribed was Abdallah Ibn Saad, a young Koreishite distinguished for wit and humor, as well as for warlike accomplishments. As he held the pen of a ready writer, Mohammed had employed him to reduce the revelations of the Koran to writing. In so doing, he had often altered and amended the text; nay, it was discovered that, through carelessness or design, he had occasionally falsified it, and rendered it absurd. He had even made his alterations and amendments matters of scoff and jest among his companions, observing that if the Koran proved Mohammed to be a prophet, he himself must be half a prophet. His interpolations being detected, he had fled from the wrath of the prophet, and returned to Mecca, where he relapsed into idolatry. On the capture of the city his foster-brother concealed him in his house until the tumult had subsided, when he led him into the presence of the prophet and supplicated for his pardon. This was the severest trial of the lenity of Mohammed. The offender had betrayed his confidence, held him up to ridicule, questioned his apostolic mission, and struck at the very foundation of his faith. For some time he maintained a stern silence, hoping, as he afterwards declared, that some zealous disciple might strike off the offender's head. No one, however, stirred; so, yielding to the entreaties of Othman, Mohammed granted a pardon. Abdallah instantly renewed his profession of faith, and continued a good Moslem. His name will be found in the wars of the Caliphs. He was one of the most dexterous horsemen of his tribe, and evinced his ruling passion to the last, for he died repeating the hundredth chapter of the Koran, entitled "The War Steeds." Perhaps it was one which had experienced his interpolations.

Another of the proscribed was Akrema Ibn Abu Jahl, who on many occasions had manifested a deadly hostility to the prophet, inherited from his father. On the entrance of Mohammed into Mecca, Akrema threw himself upon a fleet horse and escaped by an opposite gate, leaving behind him a beautiful wife, Omm Hakem, to whom he was recently married. She embraced the faith of Islam, but soon after learned that her husband, in attempting to escape by sea to Yemen, had been driven back to port. Hastening to the presenee of the prophet, she threw herself on her knees before him, loose, dishevelled, and unveiled, and implored grace for her husband. The prophet, probably more moved by her beauty than her grief, raised her gently from the earth, and told her her prayer was granted. Hurrying to the seaport, she arrived just as the vessel in which her husband had embarked was about to sail. She returned, mounted behind him, to Mecca, and brought him, a true believer, into the presence of the prophet. On this occasion, however, she was so closely veiled that her dark eyes alone were visible. Mohammed received Akrema's profession of faith, made him commander of a battalion of Hawazenites, as the dower of his beautiful and devoted wife, and bestowed liberal donations on the youthful couple. Like many other converted enemies, Akrema proved a valiant soldier in the wars of the faith, and after signalizing himself on various occasions, fell in battle, hacked and pierced by swords and lances.

The whole conduct of Mohammed on gaining possession of Mecca showed that it was a religious more than a military triumph. His heart, too, softened toward his native place, now that it was in his power; his resentments were extinguished by success, and his inclinations were all toward forgiveness.

The Ansarians, or Auxiliaries of Medina, who had aided him in his campaign, began to fear that its success might prove fatal to their own interests. They watched him anxiously, as one day, after praying on the hill Al Safa, he sat gazing down wistfully upon Mecca, the scene of his early struggles and recent glory: "Verily," said he, "thou art the best of cities, and the most beloved of Allah! Had I not been driven out from thee by my own tribe, never would I have left thee!" On hearing this, the Ansarians said, one to another, "Behold! Mohammed is conqueror and master of his native city; he will, doubtless, establish himself here, and forsake Medina!" Their words reached his ear, and he turned to them with reproachful warmth: "No!" he cried, "when you plighted to me your allegiance, I swore to live and die with you. I should not act as the servant of God, nor as his ambassador, were I to leave you."

He acted according to his words, and Medina, which had been his city of refuge, continued to be his residence to his dying day.

Mohammed did not content himself with purifying the Caaba, and abolishing idolatry from his native city; he sent forth his captains at the head of armed bands, to cast down the idols of different tribes set up in the neighboring towns and villages, and to convert their worshippers to his faith.

Of all these military apostles, none was so zealous as Khaled, whose spirit was still fermenting with recent conversion. Arriving at Naklah, the resort of the idolatrous Koreishites to worship at the shrine of Uzza, he penetrated the sacred grove, laid waste the temple, and cast the idol to the ground. A horrible hag, black and naked, with dishevelled hair, rushed forth, shrieking and wringing her hands; but Khaled severed her through the middle with one blow of his scimitar. He reported the deed to Mohammed, expressing a doubt whether she were priestess or evil spirit "Of a truth," replied the prophet, "it was Uzza herself whom thou hast destroyed."

On a similar errand into the neighboring province of Tehama, Khaled had with him three hundred and fifty men, some of them of the tribe of Suleim, and was accompanied by Abda'lrahman, one of the earliest proselytes of the faith. His instructions from the prophet were to preach peace and good will, to inculcate the faith, and to abstain from violence, unless assailed. When about two days' journey on his way to Tehama, he had to pass through the country of the tribe of Jadsima. Most of the inhabitants had embraced the faith, but some were still of the Sabean religion. On a former occasion this tribe had plundered and slain an uncle of Khaled, also the father of Abda'lrahman, and several Suleimites, as they were returning from Arabia Felix. Dreading that Khaled and his host might take vengeance for these misdeeds, they armed themselves on their approach.

Khaled was secretly rejoiced at seeing them ride forth to meet him in this military array. Hailing them with an imperious tone, he demanded whether they were Moslems or infidels. They replied, in faltering accents, "Moslems." "Why then come ye forth to meet us with weapons in your hands?" "Because we have enemies among some of the tribes who may attack us unawares."

Khaled sternly ordered them to dismount and lay by their weapons. Some complied, and were instantly seized and bound; the rest fled. Taking their flight as a confession of guilt, he pursued them with great slaughter, laid waste the country, and in the effervescence of his zeal even slew some of the prisoners.

Mohammed, when he heard of this unprovoked outrage, raised his hands to heaven, and called God to witness that he was innocent of it. Khaled, when upbraided with it on his return, would fain have shifted the blame on Abda'lrahman, but Mohammed rejected indignantly an imputation against one of the earliest and worthiest of his followers. The generous Ali was sent forthwith to restore to the people of Jadsima what Khaled had wrested from them, and to make pecuniary compensation to the relatives of the slain. It was a mission congenial with his nature, and he executed it faithfully. Inquiring into the losses and sufferings of each individual, he paid him to his full content. When every loss was made good, and all blood atoned for, he distributed the remaining money among the people, gladdening every heart by his bounty. So Ali received the thanks and praises of the prophet, but the vindictive Khaled was rebuked even by those whom he had thought to please.

"Behold!" said he, to Abda'lrahman, "I have avenged the death of thy father." "Rather say," replied the other, indignantly, "thou hast avenged the death of thine uncle. Thou hast disgraced the faith by an act worthy of an idolater."

31

Hostilities in the mountains - Enemy's camp in the valley of Autas - Battle of the pass of Honein - Capture of the enemy's camp - Interview of Mohammed with the nurse of his childhood - Division of spoils - Mohammed at his mother's grave

While the military apostles of Mohammed were spreading his doctrines at the point of the sword in the plains, a hostile storm was gathering in the mountains. A league was formed among the Thakefites, the Hawazins, the Joshmites, the Saadites, and several of the hardy mountain tribes of Bedouins, to check a power which threatened to subjugate all Arabia. The Saadites, or Beni Sad, here mentioned, are the same pastoral Arabs among whom Mohammed had been nurtured in his childhood, and in whose valley, according to tradition, his heart had been plucked forth and purified by an angel. The Thakefites, who were foremost in the league, were a powerful tribe, possessing the strong mountain town of Taif and its productive territory. They were bigoted idolaters, maintaining at their capital the far-famed shrine of the female idol Al Lat. The reader will remember the ignominious treatment of Mohammed, when he attempted to preach his doctrines at Taif: being stoned in the public square, and ultimately driven with insult from the gates. It was probably a dread of vengeance at his hands which now made the Thakefites so active in forming a league against him.

Malec Ibn Auf, the chief of the Thakefites, had the general command of the confederacy. He appointed the valley of Autas, between Honein and Taif, as the place of assemblage and encampment; and as he knew the fickle nature of the Arabs, and their proneness to return home on the least caprice, he ordered them to bring with them their families and effects. They assembled, accordingly, from various parts, to the number of four thousand fighting men; but the camp was crowded with women and children, and encumbered with flocks and herds.

The expedient of Malec Ibn Auf to secure the adhesion of the warriors was strongly disapproved by Doraid, the chief of the Joshmites. This was an ancient warrior, upwards of a hundred years old, meagre as a skeleton, almost blind, and so feeble that he had to be borne in a litter on the back of a camel. Still, though unable to mingle in the battle, he was potent in council from his military experience. This veteran of the desert advised that the women and children should be sent home forthwith, and the army relieved from all unnecessary incumbrances. His advice was not taken, and the valley of Autas continued to present rather the pastoral encampment of a tribe, than the hasty levy of an army.

In the meantime Mohammed, hearing of the gathering storm, had sallied forth to anticipate it, at the head of about twelve thousand troops, partly fugitives from Mecca and auxiliaries from Medina, partly Arabs of the desert, some of whom had not yet embraced the faith.

In taking the field he wore a polished cuirass and helmet and rode his favorite white mule Daldal, seldom mounting a charger, as he rarely mingled in actual fight. His recent successes and his superiority in numbers making him confident of an easy victory, he entered the mountains without precaution and, pushing forward for the enemy's camp at Mutas, came to a deep, gloomy valley on the confines of Honein. The troops marched without order through the rugged defile, each one choosing his own path. Suddenly they were assailed by showers of darts, stones and arrows, which lay two or three of Mohammed's soldiers dead at his feet, and wounded several others. Malec, in fact, had taken post with his ablest warriors about the heights commanding this narrow gorge. Every cliff and cavern was garrisoned with archers and slingers, and some rushed down to contend at close quarters.

Struck with a sudden panic, the Moslems turned and fled. In vain did Mohammed call upon them as their general, or appeal to them as the prophet of God. Each man sought but his own safety, and an escape from this horrible valley.

For a moment all seemed lost, and some recent but unwilling converts betrayed an exultation in the supposed reverse of fortune of the prophet.

"By heavens!" cried Abu Sofian, as he looked after the flying Moslems, "nothing will stop them until they reach the sea."

"Ay," exclaimed another, "the magic power of Mohammed is at an end! "

A third, who cherished a lurking revenge for the death of his father, slain by the Moslems in the battle of Ohod, would have killed the prophet in the confusion, had he not been surrounded and protected by a few devoted followers. Mohammed himself, in an impulse of desperation, spurred his mule upon the enemy; but Al Abbas seized the bridle, stayed him from rushing to certain death, and at the same time put up a shout that echoed through the narrow valley. Al Abbas was renowned for strength of lungs, and at this critical moment it was the salvation of the army. The Moslems rallied when they heard his well-known voice and, finding they were not pursued, returned to the combat. The enemy had descended from the heights, and now a bloody conflict ensued in the defile. "The furnace is kindling," cried Mohammed exultingly, as he saw the glitter of arms and flash of weapons. Stooping from his saddle, and grasping a handful of dust, he scattered it in the air toward the enemy. "Confusion on their faces!" cried he, "may this dust blind them!" They were blinded accordingly, and fled in confusion, say the Moslem writers, though their defeat may rather be attributed to the Moslem superiority of force, and the zeal inspired by the exclamations of the prophet. Malec and the Thakefites took refuge in the distant city of Taif; the rest retreated to the camp in the valley of Autas.

While Mohammed remained in the valley of Honein, he sent Abu Amir with a strong force to attack the camp. The Hawazins made a brave defense. Abu Amir was slain, but his nephew, Abu Musa, took the command and obtained a complete victory, killing many of the enemy. The camp afforded great booty and many captives, from the unwise expedient of Malec Ibn Auf in encumbering it with the families and effects, the flocks and herds of the confederates, and from his disregard of the sage advice of the veteran Doraid. The fate of that ancient warrior of the desert is worthy of mention. While the Moslem troops, scattered through the camp, were intent on booty, Rabia Ibn Rafi, a young Suleimite, observed a litter borne off on the back of a camel, and pursued it, supposing it to contain some beautiful female. On overtaking it and drawing the curtain, he beheld the skeleton form of the ancient Doraid. Vexed and disappointed, he struck at him with his sword, but the weapon broke in his hand. "Thy mother," said the old man sneeringly, "has furnished thee with wretched weapons; thou wilt find a better one hanging behind my saddle."

The youth seized it, but as he drew it from the scabbard, Doraid perceiving, that he was a Suleimite, exclaimed, "Tell thy mother thou hast slain Doraid Ibn Simma, who has protected many women of her tribe in the day of battle." The words were ineffectual; the skull of the veteran was cloven with his own scimitar. When Rabia, on his return to Mecca, told his mother of the deed, "Thou hast indeed slain a benefactor of thy race," said she reproachfully. "Three women of thy family has Doraid Ibn Simma freed from captivity."

Abu Musa returned in triumph to Mohammed, making a great display of the spoils of the camp of Autas, and the women and children whom he had captured. One of the female captives threw herself at the feet of the prophet, and implored his mercy as his foster-sister Al Shima, the daughter of his nurse Halêma, who had nurtured him in the Saadite valley. Mohammed sought in vain to recognize in her withered features the bright playmate of his infancy, but she laid bare her back, and showed a scar where he had bitten her in their childish gambols. He no longer doubted, but treated her with kindness, giving her the choice either to remain with him and under his protection, or to return to her home and kindred.

A scruple rose among the Moslems with respect to their female captives. Could they take to themselves such as were married, without committing the sin of adultery? The revelation of a text of the Koran put an end to the difficulty. "Ye shall not take to wife free women who are married, unless your right hand shall have made them slaves." According to this all women taken in war may be made the wives of the captors, though their former husbands be living. The victors of Honein did not fail to take immediate advantage of this law.

Leaving the captives and the booty in a secure place, and properly guarded, Mohammed now proceeded in pursuit of the Thakefites who had taken refuge in Taif. A sentiment of vengeance mingled with his pious ardor as he approached this idolatrous place, the scene of former injury and insult, and beheld the gate whence he had once been ignominiously driven forth. The walls were too strong, however, to be stormed, and there was a protecting castle; for the first time, therefore, he had recourse to catapults, battering rams, and other engines used in sieges, but unknown in Arabian warfare. These were prepared under the direction of Salmân al Farsi, the converted Persian.

The besieged, however, repulsed every attack, galling the assailants with darts and arrows, and pouring down melted iron upon the shields of bull-hides, under cover of which they approached the walls. Mohammed now laid waste the fields, the orchards, and vineyards, and proclaimed freedom to all slaves who should desert from the city. For twenty days he carried on an ineffectual siege, daily offering up prayers midway between the tents of his wives Omm Salama and Zeinab, to whom it had fallen by lot to accompany him in this campaign. His hopes of success began to fail, and he was further discouraged by a dream, which was unfavorably interpreted by Abu Beker, renowned for his skill in expounding visions. He would have raised the siege, but his troops murmured, whereupon he ordered an assault upon one of the gates. As usual, it was obstinately defended; numbers were slain on both sides. Abu Sofian, who fought valiantly on the occasion, lost an eye, and the Moslems were finally repulsed.

Mohammed now broke up his camp, promising his troops to renew the siege at a future day, and proceeded to the place where were collected the spoils of his expedition. These, say Arabian writers, amounted to twenty-four thousand camels, forty thousand sheep, four thousand ounces of silver, and six thousand captives.

In a little while appeared a deputation from the Hawazins, declaring the submission of their tribe, and begging the restoration of their families and effects. With them came Halêma, Mohammed's foster-nurse, now well stricken in years. The recollections of his childhood again pleaded with his heart. "Which is dearest to you," said he to the Hawazins, "your families or your goods?" They replied, "Our families."

"Enough," he rejoined, "as far as it concerns Al Abbas and myself, we are ready to give up our share of the prisoners; but there are others to be moved. Come to me after noontide prayer, and say, 'we implore the ambassador of God that he counsel his followers to return us our wives and children; and we implore his followers that they intercede with him in our favor.'" The envoys did as he advised. Mohammed and Al Abbas immediately renounced their share of the captives; their example was followed by all excepting the tribes of Tamim and Fazara, but Mohammed brought them to consent by promising them a sixfold share of the prisoners taken in the next expedition. Thus the intercession of Halêma procured the deliverance of all the captives of her tribe. A traditional anecdote shows the deference with which Mohammed treated this humble protector of his infancy. "I was sitting with the prophet," said one of his disciples, "when all of a sudden a woman presented herself, and he rose and spread his cloth for her to sit down upon. When she went away, it was observed, 'that woman suckled the prophet.'"

Mohammed now sent an envoy to Malec, who remained shut up in Taif, offering the restitution of all the spoils taken from him at Honein, and a present of one hundred camels, if he would submit and embrace the faith. Malec was conquered and converted by this liberal offer, and brought several of his confederate tribes with him to the standard of the prophet. He was immediately made their chief, and proved, subsequently, a severe scourge in the cause of the faith to his late associates the Thakefites.

The Moslems now began to fear that Mohammed, in these magnanimous impulses, might squander away all the gains of their recent battles; thronging around him, therefore, they clamored for a division of the spoils and captives. Regarding them, indignantly, "Have you ever," said he, "found me avaricious, or false, or disloyal?" Then plucking a hair from the back of a camel, and raising his voice, "By Allah!" cried he, "I have never taken from the common spoil the value of that camel's hair more than my fifth; and that fifth has always been expended for your good."

He then shared the booty as usual: four-fifths among the troops, but his own fifth he distributed among those whose fidelity he wished to insure. The Koreishites he considered dubious allies; perhaps he had overheard the exultation of some of them in anticipation of his defeat; he now sought to rivet them to him by gifts. To Abu Sofian he gave one hundred camels and forty okes of silver, in compensation for the eye lost in the attack on the gate of Taif. To Akrema Ibn Abu Jahl, and others of like note, he gave in due proportions, and all from his own share.

Among the lukewarm converts thus propitiated was Abbas Ibn Mardas, a poet. He was dissatisfied with his share, and vented his discontent in satirical verses. Mohammed overheard him. "Take that man hence," said he, "and cut out his tongue." Omar, ever ready for rigorous measures, would have executed the sentence literally, and on the spot; but others, better instructed in the prophet's meaning, led Abbas, all trembling, to the public square where the captured cattle were collected, and bade him choose what he liked from among them.

"What!" cried the poet joyously, relieved from the horrors of mutilation, "is this the way the prophet would silence my tongue? By Allah! I will take nothing." Mohammed, however, persisted in his politic generosity, and sent him sixty camels. From that time forward the poet was never weary of chanting the liberality of the prophet.

While thus stimulating the goodwill of lukewarm proselytes of Mecca, Mohammed excited the murmurs of his auxiliaries of Medina, "See," they said, "how he lavishes gifts upon the treacherous Koreishites, while we, who have been loyal to him through all dangers, receive nothing but our naked share. What have we done that we should be thus thrown into the background?"

Mohammed was told of their murmurs, and summoned their leaders to his tent. "Hearken, ye men of Medina," said he; "were ye not in discord among yourselves, and have I not brought you into harmony? Were ye not in error, and have I not brought you into the path of truth? Were ye not poor, and have I not made you rich?"

They acknowledged the truth of his words. "Look ye!" he continued, "I came among you stigmatized as a liar, yet you believed in me; persecuted, yet you protected me; a fugitive, yet you sheltered me; helpless, yet you aided me. Think you I do not feel all this? Think you I can be ungrateful? You complain that I bestow gifts upon these people, and give none to you. It is true, I give them worldly gear, but it is to win their worldly hearts. To you, who have been true, I give myself! They return home with sheep and camels; ye return with the prophet of God among you. For by him in whose hands is the soul of Mohammed, though the whole world should go one way and ye another, I would remain with you! Which of you, then, have I most rewarded? "

The auxiliaries were moved even to tears by this appeal. "O prophet of God," they exclaimed, "we are content with our lot!"

The booty being divided, Mohammed returned to Mecca, not with the parade and exultation of a conqueror, but in pilgrim garb, to complete the rites of his pilgrimage. All these being scrupulously performed, he appointed Moad Ibn Jabal as imam, or pontiff, to instruct the people in the doctrines of Islam, and gave the government of the city into the hands of Otab, a youth but eighteen years of age; after which he bade farewell to his native place, and set out with his troops on the return to Medina.

When Mohammed arrived at the village of Al Abwa, where his mother was buried, his heart yearned to pay a filial tribute to her memory, but his own revealed law forbade any respect to the grave of one who had died in unbelief. In the strong agitation of his feelings he implored from heaven a relaxation of this law. If there was any deception on an occasion of this kind, one would imagine it must have been self-deception, and that he really believed in a fancied intimation from heaven relaxing the law, in part, in the present instance, and permitting him to visit the grave. He burst into tears on arriving at this trying place of the tenderest affections; but tears were all the filial tribute he was permitted to offer. "I asked leave of God," said he, mournfully, "to visit my mother's grave, and it was granted; but when I asked leave to pray for her, it was denied me!"

32

Death of the prophet's daughter Zeinab - Birth of his son Ibrahim - Deputations from distant tribes - Poetical contest in presence of the prophet - His susceptibility to the charms of poetry - Reduction of the city of Taif; destruction of its idols - Negotiation with Amir Ibn Tufiel, a proud Bedouin chief; independent spirit of the latter - Interview of Adi, another chief, with Mohammed

Shortly after his return to Medina, Mohammed was afflicted by the death of his daughter Zeinab, the same who had been given up to him in exchange for her husband Abul Aass, the unbeliever captured at the battle of Beder. The domestic affections of the prophet were strong, and he felt deeply this bereavement; he was consoled, however, by the birth of a son, by his favorite concubine Mariyah. He called the child Ibrahim, and rejoiced in the hope that this son of his old age, his only male issue living, would continue his name to after generations.

His fame, either as a prophet or a conqueror, was now spreading to the uttermost parts of Arabia, and deputations from distant tribes were continually arriving at Medina, some acknowledging him as a prophet and embracing Islam, others submitting to him as a temporal sovereign, and agreeing to pay tribute. The talents of Mohammed rose to the exigency of the moment; his views expanded with his fortunes, and he now proceeded with statesmanlike skill to regulate the fiscal concerns of his rapidly growing empire. Under the specious appellation of alms, a contribution was levied on true believers, amounting to a tithe of the productions of the earth, where it was fertilized by brooks and rain; and a twentieth part where its fertility was the result of irrigation. For every ten camels, two sheep were required; for forty head of cattle, one cow; for thirty head, a two years' calf; for every forty sheep, one; whoever contributed more than at this rate would be considered so much the more devout, and would gain a proportionate favor in the eyes of God.

The tribute exacted from those who submitted to temporal sway, but continued in unbelief, was at the rate of one dinar in money or goods, for each adult person, bond or free.

Some difficulty occurred in collecting the charitable contributions; the proud tribe of Tamim openly resisted them, and drove away the collector. A troop of Arab horse was sent against them, and brought away a number of men, women and children, captives. A deputation of the Tamimites came to reclaim the prisoners. Four of the deputies were renowned as orators and poets, and instead of humbling themselves before Mohammed, proceeded to declaim in prose and verse, defying the Moslems to a poetical contest.

"I am not sent by God as a poet," replied Mohammed, "neither do I seek fame as an orator."

Some of his followers, however, accepted the challenge, and a war of ink ensued, in which the Tamimites acknowledged themselves vanquished. So well pleased was Mohammed with the spirit of their defiance, with their poetry, and with their frank acknowledgment of defeat, that he not merely gave them up the prisoners, but dismissed them with presents.

Another instance of his susceptibility to the charms of poetry is recorded in the case of Caab Ibn Zohair, a celebrated poet of Mecca, who had made him the subject of satirical verses, and had consequently been one of the proscribed, but had fled on the capture of the sacred city. Caab now came to Medina to make his peace, and approaching Mohammed when in the mosque, began chanting his praises in a poem afterwards renowned among the Arabs as a masterpiece. He concluded by especially extolling his clemency, "for with the prophet of God the pardon of injuries is, of all his virtues, that on which one can rely with the greatest certainty."

Captivated with the verse, and soothed by the flattery, Mohammed made good the poet's words, for he not merely forgave him, but taking off his own mantle, threw it upon his shoulders. The poet preserved the sacred garment to the day of his death, refusing golden offers for it. The Caliph Moawyah purchased it of his heirs for ten thousand drachmas, and it continued to be worn by the Caliphs in processions and solemn ceremonials, until the thirty-sixth Caliphat, when it was torn from the back of the Caliph Al-Most'-asem Billah, by Holâgu, the Tartar conqueror, and burnt to ashes.

While town after town and castle after castle of the Arab tribes were embracing the faith, and professing allegiance to Mohammed, Taif, the stronghold of the Thakefites, remained obstinate in the worship of its boasted idol Al Lat. The inhabitants confided in their mountain position, and in the strength of their walls and castle. But, though safe from assault, they found themselves gradually hemmed in and isolated by the Moslems, so that at length they could not stir beyond their walls without being attacked. Thus threatened and harassed, they sent ambassadors to Mohammed to treat for peace.

The prophet cherished a deep resentment against this stiff-necked and most idolatrous city, which had at one time ejected him from its gates, and at another time repulsed him from its walls. His terms were conversion and unqualified submission. The ambassadors readily consented to embrace Islam themselves, but pleaded the danger of suddenly shocking the people of Taif by a demand to renounce their ancient faith. In their name, therefore, they entreated permission for three years longer to worship their ancient idol Al Lat. The request was peremptorily denied. They then asked at least one month's delay, to prepare the public mind. This likewise was refused, all idolatry being incompatible with the worship of God. They then entreated to be excused from the observance of the daily prayers.

"There can be no true religion without prayer," replied Mohammed. In fine, they were compelled to make an unconditional submission.

Abu Sofian, Ibn Harb, and Al Mogheira were sent to Taif to destroy the idol Al Lat, which was of stone. Abu Sofian struck at it with a pickaxe but, missing his blow, fell prostrate on his face. The populace set up a shout, considering it a good augury; but Al Mogheira demolished their hopes, and the statue, at one blow of a sledgehammer. He then stripped it of the costly robes, the bracelets, the necklace, the earrings, and other ornaments of gold and precious stones wherewith it had been decked by its worshippers, and left it in fragments on the ground, with the women of Taif weeping and lamenting over it.[1]

Among those who still defied the power of Mohammed was the Bedouin chief Amir Ibn Tufiel, head of the powerful tribe of Amir. He was renowned for personal beauty and princely magnificence, but was of a haughty spirit, and his magnificence partook of ostentation. At the great fair of Okaz, between Taif and Naklah, where merchants, pilgrims and poets were accustomed to assemble from all parts of Arabia, a herald would proclaim: "Whoso wants a beast of burden, let him come to Amir; is anyone hungry, let him come to Amir, and he will be fed; is he persecuted, let him fly to Amir, and he will be protected."

Amir had dazzled everyone by his generosity, and his ambition had kept pace with his popularity. The rising power of Mohammed inspired him with jealousy. When advised to make terms with him, "I have sworn," replied he haughtily, "never to rest until I had won all Arabia; and shall I do homage to this Koreishite?"

The recent conquests of the Moslems, however, brought him to listen to the counsels of his friends. He repaired to Medina and, coming into the presence of Mohammed, demanded frankly, "Wilt thou be my friend?"

"Never, by Allah!" was the reply, "unless thou dost embrace the faith of Islam."

"And if I do, wilt thou content thyself with the sway over the Arabs of the cities, and leave to me the Bedouins of the deserts?"

Mohammed replied in the negative.

"What then will I gain by embracing thy faith?"

"The fellowship of all true believers."

"I covet no such fellowship!" replied the proud Amir; and with a warlike menace he returned to his tribe.

A Bedouin chieftain of a different character was Adi, a prince of the tribe of Taï. His father Hatim had been famous, not merely for warlike deeds, but for boundless generosity, insomuch that the Arabs were accustomed to say, "as generous as Hatim." Adi the son was a Christian; and, however he might have inherited his father's generosity, was deficient in his valor. Alarmed at the ravaging expeditions of the Moslems, he ordered a young Arab, who tended his camels in the desert, to have several of the strongest and fleetest at hand, and to give instant notice of the approach of an enemy.

It happened that Ali, who was scouring that part of the country with a band of horsemen, came in sight, bearing with him two banners, one white, the other black. The young Bedouin beheld them from afar, and ran to Adi, exclaiming, "the Moslems are at hand. I see their banners at a distance!" Adi instantly placed his wife and children on the camels, and fled to Syria. His sister, surnamed Saffana, or the Pearl, fell into the hands of the Moslems, and was carried with other captives to Medina. Seeing Mohammed pass near to the place of her confinement, she cried to him:

"Have pity upon me, O ambassador of God! My father is dead, and he who should have protected has abandoned me. Have pity upon me, O ambassador of God, as God may have pity upon thee!"

"Who is thy protector?" asked Mohammed.

"Adi, the son of Hatim."

"He is a fugitive from God and his prophet," replied Mohammed, and passed on.

On the following day, as Mohammed was passing by, Ali, who had been touched by the woman's beauty and her grief, whispered to her to arise and entreat the prophet once more. She accordingly repeated her prayer. "O prophet of God! my father is dead; my brother, who should have been my protector, has abandoned me. Have mercy upon me, as God will have mercy upon thee."

Mohammed turned to her benignantly. "Be it so," said he; and he not only set her free, but gave her raiment and a camel, and sent her by the first caravan bound to Syria.

Arriving in the presence of her brother, she upbraided him with his desertion. He acknowledged his fault and was forgiven. She then urged him to make his peace with Mohammed. "He is truly a prophet," said she, "and will soon have universal sway; hasten, therefore, in time to win his favor."

The politic Adi listened to her counsel and, hastening to Medina, greeted the prophet, who was in the mosque. His own account of the interview presents a striking picture of the simple manners and mode of life of Mohammed, now in the full exercise of sovereign power, and the career of rapid conquest. "He asked me," says Adi, "my name, and when I gave it, invited me to accompany him to his home. On the way a weak emaciated woman accosted him. He stopped and talked to her of her affairs. This, thought I to myself, is not very kingly. When we arrived at his house, he gave me a leathern cushion stuffed with palm leaves to sit upon, while he sat upon the bare ground. This, thought I, is not very princely!

"He then asked me three times to embrace Islam. I replied, 'I have a faith of my own.' 'I know thy faith,' said he, 'better than thou dost thyself. As prince, thou takest one fourth of the booty from thy people. Is this Christian doctrine?' By these words I perceived him to be a prophet, who knew more than other men.

"'Thou dost not incline to Islam,' continued he, 'because thou seest we are poor. The time is at hand when true believers will have more wealth than they will know how to manage. Perhaps thou art deterred by seeing the small number of the Moslems in comparison with the hosts of their enemies. By Allah! in a little while a Moslem woman will be able to make a pilgrimage on her camel, alone and fearless, from Kadesia to God's temple at Mecca. Thou thinkest, probably, that the might is in the hands of the unbelievers; know that the time is not far off when we will plant our standards on the white castles of Babylon."[2]

The politic Adi believed in the prophecy, and forthwith embraced the faith.

33

Preparations for an expedition against Syria - Intrigues
of Abdallah Ibn Obba - Contributions of the faithful -
March of the army - The accursed region of Hajar -
Encampment at Tabuc - Subjugation of the neighboring
provinces - Khaled surprises Okaïder and his castle -
Return of the army to Medina

Mohammed had now, either by conversion or conquest, made himself sovereign of almost all Arabia. The scattered tribes, heretofore dangerous to each other, but by their disunion powerless against the rest of the world, he had united into one nation, and thus fitted for external conquest. His prophetic character gave him absolute control of the formidable power thus conjured up in the desert, and he was now prepared to lead it forth for the propagation of the faith, and the extension of the Moslem power in foreign lands.

His numerous victories, and the recent affair at Muta, had at length, it is said, roused the attention of the Emperor Heraclius, who was assembling an army on the confines of Arabia to crush this new enemy. Mohammed determined to anticipate his hostilities, and to carry the standard of the faith into the very heart of Syria.

Hitherto he had undertaken his expeditions with secrecy, imparting his plans and intentions to none but his most confidential officers, and beguiling his followers into enterprises of danger. The present campaign, however, so different from the brief predatory excursions of the Arabs, would require great preparations; an unusual force was to be assembled, and all kinds of provision made for distant marches and a long absence. He proclaimed openly, therefore, the object and nature of the enterprise.

There was not the usual readiness to flock to his standard. Many remembered the disastrous affair at Muta, and dreaded to come again in conflict with disciplined Roman troops. The time of year also was unpropitious for such a distant and prolonged expedition. It was the season of summer heat; the earth was parched, and the springs and brooks were dried up. The date harvest too was approaching, when the men should be at home to gather the fruit, rather than abroad on predatory enterprises.

All these things were artfully urged upon the people by Abdallah Ibn Obba, the Khazradite, who continued to be the covert enemy of Mohammed, and seized every occasion to counteract his plans. "A fine season this," would he cry, "to undertake such a distant march in defiance of dearth and drought, and the fervid heat of the desert! Mohammed seems to think a war with Greeks quite a matter of sport; trust me, you will find it very different from a war of Arab against Arab. By Allah! methinks I already see you all in chains."

By these and similar scoffs and suggestions, he wrought upon the fears and feelings of the Khazradites, his partisans, and rendered the enterprise generally unpopular. Mohammed, as usual, had resort to revelation. "Those who would remain behind, and refuse to devote themselves to the service of God," said a timely chapter of the Koran, "allege the summer heat as an excuse. Tell them the fire of hell is hotter! They may hug themselves in the enjoyment of present safety, but endless tears will be their punishment hereafter."

Some of his devoted adherents manifested their zeal at this lukewarm moment. Omar, Al Abbas, and Abda'lrahman gave large sums of money; several female devotees brought their ornaments and jewels. Othman delivered one thousand, some say ten thousand, dinars to Mohammed, and was absolved from his sins, past, present, or to come. Abu Beker gave four thousand drachmas; Mohammed hesitated to accept the offer, knowing it to be all that he possessed. "What will remain," said he, "for thee and thy family?" "God and his prophet," was the reply.

These devout examples had a powerful effect; yet it was with much difficulty that an army of ten thousand horse and twenty thousand foot was assembled. Mohammed now appointed Ali governor of Medina during his absence, and guardian of both their families. He accepted the trust with great reluctance, having been accustomed always to accompany the prophet, and share all his perils. All arrangements being completed,

Mohammed marched forth from Medina on this momentous expedition. A part of his army was composed of Khazradites and their confederates, led by Abdallah Ibn Obba. This man, whom Mohammed had well denominated the Chief of the Hypocrites, encamped separately with his adherents at night, at some distance in the rear of the main army; and when the latter marched forward in the morning, he lagged behind and led his troops back to Medina. Repairing to Ali, whose dominion in the city was irksome to him and his adherents, he endeavored to make him discontented with his position, alleging that Mohammed had left him in charge of Medina solely to rid himself of an incumbrance. Stung by the suggestion, Ali hastened after Mohammed, and demanded if what Abdallah and his followers said were true.

"These men," replied Mohammed, "are liars. They are the party of Hypocrites and Doubters, who would breed sedition in Medina. I left thee behind to keep watch over them, and to be a guardian to both our families. I would have thee to be to me what Aaron was to Moses; excepting that thou canst not be, like him, a prophet, I being the last of the prophets." With this explanation Ali returned contented to Medina.

Many have inferred from the foregoing that Mohammed intended Ali for his Caliph or successor, that being the signification of the Arabic word used to denote the relation of Aaron to Moses.

The troops who had continued on with Mohammed soon began to experience the difficulties of braving the desert in this sultry season. Many turned back on the second day, and others on the third and fourth. Whenever word was brought to the prophet of their desertion, "Let them go," would be the reply; "if they are good for anything God will bring them back to us; if they are not, we are relieved from so many incumbrances."

While some thus lost heart upon the march, others who had remained at Medina repented of their faintheartedness. One, named Abu Khaithama, entering his garden during the sultry heat of the day, beheld a repast of viands and fresh water spread for him by his two wives in the cool shade of a tent. Pausing at the threshold, "At this moment," exclaimed he, "the prophet of God is exposed to the winds and heats of the desert, and shall Khaithama sit here in the shade beside his beautiful wives? By Allah! I will not enter the tent!" He immediately armed himself with sword and lance and, mounting his camel, hastened off to join the standard of the faith.

In the meantime the army, after a weary march of seven days, entered the mountainous district of Hajar, inhabited in days of old by the Thamudites, one of the lost tribes of Arabia. It was the accursed region, the tradition concerning which has already been related. The advance of the army, knowing nothing of this tradition, and being heated and fatigued, beheld, with delight, a brook running through a verdant valley, and cool caves cut in the sides of the neighboring hills, once the abodes of the heaven-smitten Thamudites. Halting along the brook, some prepared to bathe, others began to cook and make bread, while all promised themselves cool quarters for the night in the caves.

Mohammed, in marching, had kept, as was his wont, in the rear of the army to assist the weak, occasionally taking up a wayworn laggard behind him. Arriving at the place where the troops had halted, he recollected it of old, and the traditions concerning it, which had been told to him when he passed here in the days of his boyhood. Fearful of incurring the ban which hung over the neighborhood, he ordered his troops to throw away the meat cooked with the water of the brook, to give the bread kneaded with it to the camels, and to hurry away from the heaven-accursed place. Then wrapping his face in the folds of his mantle, and setting spurs to his mule, he hastened through that sinful region, the army following him as if flying from an enemy.

The succeeding night was one of great suffering: the army had to encamp without water; the weather was intensely hot, with a parching wind from the desert; and intolerable thirst prevailed throughout the camp, as though the Thamudite ban still hung over it. The next day, however, an abundant rain refreshed and invigorated both man and beast. The march was resumed with a new ardor, and the army arrived, without further hardship, at Tabuc, a small town on the confines of the Roman empire, about half way between Medina and Damascus, and about ten days' journey from either city.

Here Mohammed pitched his camp in the neighborhood of a fountain, and in the midst of groves and pasturage. Arabian traditions affirm that the fountain was nearly dry, insomuch that, when a small vase was filled for the prophet, not a drop was left. Having assuaged his thirst, however, and made his ablutions, Mohammed threw what remained in the vase back into the fountain; whereupon a stream gushed forth sufficient for the troops and all the cattle.

From this encampment Mohammed sent out his captains to proclaim and enforce the faith, or to exact tribute. Some of the neighboring princes sent embassies, either acknowledging the divinity of his mission, or submitting to his temporal sway. One of these was Johanna Ibn Ruba, prince of Eyla, a Christian city near the Red Sea. This was the same city about which the tradition is told that in days of old, when its inhabitants were Jews, the old men were turned into swine and the young men into monkeys, for fishing on the Sabbath, a judgment solemnly recorded in the Koran.

The prince of Eyla made a covenant of peace with Mohammed, agreeing to pay an annual tribute of three thousand dinars or crowns of gold. The form of the covenant became a precedent in treating with other powers.

Among the Arab princes who professed the Christian faith, and refused to pay homage to Mohammed, was Okaïder Ibn Malec, of the tribe of Kenda. He resided in a castle at the foot of a mountain, in the midst of his domain. Khaled was sent with a troop of horse to bring him to terms. Seeing the castle was too strong to be carried by assault, he had recourse to stratagem. One moonlit night, as Okaïder and his wife were enjoying the fresh air on the terraced roof of the castle, they beheld an animal grazing, which they supposed to be a wild ass from the neighboring mountains. Okaïder, who was a keen huntsman, ordered horse and lance and sallied forth to the chase, accompanied by his brother Hassan and several of his people. The wild ass proved to be a decoy. They had not ridden far before Khaled and his men rushed from ambush and attacked them. They were too lightly armed to make much resistance. Hassan was killed on the spot, and Okaïder taken prisoner; the rest fled back to the castle, which, however, was soon surrendered. The prince was ultimately set at liberty on paying a heavy ransom and becoming a tributary.

As a trophy of the victory, Khaled sent to Mohammed the vest stripped from the body of Hassan. It was of silk, richly embroidered with gold. The Moslems gathered round, and examined it with admiration. "Do you admire this vest?" said the prophet. "I swear by him in whose hands is the soul of Mohammed, the vest which Saad, the son of Maadi, wears at this moment in paradise, is far more precious." This Saad was the judge who passed sentence of death on seven hundred Jewish captives at Medina, at the conclusion of a former campaign.

His troops being now refreshed by the sojourn at Tabuc, and the neighboring country being brought into subjection, Mohammed was bent upon prosecuting the object of his campaign, and pushing forward into the heart of Syria. His ardor, however, was not shared by his followers. Intelligence of immense bodies of hostile troops, assembled on the Syrian borders, had damped the spirits of the army. Mohammed remarked the general discouragement, yet was loath to abandon the campaign when it was but half completed. Calling a council of war, he propounded the question whether or not to continue forward. To this Omar replied dryly, "If thou hast the command of God to proceed further, do so." "If I had the command of God to proceed further," observed Mohammed, "I should not have asked thy counsel."

Omar felt the rebuke. He then, in a respectful tone, represented the impolicy of advancing in the face of the overwhelming force said to be collected on the Syrian frontier; he represented, also, how much Mohammed had already effected in this campaign. He had checked the threatened invasion of the imperial arms, and had received the homage and submission of various tribes and people, from the head of the Red Sea to the Euphrates. Omar advised him, therefore, to be content for the present year with what he had achieved, and to defer the completion of the enterprise to a future campaign.

His counsel was adopted: for, whenever Mohammed was not under strong excitement, or fancied inspiration., he was rather prone to yield up his opinion in military matters to that of his generals. After a sojourn of about twenty days, therefore, at Tabuc, he broke up his camp and conducted his army back to Medina.

34

*Triumphal entry into Medina - Punishment of those who
had refused to join the campaign - Effects of
excommunication - Death of Abdallah Ibn Obba -
Dissensions in the prophet's harem*

The entries of Mohammed into Medina on returning from his
warlike triumphs partook of the simplicity and absence of
parade which characterized all his actions. On approaching the
city, when his household came forth with the multitude to meet
him, he would stop to greet them, and take up the children of the
house behind him on his horse. It was in this simple way that he
entered Medina, on returning from the campaign against
Tabuc.

The arrival of an army laden with spoil, gathered in the
most distant expedition ever undertaken by the soldiers of
Islam, was an event of too great moment not to be hailed with
triumphant exultation by the community. Those alone were cast
down in spirit who had refused to march forth with the army, or
had deserted it when on the march. All these were at first placed
under an interdict, Mohammed forbidding his faithful
followers to hold any intercourse with them. Mollified, however,
by their contrition or excuses, he gradually forgave the greater
part of them. Seven of those who continued under interdict,
finding themselves cut off from communion with their
acquaintance, and marked with opprobrium amid an exulting
community, became desperate, and chained themselves to the
walls of the mosque, swearing to remain there until pardoned.
Mohammed, on the other hand, swore he would leave them there
unless otherwise commanded by God. Fortunately he received
the command in a revealed verse of the Koran; but, in freeing

them from their self-imposed fetters, he exacted one third of their possessions, to be expended in the service of the faith.

Among those still under interdict were Kaab Ibn Malec, Murara Ibn Rabia, and Hilal Ibn Omeya. These had once been among the most zealous of professing Moslems; their defection was, therefore, ten times more heinous in the eyes of the prophet than that of their neighbors, whose faith had been lukewarm and dubious. Toward them, therefore, he continued implacable. Forty days they remained interdicted, and the interdict extended to communication with their wives.

The account given by Kaab Ibn Malec of his situation, while thus excommunicated, presents a vivid picture of the power of Mohammed over the minds of his adherents. Kaab declared that everybody shunned him, or regarded him with an altered mien. His two companions in disgrace did not leave their home; he, however, went about from place to place, but no one spoke to him. He sought the mosque, sat down near the prophet and saluted him, but his salutation was not returned. On the forty-first day came a command that he should separate from his wife. He now left the city and pitched a tent on the hill of Sala, determined there to undergo in its severest rigor the punishment meted out to him. His heart, however, was dying away; the wide world, he said, appeared to grow narrow to him. On the fifty-first day came a messenger holding out the hope of pardon. He hastened to Medina, and sought the prophet at the mosque, who received him with a radiant countenance, and said that God had forgiven him. The soul of Kaab was lifted up from the depths of despondency, and in the transports of his gratitude he gave a portion of his wealth in atonement of his error.

Not long after the return of the army to Medina, Abdallah Ibn Obba, the Khazradite, "the chief of the Hypocrites," fell ill, so that his life was despaired of. Although Mohammed was well aware of the perfidy of this man, and of the secret arts he had constantly practiced against him, he visited him repeatedly during his illness, was with him at his dying hour, and followed his body to the grave. There, at the urgent entreaty of the son of the deceased, he put up prayers that his sins might be forgiven.

Omar privately remonstrated with Mohammed for praying for a hypocrite, reminding him how often he had been slandered by Abdallah; but he was shrewdly answered by a text of the Koran: "Thou mayst pray for the 'Hypocrites' or not, as thou wilt; but though thou shouldst pray seventy times, yet will they not be forgiven."

The prayers at Abdallah's grave, therefore, were put up out of policy, to win favor with the Khazradites, and the powerful friends of the deceased; and in this respect the prayers were successful, for most of the adherents of the deceased became devoted to the prophet, whose sway was thenceforth undisputed in Medina. Subsequently he announced another revelation, which forbade him to pray by the deathbed or stand by the grave of any one who died in unbelief.

But though Mohammed exercised such dominion over his disciples, and the community at large, he had great difficulty in governing his wives, and maintaining tranquillity in his harem. He appears to have acted with tolerable equity in his connubial concerns, assigning to each of his wives a separate habitation, of which she was sole mistress, and passing the twenty-four hours with them by turns. It so happened that on one occasion, when he was sojourning with Hafsa, the latter left her dwelling to visit her father. Returning unexpectedly, she surprised the prophet with his favorite and fortunate slave Mariyah, the mother of his son Ibrahim. The jealousy of Hafsa was vociferous. Mohammed endeavored to pacify her, dreading lest her outcries should rouse his whole harem to rebellion; but she was only to be appeased by an oath on his part never more to cohabit with Mariyah. On these terms she forgave the past, and promised secrecy.

She broke her promise, however, and revealed to Ayesha the infidelity of the prophet, and in a little while it was known throughout the harem. His wives now united in a storm of reproaches until, his patience being exhausted, he repudiated Hafsa, and renounced all intercourse with the rest. For a month he lay alone on a mat in a separate apartment; but Allah, at length, in consideration of his lonely state, sent down the first and sixth chapters of the Koran, absolving him from the oath respecting Mariyah, who forthwith became the companion of his solitary chamber.

The refractory wives were now brought to a sense of their error, and apprised by the same revelation that the restrictions imposed on ordinary men did not apply to the prophet. In the end he took back Hafsa, who was penitent; and he was reconciled to Ayesha, whom he tenderly loved, and all the rest were in due time received into favor; but he continued to cherish Mariyah, for she was fair to look upon, and was the mother of his only son.

35

Abu Beker conducts the yearly pilgrimage to Mecca -
Mission of Ali to announce a revelation

The sacred month of yearly pilgrimage was now at hand, but
Mohammed was too much occupied with public and domestic
concerns to absent himself from Medina; he deputed Abu Beker,
therefore, to act in his place as emir or commander of the
pilgrims, who were to resort from Medina to the holy city. Abu
Beker accordingly departed at the head of three hundred
pilgrims, with twenty camels for sacrifice.

Not long afterwards Mohammed summoned his son-in-law
and devoted disciple Ali and, mounting him on Al Adha, or the
slit-eared, the swiftest of his camels, urged him to hasten with
all speed to Mecca, there to promulgate before the multitude of
pilgrims assembled from all parts an important sura, or chapter
of the Koran, just received from heaven.

Ali executed his mission with his accustomed zeal and
fidelity. He reached the sacred city in the height of the great
religious festival. On the day of sacrifice, when the ceremonies
of pilgrimage were completed by the slaying of the victims in the
valley of Mina, and when Abu Beker had preached and
instructed the people in the doctrines and rites of Islam, Ali rose
before an immense multitude assembled at the hill Al Akaba,
and announced himself a messenger from the prophet, bearing
an important revelation. He then read the sura, or chapter of the
Koran, of which he was the bearer, in which the religion of the
sword was declared in all its rigor. It absolved Mohammed
from all truce or league with idolatrous and other unbelievers,
should they in anywise have been false to their stipulations, or
given aid to his enemies. It allowed unbelievers four months of
toleration from the time of this announcement, during which

months they might "go to and fro about the earth securely," but at the expiration of that time all indulgence would cease; war would then be made in every way, at every time and in every place, by open force or by stratagem, against those who persisted in unbelief: no alternative would be left them but to embrace the faith, or pay tribute. The holy months and the holy places would no longer afford them protection. "When the months wherein ye are not allowed to attack them shall be passed," said the revelation, "kill the idolatrous wherever ye shall find them, or take them prisoners; besiege them, or lie in wait for them." The ties of blood and friendship were to be alike disregarded; the faithful were to hold no communion with their nearest relatives and dearest friends, should they persist in idolatry. After the expiration of the current year, no unbeliever was to be permitted to tread the sacred bounds of Mecca, nor to enter the temple of Allah, a prohibition which continues to the present day.

This stringent chapter of the Koran is thought to have been provoked, in a great measure, by the conduct of some of the Jewish and idolatrous Arabs, with whom Mohammed had made covenants, but who had repeatedly played him false, and even made treacherous attempts upon his life. It evinces, however, the increased confidence he felt in consequence of the death of his insidious and powerful foe, Abdallah Ibn Obba, and the rapid conversion or subjugation of the Arab tribes. It was, in fact, a decisive blow for the exclusive domination of his faith.

When Abu Beker and Ali returned to Mecca, the former expressed surprise and dissatisfaction that he had not been made the promulgator of so important a revelation, as it seemed to be connected with his recent mission, but he was pacified by the assurance that all new revelations must be announced by the prophet himself, or by some one of his immediate family.

36

*Mohammed sends his captains on distant enterprises -
Appoints lieutenants to govern in Arabia Felix - Sends
Ali to suppress an insurrection in that province - Death
of the prophet's only son Ibrahim - His conduct at the
deathbed and the grave - His growing infirmities - His
valedictory pilgrimage to Mecca, and his conduct and
preaching while there*

The promulgation of the last-mentioned chapter of the Koran,
with the accompanying declaration of exterminating war
against all who should refuse to believe or submit, produced
hosts of converts and tributaries; so that, towards the close of the
month, and in the beginning of the tenth year of the Hegira, the
gates of Medina were thronged with envoys from distant tribes
and princes. Among those who bowed to the temporal power of the
prophet was Farwa, lieutenant of Heraclius, in Syria, and
governor of Amon, the ancient capital of the Ammonites. His
act of submission, however, was disavowed by the emperor, and
punished with imprisonment.

Mohammed felt and acted more and more as a sovereign,
but his grandest schemes as a conqueror were always sanctified
by his zeal as an apostle. His captains were sent on more distant
expeditions than formerly, but it was always with a view to
destroy idols, and bring idolatrous tribes to subjection, so that
his temporal power but kept pace with the propagation of his
faith. He appointed two lieutenants to govern in his name in
Arabia Felix; but a portion of that rich and important country
having shown itself refractory, Ali was ordered to repair thither
at the head of three hundred horsemen, and bring the
inhabitants to reason.

The youthful disciple expressed a becoming diffidence to
undertake a mission where he would have to treat with men far

older and wiser than himself; but Mohammed laid one hand upon his lips, and the other upon his breast, and raising his eyes to heaven, exclaimed, "O, Allah! loosen his tongue aud guide his heart!" He gave him one rule for his conduct as a judge: "When two parties come before thee, never pronounce in favor of one until thou hast heard the other." Then, giving into his hands the standard of the faith, and placing the turban on his head, he bade him farewell.

When the military missionary arrived in the heretical region of Yemen, his men, indulging their ancient Arab propensities, began to sack, to plunder, and destroy. Ali checked their excesses and, arresting the fugitive inhabitants, began to expound to them the doctrines of Islam. His tongue, though so recently consecrated by the prophet, failed to carry conviction, for he was answered by darts and arrows; whereupon he returned to the old argument of the sword, which he urged with such efficacy that, after twenty unbelievers had been slain, the rest avowed themselves thoroughly convinced. This zealous achievement was followed by others of a similar kind, after each of which he despatched messengers to the prophet announcing a new triumph of the faith.

While Mohammed was exulting in the tidings of success from every quarter, he was stricken to the heart by one of the severest domestic bereavements. Ibrahim, his son by his favorite concubine Mariyah, a child but fifteen months old, his only male issue, on whom reposed his hope of transmitting his name to posterity, was seized with a mortal malady, and expired before his eyes. Mohammed could not control a father's feelings as he bent in agony over this blighted blossom of his hopes. Yet even in his trying hour he showed that submission to the will of God which formed the foundation of his faith. "My heart is sad," murmured he, "and mine eyes overflow with tears at parting with thee, O my son! And still greater would be my grief, did I not know that I must soon follow thee; for we are of God, from him we came, and to him we must return."

Abd'lrahman, seeing him in tears, demanded, "Hast thou not forbidden us to weep for the dead?" "No," replied the prophet. "I have forbidden ye to utter shrieks and outcries, to beat your faces, and rend your garments; these are suggestions of the evil one—but tears shed for a calamity are as balm to the heart, and are sent in mercy."

He followed his child to the grave, where, amidst the agonies of separation, he gave another proof that the elements of his religion were ever present to his mind. "My son! my son!" he exclaimed, as the body was committed to the tomb, "say God is my Lord! the prophet of God was my father, and Islamism is my faith!" This was to prepare his child for the questioning by examining angels as to religious belief, which, according to Moslem creed, the deceased would undergo while in the grave.[1]

An eclipse of the sun which happened about that time was interpreted by some of his zealous followers as a celestial sign of mourning for the death of Ibrahim, but the afflicted father rejected such obsequious flattery. "The sun and moon," he said, "are among the wonders of God, through which at times he signifies his will to his servants; but their eclipse has nothing to do either with the birth or death of any mortal."

The death of Ibrahim was a blow which bowed him toward the grave. His constitution was already impaired by the extraordinary excitements and paroxysms of his mind, and the physical trials to which he had been exposed; the poison, too, administered to him at Khaïbar, had tainted the springs of life, subjected him to excruciating pains, and brought on a premature old age. His religious zeal took the alarm from the increase of bodily infirmities, and he resolved to expend his remaining strength in a final pilgrimage to Mecca, intended to serve as a model for all future observances of the kind.

The announcement of his pious intention brought devotees from all parts of Arabia to follow the pilgrim-prophet. The streets of Medina were crowded with the various tribes from the towns and cities, from the fastnesses of the mountains, and the remote parts of the desert, and the surrounding valleys were studded with their tents. It was a striking picture of the triumph of a faith—these recently disunited, barbarous, and warring tribes, brought together as brethren, and inspired by one sentiment of religious zeal.

Mohammed was accompanied on this occasion by his nine wives, who were transported on litters. He departed at the head of an immense train, some say of fifty-five, others ninety, and others a hundred and fourteen thousand pilgrims. There was a large number of camels also, decorated with garlands of flowers and fluttering streamers, intended to be offered up in sacrifice.

The first night's halt was a few miles from Medina, at the village of Dhu'l Holaïfa, where, on a former occasion, he and his followers had laid aside their weapons and assumed the pilgrim garb. Early on the following morning, after praying in the mosque, he mounted his camel Al Aswa and, entering the plain of Baïda, uttered the prayer or invocation called in Arabic Talbijah, in which he was joined by all his followers. The following is the import of this solemn invocation: "Here am I in thy service, O God! Here am I in thy service! Thou hast no companion. To thee alone belongeth worship. From thee cometh all good. Thine alone is the kingdom. There is none to share it with thee."

This prayer, according to Moslem tradition, was uttered by the patriarch Abraham when, from the top of the hill of Kubeis, near Mecca, he preached the true faith to the whole human race, and so wonderful was the power of his voice that it was heard by every living being throughout the world; insomuch that the very child in the womb responded, "Here am I in thy service, O God!"

In this way the pilgrim host pursued its course, winding in a lengthened train of miles, over mountain and valley, and making the deserts vocal at times with united prayers and ejaculations. There were no longer any hostile armies to impede or molest it, for by this time the Islam faith reigned serenely over all Arabia. Mohammed approached the sacred city over the same heights which he had traversed in capturing it, and he entered through the gate Beni Scheiba, which still bears the name of The Holy.

A few days after his arrival, he was joined by Ali, who had hastened back from Yemen, and who brought with him a number of camels to be slain in sacrifice.

As this was to be a model pilgrimage, Mohammed rigorously observed all the rites which he had continued in compliance with patriarchal usage, or introduced in compliance with revelation. Being too weak and infirm to go on foot, he mounted his camel, and thus performed the circuits round the Caaba, and the journeyings to and fro between the hills of Safa and Merwa.

When the camels were to be offered up in sacrifice, he slew sixty-three with his own hand, one for each year of his age, and Ali, at the same time, slew thirty-seven on his own account.

Mohammed then shaved his head, beginning on the right side and ending on the left. The locks thus shorn away were equally divided among his disciples, and treasured up as sacred relics. Khaled ever afterwards wore one in his turban, and affirmed that it gave him supernatural strength in battle.

Conscious that life was waning away within him, Mohammed, during this last sojourn in the sacred city of his faith, sought to engrave his doctrines deeply in the minds and hearts of his followers. For this purpose he preached frequently in the Caaba from the pulpit, or in the open air from the back of his camel. "Listen to my words," would he say, "for I know not whether, after this year, we shall ever meet here again. O, my hearers, I am but a man like yourselves: the angel of death may at any time appear, and I must obey his summons."

He would then proceed to inculcate not merely religious doctrines and ceremonies, but rules for conduct in all the concerns of life, public and domestic; and the precepts laid down and enforced on this occasion have had a vast and durable influence on the morals, manners, and habitudes of the whole Moslem world.

It was doubtless in view of his approaching end, and in solicitude for the welfare of his relatives and friends after his death, and especially of his favorite Ali, who, he perceived, had given dissatisfaction in the conduct of his recent campaign in Yemen, that he took occasion, during a moment of strong excitement and enthusiasm among his hearers, to address to them a solemn adjuration.

"Ye believe," said he, "that there is but one God; that Mohammed is his prophet and apostle; that paradise and hell are truths; that death and the resurrection are certain; and that there is an appointed time when all who rise from the grave must be brought to judgment."

They all answered, "We believe these things." He then adjured them solemnly by these dogmas of their faith ever to hold his family, and especially Ali, in love and reverence. "Whoever loves me," said he, "let him receive Ali as his friend. May God uphold those who befriend him, and may he turn from his enemies."

It was at the conclusion of one of his discourses in the open air, from the back of his camel, that the famous verse of the Koran is said to have come down from heaven in the very voice of the Deity. "Evil to those, this day, who have denied your religion. Fear them not, fear me. This day I have perfected your religion, and accomplished in you my grace. It is my good pleasure that Islamism be your faith."

On hearing these words, say the Arabian historians, the camel Al Kaswa, on which the prophet was seated, fell on its knees in adoration. These words, they add, were the seal and conclusion of the law, for after them there were no further revelations.

Having thus fulfilled all the rites and ceremonies of pilgrimage, and made a full exposition of his faith, Mohammed bade a last farewell to his native city and, putting himself at the head of his pilgrim army, set out on his return to Medina.

As he came in sight of it, he lifted up his voice and exclaimed, "God is great; God is great! There is but one God; he has no companion. His is the kingdom. To him alone belongeth praise. He is almighty. He hath fulfilled his promise. He has stood by his servant, and alone dispersed his enemies. Let us return to our homes, and worship and praise him!"

Thus ended what has been termed the valedictory pilgrimage, being the last made by the prophet.

37

The two false prophets: Al Aswad and Moseïlma

The health of Mohammed continued to decline after his return to
Medina; nevertheless his ardor to extend his religious empire
was unabated, and he prepared, on a great scale, for the
invasion of Syria and Palestine. While he was meditating
foreign conquest, however, two rival prophets arose to dispute his
sway in Arabia. One was named Al Aswad, the other
Moseïlma; they received from the faithful the well-merited
appellation of "The Two Liars." Al Aswad, a quick-witted man,
and gifted with persuasive eloquence, was originally an
idolater, then a convert to Islam, from which he apostatized to set
up for a prophet, and establish a religion of his own. His
fickleness in matters of faith gained him the appellation of
Ailhala, or "The Weathercock." In emulation of Mohammed he
pretended to receive revelations from heaven through the
medium of two angels. Being versed in juggling arts and
natural magic, he astonished and confounded the multitude
with spectral illusions, which he passed off as miracles,
insomuch that certain Moslem writers believe he was really
assisted by two evil genii or demons. His schemes, for a time,
were crowned with great success, which shows how unsettled the
Arabs were in those days in matters of religion, and how ready
to adopt any new faith.

Budhan, the Persian whom Mohammed had continued as
viceroy of Arabia Felix, died in this year; whereupon Al Aswad,
now at the head of a powerful sect, slew his son and successor,
espoused his widow after putting her father to death, and seized
upon the reins of government. The people of Najran invited him
to their city; the gates of Sanaa, the capital of Yemen, were

likewise thrown open to him, so that, in a little while, all Arabia Felix submitted to his sway.

The news of this usurpation found Mohammed suffering in the first stages of a dangerous malady, and engrossed by preparations for the Syrian invasion. Impatient of any interruption to his plans, and reflecting that the whole danger and difficulty in question depended upon the life of an individual, he sent orders to certain of his adherents, who were about Al Aswad, to make way with him openly or by stratagem, either way being justifiable against enemies of the faith, according to the recent revelation promulgated by Ali. Two persons undertook the task, less, however, through motives of religion than revenge. One, named Rais, had received a mortal offense from the usurper; the other, named Firuz the Daïlemite, was cousin to Al Aswad's newly espoused wife, and nephew of her murdered father. They repaired to the woman, whose marriage with the usurper had probably been compulsory, and urged upon her the duty, according to the Arab law of blood, of avenging the deaths of her father and her former husband. With much difficulty they prevailed upon her to facilitate their entrance at the dead of night in the chamber of Al Aswad, who was asleep. Firuz stabbed him in the throat with a poniard. The blow was not effectual. Al Aswad started up, and his cries alarmed the guard. His were, however, went forth and quieted them. "The prophet," said she, "is under the influence of divine inspiration." By this time the cries had ceased, for the assassins had stricken off the head of their victim. When the day dawned the standard of Mohammed floated once more on the walls of the city, and a herald proclaimed, by sound of trumpet, the death of Al Aswad, otherwise called the Liar and Impostor. His career of power began, and was terminated, within the space of four months. The people, easy of faith, resumed Islamism with as much facility as they had abandoned it.

Moseïlma, the other impostor, was an Arab of the tribe of Honeifa, and ruled over the city and province of Yamama, situated between the Red Sea and the Gulf of Persia. In the ninth year of the Hegira he had come to Mecca at the head of an embassy from his tribe, and had made profession of faith between the hands of Mohammed; but, on returning to his own country, had proclaimed that God had gifted him likewise with prophecy, and appointed him to aid Mohammed in converting the human race. To this effect he likewise wrote a Koran, which he gave forth as a volume of inspired truth. His creed was noted for giving the soul a humiliating residence in the region of the abdomen.

Being a man of influence and address, he soon made hosts of converts among his credulous countrymen. Rendered confident by success, he addressed an epistle to Mohammed, beginning as follows:

"From Moseïlma the prophet of Allah, to Mohammed the prophet of Allah! Come, now, and let us make a partition of the world, and let half be thine and half be mine."

This letter came to the hands of Mohammed while he was bowed down by infirmities and engrossed by military preparations. He contented himself for the present with the following reply:

"From Mohammed the prophet of God, to Moseïlma the Liar! The earth is the Lord's, and he giveth it as an inheritance to such of his servants as find favor in his sight. Happy shall those be who live in his fear."

In the urgency of other affairs, the usurpation of Moseïlma remained unchecked. His punishment was reserved for a future day.

38

*An army prepared to march against Syria - Command
given to Osama - The prophet's farewell address to the
troops - His last illness - His sermons in the mosque -
His death and the attending circumstances*

It was early in the eleventh year of the Hegira that, after
unusual preparations, a powerful army was ready to march for
the invasion of Syria. It would almost seem a proof of the failing
powers of Mohammed's mind that he gave the command of such
an army, on such an expedition, to Osama, a youth but twenty
years of age, instead of some one of his veteran and well-tried
generals. It seems to have been a matter of favor, dictated by
tender and grateful recollections. Osama was the son of Zeid,
Mohammed's devoted freedman, who had given the prophet such
a signal and acceptable proof of devotion in relinquishing to
him his beautiful wife Zeinab. Zeid had continued to the last the
same zealous and self-sacrificing disciple, and had fallen
bravely fighting for the faith in the battle of Muta.

Mohammed was aware of the hazard of the choice he had
made, and feared the troops might be insubordinate under so
young a commander. In a general review, therefore, he
exhorted them to obedience, reminding them that Osama's
father, Zeid, had commanded an expedition of this very kind,
against the very same people, and had fallen by their hands; it
was but a just tribute to his memory, therefore, to give his son an
opportunity of avenging his death. Then placing his banner in
the hands of the youthful general, he called upon him to fight
valiantly the fight of the faith against all who should deny the
unity of God. The army marched forth that very day, and
encamped at Djorf, a few miles from Medina; but
circumstances occurred to prevent its further progress.

That very night Mohammed had a severe access of the malady which for some time past had affected him, and which was ascribed by some to the lurking effects of the poison given to him at Khaïbar. It commenced with a violent pain in the head, accompanied by vertigo, and the delirium which seems to have mingled with all his paroxysms of illness. Starting up in the mid-watches of the night from a troubled dream, he called upon an attendant slave to accompany him, saying he was summoned by the dead who lay interred in the public burying-place of Medina to come and pray for them. Followed by the slave, he passed through the dark and silent city, where all were sunk in sleep, to the great burying-ground, outside of the walls.

Arrived in the midst of the tombs, he lifted up his voice and made a solemn apostrophe to their tenants. "Rejoice, ye dwellers in the grave!" exclaimed he. "More peaceful is the morning to which ye shall awaken than that which attends the living. Happier is your condition than theirs. God has delivered you from the storms with which they are threatened, and which shall follow one another like the watches of a stormy night, each darker than that which went before."

After praying for the dead, he turned and addressed his slave. "The choice is given me," said he, "either to remain in this world to the end of time, in the enjoyment of all its delights, or to return sooner to the presence of God; and I have chosen the latter."

From this time his illness rapidly increased, though he endeavored to go about as usual, and shifted his residence from day to day, with his different wives, as he had been accustomed to do. He was in the dwelling of Maïmona when the violence of his malady became so great that he saw it must soon prove fatal. His heart now yearned to be with his favorite wife Ayesha, and to pass with her the fleeting residue of life. With his head bound up, and his tottering frame supported by Ali, and Fadhl the son of Al Abbas, he repaired to her abode. She, likewise, was suffering with a violent pain in the head, and entreated of him a remedy.

"Wherefore a remedy?" said he. "Better that thou shouldst die before me. I could then close thine eyes, wrap thee in thy funeral garb, lay thee in the tomb, and pray for thee."

"Yes," replied she, "and then return to my house and dwell with one of thy other wives, who would profit by my death."

Mohammed smiled at this expression of jealous fondness, and resigned himself into her care. His only remaining child, Fatima, the wife of Ali, came presently to see him. Ayesha used to say that she never saw any one resemble the prophet more in sweetness of temper than this his daughter. He treated her always with respectful tenderness. When she came to him, he used to rise up, go towards her, take her by the hand and kiss it, and would seat her in his own place. Their meeting on this occasion is thus related by Ayesha, in the traditions preserved by Abulfeda.

"'Welcome, my child,' said the prophet, and made her sit beside him! He then whispered something in her ear, at which she wept. Perceiving her affliction, he whispered something more, and her countenance brightened with joy.

"'What is the meaning of this?' said I to Fatima. 'The prophet honors thee with a mark of confidence never bestowed on any of his wives.' 'I cannot disclose the secret of the prophet of God,' replied Fatima. Nevertheless, after his death, she declared that at first he announced to her his impending death; but, seeing her weep, consoled her with the assurance that she would shortly follow him, and become a princess in heaven, among the faithful of her sex."

In the second day of his illness Mohammed was tormented by a burning fever, and caused vessels of water to be emptied on his head and over his body, exclaiming amidst his paroxysms, "Now I feel the poison of Khaïbar rending my entrails."

When somewhat relieved, he was aided in repairing to the mosque, which was adjacent to his residence. Here, seated in his chair, or pulpit, he prayed devoutly; after which, addressing the congregation, which was numerous, "If any of you," said he, "have aught upon his conscience, let him speak out, that I may ask God's pardon for him."

Upon this, a man who had passed for a devout Moslem stood forth and confessed himself a hypocrite, a liar, and a weak disciple. "Out upon thee!" cried Omar, "why dost thou make known what God had suffered to remain concealed?" But Mohammed turned rebukingly to Omar. "O son of Khattâb," said he, "better is it to blush in this world than suffer in the next." Then lifting his eyes to heaven, and praying for the self-accused, "O God," he exclaimed, "give him rectitude and faith, and take from him all weakness in fulfilling such of thy commands as his conscience dictates."

Again addressing the congregation, "Is there anyone among you," he said, "whom I have stricken? Here is my back; let him strike me in return. Is there anyone whose character I have aspersed? Let him now cast reproach upon me. Is there anyone from whom I have taken aught unjustly? Let him now come forward and be indemnified."

Upon this, a man among the throng reminded Mohammed of a debt of three dishes of silver, and was instantly repaid with interest. "Much easier is it," said the prophet, "to bear punishment in this world than throughout eternity."

He now prayed fervently for the faithful who had fallen by his side in the battle of Ohod, and for those who had suffered for the faith in other battles, interceding with them in virtue of the pact which exists between the living and the dead.

After this he addressed the Mohadjerins or Exiles, who had accompanied him from Mecca, exhorting them to hold in honor the Ansarians, or allies of Medina. "The number of believers," said he, "will increase, but that of the allies never can. They were my family with whom I found a home. Do good to those who do good to them, and break friendship with those who are hostile to them."

He then gave three parting commands:

First: Expel all idolaters from Arabia.

Second: Allow all proselytes equal privileges with yourselves.

Third: Devote yourselves incessantly to prayer.

His sermon and exhortation being finished, he was affectionately supported back to the mansion of Ayesha, but was so exhausted on arriving there that he fainted.

His malady increased from day to day, apparently with intervals of delirium, for he spoke of receiving visits from the angel Gabriel, who came from God to inquire after the state of his health, and told him that it rested with himself to fix his dying moment, the angel of death being forbidden by Allah to enter his presence without his permission.

In one of his paroxysms he called for writing implements, that he might leave some rules of conduct for his followers. His attendants were troubled, fearing he might do something to impair the authority of the Koran. Hearing them debate among themselves whether to comply with his request, he ordered them to leave the room, and when they returned said nothing more on the subject.

On Friday, the day of religious assemblage, he prepared, notwithstanding his illness, to officiate in the mosque, and had water again poured over him to refresh and strengthen him, but on making an effort to go forth, fainted. On recovering, he requested Abu Beker to perform the public prayers, observing, "Allah has given his servant the right to appoint whom he pleases in his place." It was afterwards maintained by some that he thus intended to designate this long tried friend and adherent as his successor in office, but Abu Beker shrank from construing the words too closely.

Word was soon brought to Mohammed that the appearance of Abu Beker in the pulpit had caused great agitation, a rumor being circulated that the prophet was dead. Exerting his remaining strength, therefore, and leaning on the shoulders of Ali and Al Abbas, he made his way into the mosque, where his appearance spread joy throughout the congregation. Abu Beker ceased to pray, but Mohammed bade him proceed and, taking his seat behind him in the pulpit, repeated the prayers after him. Then addressing the congregation, "I have heard," said he, "that a rumor of the death of your prophet filled you with alarm; but has any prophet before me lived for ever, that ye think I would never leave you? Everything happens according to the will of God, and has its appointed time, which is not to be hastened nor avoided. I return to him who sent me; and my last command to you is, that ye remain united; that ye love, honor, and uphold each other; that ye exhort each other to faith and constancy in belief, and to the performance of pious deeds; by these alone men prosper; all else leads to destruction."

In concluding his exhortation, he added, "I do but go before you; you will soon follow me. Death awaits us all; let no one then seek to turn it aside from me. My life has been for your good; so will be my death."

These were the last words he spoke in public; he was again conducted back by Ali and Abbas to the dwelling of Ayesha.

On a succeeding day there was an interval during which he appeared so well that Ali, Abu Beker, Omar, and the rest of those who had been constantly about him, absented themselves for a time to attend to their affairs. Ayesha alone remained with him. The interval was but illusive. His pains returned with redoubled violence. Finding death approaching, he gave orders that all his slaves should be restored to freedom, and all the money in the house distributed among the poor; then raising his eyes to heaven, "God be with me in the death struggle," he exclaimed.

Ayesha now sent in haste for her father and Hafza. Left alone with Mohammed, she sustained his head on her lap, watching over him with tender assiduity, and endeavoring to soothe his dying agonies. From time to time he would dip his hand in a vase of water, and with it feebly sprinkle his face. At length raising his eyes and gazing upward for a time with unmoving eyelids, "O Allah!" ejaculated he, in broken accents, "be it so!—among the glorious associates in paradise!"

"I knew by this," said Ayesha, who related the dying scene, "that his last moment had arrived, and that he had made choice of supernal existence."

In a few moments his hands were cold, and life was extinct. Ayesha laid his head upon the pillow and, beating her head and breast, gave way to loud lamentations. Her outcries brought the other wives of Mohammed, and their clamorous grief soon made the event known throughout the city. Consternation seized upon the people, as if some prodigy had happened. All business was suspended. The army which had struck its tents was ordered to halt, and Osama, whose foot was in the stirrup for the march, turned his steed to the gates of Medina, and planted his standard at the prophet's door.

The multitude crowded to contemplate the corpse, and agitation and dispute prevailed even in the chamber of death. Some discredited the evidence of their senses. "How can he be dead ?" they cried. "Is he not our mediator with God? How then can he be dead? Impossible! He is but in a trance, and carried up to heaven like Isa (Jesus) and the other prophets."

The throng augmented about the house, declaring with clamor that the body should not be interred, when Omar, who had just heard the tidings, arrived. He drew his scimitar and, passing through the crowd, threatened to strike off the hands and feet of anyone who should affirm that the prophet was dead. "He has but departed for a time," he said, "as Musa (Moses) the son of Imram went up forty days into the mountain; and like him he will return again."

Abu Beker, who had been in a distant part of the city, arrived in time to soothe the despair of the people and calm the transports of Omar. Passing into the chamber he raised the cloth which covered the corpse and, kissing the pale face of Mohammed, "O thou!" he exclaimed, "who wert to me as my father and my mother; sweet art thou even in death, and living odors dost thou exhale! Now livest thou in everlasting bliss, for never will Allah subject thee to a second death."

Then covering the corpse he went forth, and endeavored to silence Omar, but finding it impossible, he addressed the multitude. "Truly if Mohammed is the sole object of your adoration, he is dead; but if it be God you worship, he cannot die. Mohammed was but the prophet of God, and has shared the fate of the apostles and holy men who have gone before him. Allah, himself, has said in his Koran that Mohammed was but his ambassador, and was subject to death. What then! will you turn the heel upon him, and abandon his doctrine because he is dead? Remember your apostasy harms not God, but insures your own condemnation; while the blessings of God will be poured out upon those who continue faithful to him."

The people listened to Abu Beker with tears and sobbings, and as they listened their despair subsided. Even Omar was convinced but not consoled, throwing himself on the earth and bewailing the death of Mohammed, whom he remembered as his commander and his friend.

The death of the prophet, according to the Moslem historians Abulfeda and Al Jannabi, took place on his birthday, when he had completed his sixty-third year. It was in the eleventh year of the Hegira, and the 632nd year of the Christian era.

The body was prepared for sepulture by several of the dearest relatives and disciples. They affirmed that a marvelous fragrance which, according to the evidence of his wives and daughters, emanated from his person during life, still continued; so that, to use the words of Ali, "it seemed as if he were, at the same time, dead and living."

The body, having been washed and perfumed, was wrapped in three coverings: two white, and the third of the striped cloth of Yemen. The whole was then perfumed with amber, musk, aloes, and odoriferous herbs. After this it was exposed in public, and seventy-two prayers were offered up.

The body remained three days unburied, in compliance with oriental custom, and to satisfy those who still believed in the possibility of a trance. When the evidences of mortality could no longer be mistaken, preparations were made for interment. A dispute now arose as to the place of sepulture. The Mohadjerins or disciples from Mecca contended for that city, as being the place of his nativity; the Ansarians claimed for Medina, as his asylum and the place of his residence during the last ten years of his life. A third party advised that his remanas should be transported to Jerusalem, as the place of sepulture of the prophets. Abu Beker, whose word had always the greatest weight, declared it to have been the expressed opinion of Mohammed that a prophet should be buried in the place where he died. This in the present instance was complied with to the very letter, for a grave was dug in the house of Ayesha, beneath the very bed on which Mohammed had expired.[1]

39

Person and character of Mohammed, and speculations on his prophetic career

Mohammed, according to accounts handed down by tradition from his contemporaries, was of the middle stature, square built and sinewy, with large hands and feet. In his youth he was uncommonly strong and vigorous; in the latter part of his life he inclined to corpulency. His head was capacious, well shaped, and well set on a neck which rose like a pillar from his ample chest. His forehead was high, broad at the temples, and crossed by veins extending down to the eyebrows, which swelled whenever he was angry or excited. He had an oval face, marked and expressive features, an aquiline nose, black eyes, arched eyebrows which nearly met, a mouth large and inflexible, indicative of eloquence; very white teeth, somewhat parted and irregular; black hair which waved without a curl on his shoulders, and a long and very full beard.

His deportment, in general, was calm and equable; he sometimes indulged in pleasantry, but more commonly was grave and dignified, though he is said to have possessed a smile of captivating sweetness. His complexion was more ruddy than is usual with Arabs, and in his excited and enthusiastic moments there was a glow and radiance in his countenance, which his disciples magnified into the supernatural light of prophecy.

His intellectual qualities were undoubtedly of an extraordinary kind. He had a quick apprehension, a retentive memory, a vivid imagination, and an inventive genius. Owing but little to education, he had quickened and informed his mind by close observation, and stored it with a great variety of knowledge concerning the systems of religion current in his day, or handed down by tradition from antiquity. His ordinary discourse was grave and sententious, abounding with those aphorisms and apologues so popular among the Arabs; at times he was excited and eloquent, and his eloquence was aided by a voice musical and sonorous.

He was sober and abstemious in his diet, and a rigorous observer of fasts. He indulged in no magnificence of apparel, the ostentation of a petty mind; neither was his simplicity in dress affected, but the result of a real disregard to distinction from so trivial a source. His garments were sometimes of wool, sometimes of the striped cotton of Yemen, and were often patched. He wore a turban, for he said turbans were worn by the angels; and in arranging it he let one end hang down between his shoulders, which he said was the way they wore it. He forbade the wearing of clothes entirely of silk, but permitted a mixture of thread and silk. He forbade also red clothes and the use of gold rings. He wore a seal ring of silver, the engraved part under his finger close to the palm of his hand bearing the inscription, "Mohammed the messenger of God." He was scrupulous as to personal cleanliness, and observed frequent ablutions. In some respects he was a voluptuary. "There are two things in this world," he would say, "which delight me: women and perfumes. These two things rejoice my eyes and render me more fervent in devotion." From his extreme cleanliness, and the use of perfumes and sweet-scented oil for his hair, probably arose that sweetness and fragrance of person which his disciples considered innate and miraculous. His passion for the sex had an influence over all his affairs. It is said that when in the presence of a beautiful female, he was continually smoothing his brow and adjusting his hair, as if anxious to appear to advantage.

The number of his wives is uncertain. Abulfeda, who writes with more caution than other of the Arabian historians, limits it to fifteen, though some make it as much as twenty-five. At the time of his death he had nine, each in her separate dwelling, and all in the vicinity of the mosque at Medina. The plea alleged for his indulging in a greater number of wives than he permitted to his followers was a desire to beget a race of prophets for his people. If such indeed were his desire, it was disappointed. Of all his children, Fatima the wife of Ali alone survived him, and she died within a short time after his death.

Of her descendants, none excepting her eldest son Hassan ever sat on the throne of the Caliphs.

In his private dealings he was just. He treated friends and strangers, the rich and poor, the powerful and the weak, with equity, and was beloved by the common people for the affability with which he received them, and listened to their complaints.

He was naturally irritable, but had brought his temper under great control, so that even in the self-indulgent intercourse of domestic life he was kind and tolerant. "I served him from the time I was eight years old," said his servant Anas, "and he never scolded me for anything, though things were spoiled by me."

The question now occurs, was he the unprincipled impostor that he has been represented? Were all his visions and revelations deliberate falsehoods, and was his whole system a tissue of deceit? In considering this question we must bear in mind that he is not chargeable with many extravagances which exist in his name. Many of the visions and revelations handed down as having been given by him are spurious. The miracles ascribed to him are all fabrications of Moslem zealots. He expressly and repeatedly disclaimed all miracles excepting the Koran—which, considering its incomparable merit, and the way in which it had come down to him from heaven, he pronounced the greatest of miracles. And here we must indulge a few observations on this famous document. While zealous Moslems and some of the most learned doctors of the faith draw proofs of its divine origin from the inimitable excellence of its style and composition, and the avowed illiteracy of Mohammed, less devout critics have pronounced it a chaos of beauties and defects; without method or arrangement; full of obscurities, incoherencies, repetitions, false versions of Scriptural stories, and direct contradictions.

The truth is that the Koran as it now exists is not the same Koran delivered by Mohammed to his disciples, but has undergone many corruptions and interpolations. The revelations contained in it were given at various times, in various places, and before various persons; sometimes they were taken down by his secretaries or disciples on parchment, on palm leaves, or the shoulder blades of sheep, and thrown together in a chest, of which one of his wives had charge; sometimes they were merely treasured up in the memories of those who heard them. No care appears to have been taken to

systematize and arrange them during his life; and at his death
they remained in scattered fragments, many of them at the
mercy of fallacious memories. It was not until some time after
his death that Abu Beker undertook to have them gathered
together and transcribed. Zeid Ibn Thabet, who had been one of
the secretaries of Mohammed, was employed for the purpose. He
professed to know many parts of the Koran by heart, having
written them down under the dictation of the prophet; other parts
he collected piecemeal from various hands, written down in the
rude way we have mentioned, and many parts he took down as
repeated to him by various disciples who professed to have heard
them uttered by the prophet himself. The heterogeneous
fragments thus collected were thrown together without selection,
without chronological order, and without system of any kind.
The volume thus formed during the Caliphat of Abu Beker was
transcribed by different hands, and many professed copies put
in circulation and dispersed throughout the Moslem cities. So
many errors, interpolations, and contradictory readings soon
crept into these copies that Othman, the third Caliph, called in
the various manuscripts, and forming what he pronounced the
genuine Koran, caused all the others to be destroyed.

This simple statement may account for many of the
incoherencies, repetitions, and other discrepancies charged
upon this singular document. Mohammed, as has justly been
observed, may have given the same precepts, or related the same
apologue at different times, to different persons in different
words; or various persons may have been present at one time,
and given various versions of his words, and reported his
apologues and scriptural stories in different ways, according to
their imperfect memoranda or fallible recollections. Many
revelations given by him as having been made in foregone
times to the prophets, his predecessors, may have been reported
as having been given as relations made to himself. It has been
intimated that Abu Beker, in the early days of his Caliphat, may
have found it politic to interpolate many things in the Koran,
calculated to aid him in emergencies, and confirm the empire
of Islamism. What corruptions and interpolations may have
been made by other and less scrupulous hands, after the
prophet's death, we may judge by the daring liberties of the kind
taken by Abdallah Ibn Saad, one of his secretaries, during his
lifetime.

From all these circumstances it will appear that even the documentary memorials concerning Mohammed abound with vitiations, while the traditional are full of fable. These increase the difficulty of solving the enigma of his character and conduct. His history appears to resolve itself into two grand divisions. During the first part, up to the period of middle life, we cannot perceive what adequate object he had to gain by the impious and stupendous imposture with which he stands charged. Was it riches? His marriage with Cadijah had already made him wealthy, and for years preceding his pretended vision he had manifested no desire to increase his store. Was it distinction? He already stood high in his native place, as a man of intelligence and probity. He was of the illustrious tribe of Koreish, and of the most honored branch of that tribe. Was it power? The guardianship of the Caaba, and with it the command of the sacred city, had been for generations in his immediate family, and his situation and circumstances entitled him to look forward with confidence to that exalted trust. In attempting to subvert the faith in which he had been brought up, he struck at the root of all these advantages. On that faith were founded the fortunes and dignities of his family. To assail it must draw on himself the hostility of his kindred, the indignation of his fellow-citizens, and the horror and odium of all his countrymen, who were worshippers at the Caaba.

Was there anything brilliant in the outset of his prophetic career to repay him for these sacrifices, and to lure him on? On the contrary, it was begun in doubt and secrecy. For years it was not attended by any material success. In proportion as he made known his doctrines and proclaimed his revelations, they subjected him to ridicule, scorn, obloquy, and finally to an inveterate persecution, which ruined the fortunes of himself and his friends; compelled some of his family and followers to take refuge in a foreign land; obliged him to hide from sight in his native city; and finally drove him forth a fugitive to seek an uncertain home elsewhere. Why should he persist for years in a course of imposture which was thus prostrating all his worldly fortunes, at a time of life when it was too late to build them up anew?

In the absence of sufficient worldly motives, we are compelled to seek some other explanation of his conduct in this stage of his most enigmatical history; and this we have endeavored to set forth in the early part of this work, where we have shown his enthusiastic and visionary spirit gradually wrought up by solitude, fasting, prayer, and meditation, and irritated by bodily disease into a state of temporary delirium, in which he fancies he receives a revelation from heaven, and is declared a prophet of the Most High. We cannot but think there was self-deception in this instance, and that he believed in the reality of the dream or vision, especially after his doubts had been combated by the zealous and confiding Cadijah, and the learned and crafty Waraka.

Once he had been persuaded of his divine mission to go forth and preach the faith, all subsequent dreams and impulses might be construed to the same purport; all might be considered intimations of the divine will, imparted in their several ways to him as a prophet. We find him repeatedly subject to trances and ecstasies in times of peculiar agitation and excitement, when he may have fancied himself again in communication with the Deity, and these were almost always followed by revelations.

The general tenor of his conduct up to the time of his flight from Mecca is that of an enthusiast acting under a species of mental delusion, deeply imbued with a conviction of his being a divine agent for religious reform. And there is something striking and sublime in the luminous path which his enthusiastic spirit struck out for itself through the bewildering maze of adverse faiths and wild traditions—the pure and spiritual worship of the one true God, which he sought to substitute for the blind idolatry of his childhood.

All the parts of the Koran supposed to have been promulgated by him at this time, incoherently as they have come down to us, and marred as their pristine beauty must be in passing through various hands, are of a pure and elevated character, and breathe poetical, if not religious, inspiration. They show that he had drunk deep of the living waters of Christianity, and if he had failed to imbibe them in their crystal purity, it might be because he had to drink from broken cisterns, and streams troubled and perverted by those who should have been their guardians. The faith he had hitherto inculcated was purer than that held forth by some of the pseudo-Christians of Arabia, and his life, so far, had been regulated according to its tenets.

Such is our view of Mohammed and his conduct during the early part of his career, while he was a persecuted and ruined man in Mecca. A signal change, however, took place, as we have shown in the foregoing chapters, after his flight to Medina, when, in place of the mere shelter and protection which he sought, he finds himself revered as a prophet, implicitly obeyed as a chief, and at the head of a powerful, growing, and warlike host of votaries. From this time worldly passions and worldly schemes too often give the impulse to his actions, instead of that visionary enthusiasm which, even if mistaken, threw a glow of piety on his earlier deeds. The old doctrines of forbearance, long-suffering, and resignation, are suddenly dashed aside; he becomes vindictive towards those who have hitherto oppressed him, and ambitious of extended rule. His doctrines, precepts, and conduct become marked by contradictions, and his whole course is irregular and unsteady. His revelations, henceforth, are so often opportune, and fitted to particular emergencies, that we are led to doubt his sincerity, and that he is any longer under the same delusion concerning them. Still, it must be remembered, as we have shown, that the records of these revelations are not always to be depended upon. What he may have uttered as from his own will may have been reported as if given by the will of God. Often, too, as we have already suggested, he may have considered his own impulses as divine intimations; and that, being an agent ordained to propagate the faith, all impulses and conceptions toward that end might be part of a continued and divine inspiration.

If we are far from considering Mohammed the gross and impious impostor that some have represented him, so also are we indisposed to give him credit for vast forecast, and for that deeply concerted scheme of universal conquest which has been ascribed to him. He was, undoubtedly, a man of great genius and a suggestive imagination, but it appears to us that he was, in a great degree, the creature of impulse and excitement, and very much at the mercy of circumstances. His schemes grew out of his fortunes, and not his fortunes out of his schemes. He was forty years of age before he first broached his doctrines. He suffered year after year to steal away before he promulgated them out of his own family. When he fled from Mecca thirteen years had elapsed from the announcement of his mission, and from being a wealthy merchant he had sunk to be a ruined fugitive. When he reached Medina he had no idea of the worldly power that awaited him; his only thought was to build a humble mosque where he might preach, and his only hope that he might be suffered to preach with impunity. When power suddenly broke upon him, he used it for a time in petty forays and local feuds. His military plans expanded with his resources, but were by no means masterly, and were sometimes unsuccessful. They were not struck out with boldness, nor executed with decision; but were often changed in deference to the opinions of warlike men about him, and sometimes at the suggestion of inferior minds, who occasionally led him wrong. Had he, indeed, conceived from the outset the idea of binding up the scattered and conflicting tribes of Arabia into one nation by a *brotherhood of faith*, for the purpose of carrying out a scheme of external conquest, he would have been one of the first of military projectors; but the idea of extended conquest seems to have been an afterthought, produced by success. The moment he proclaimed the religion of the sword, and gave the predatory Arabs a taste of foreign plunder, that moment he was launched in a career of conquest, which carried him forward with its own irresistible impetus. The fanatic zeal with which he had inspired his followers did more for his success than his military science; their belief in his doctrine of predestination produced victories which no military calculation could have anticipated. In his dubious outset as a prophet, he had been encouraged by the crafty counsels of his scriptural oracle Waraka; in his career as a conqueror, he had Omar, Khaled, and other fiery spirits by his side to urge him on, and to aid him in managing the tremendous power which he had evoked into action. Even with all their aid, he had occasionally to avail himself of his supernatural machinery as a prophet, and in so doing may have reconciled himself to the fraud by considering the pious end to be obtained.

His military triumphs awakened no pride, no vainglory, as they would have done had they been effected for selfish purposes. In the time of his greatest power, he maintained the same simplicity of manners and appearance as in the days of his adversity. So far from affecting regal state, he was displeased if, on entering a room, any unusual testimonial of respect were shown him. If he aimed at universal dominion, it was the dominion of the faith. As to the temporal rule which grew up in his hands, as he used it without ostentation, so he took no step to perpetuate it in his family.

The riches which poured in upon him from tribute and the spoils of war, were expended in promoting the victories of the faith, and in relieving the poor among its votaries, insomuch that his treasury was often drained of its last coin. Omar Ibn Al

Hareth declares that Mohammed, at his death, did not leave a golden dinar nor a silver dirhem, a slave nor a slave girl, nor anything but his gray mule Daldal, his arms, and the ground which he bestowed upon his wives, his children, and the poor. "Allah," says an Arabian writer, "offered him the keys of all the treasures of the earth, but he refused to accept them."

It is this perfect abnegation of self, connected with this apparently heartfelt piety, running throughout the various phases of his fortune, which perplex one in forming a just estimate of Mohammed's character. However he betrayed the alloy of earth after he had worldly power at his command, the early aspirations of his spirit continually returned and bore him above all earthly things. Prayer, that vital duty of Islamism, and that infallible purifier of the soul, was his constant practice. "Trust in God," was his comfort and support in times of trial and despondency. On the clemency of God, we are told, he reposed all his hopes of supernal happiness. Ayesha relates that on one occasion she inquired of him, "O prophet, do none enter paradise but through God's mercy ?" "None! none!" he replied, with earnest and emphatic repetition. "But you, O prophet, will not *you* enter excepting through his compassion?" Then Mohammed put his hand upon his head, and replied three times, with great solemnity, "Neither shall I enter paradise unless God cover me with his mercy!"

When he hung over the deathbed of his infant son Ibrahim, resignation to the will of God was exhibited in his conduct under this keenest of afflictions, and the hope of soon rejoining his child in paradise was his consolation. When he followed him to the grave, he invoked his spirit, in the awful examination of the tomb, to hold fast to the foundations of the faith, the unity of God, and his own mission as a prophet. Even in his own dying hour, when there could be no longer a worldly motive for deceit, he still breathed the same religious devotion, and the same belief in his apostolic mission. The last words that trembled on his lips ejaculated a trust of soon entering into blissful companionship with the prophets who had gone before him.

It is difficult to reconcile such ardent, persevering piety with an incessant system of blasphemous imposture; nor such pure and elevated and benignant precepts as are contained in the Koran, with a mind haunted by ignoble passions, and devoted to the grovelling interests of mere mortality; and we find no other satisfactory mode of solving the enigma of his character and conduct than by supposing that the ray of mental hallucination which flashed upon his enthusiastic spirit during his religious ecstasies in the midnight cavern of Mount Hara, continued more or less to bewilder him with a species of monomania to the end of his career, and that he died in the delusive belief of his mission as a prophet.

Appendix

The faith of Islam

In an early chapter of this work we have given such particulars of the faith inculcated by Mohammed as we deemed important to the understanding of the succeeding narrative. We now, though at the expense of some repetition, subjoin a more complete summary, accompanied by a few observations.

The religion of Islam, as we observed, is divided into two parts: FAITH AND PRACTICE: — and first of Faith. This is distributed under six different heads, or articles: 1st, faith in God; 2nd, in his angels; 3rd, in his Scriptures or Koran; 4th, in his prophets; 5th, in the resurrection and final judgment; 6th, in predestination. Of these we will briefly treat in the order we have enumerated them.

FAITH IN GOD. Mohammed inculcated the belief that there is, was, and ever will be, one only God, the creator of all things; who is single, immutable, omniscient, omnipotent, all-merciful, and eternal. The unity of God was specifically and strongly urged, in contradistinction to the Trinity of the Christians. It was designated, in the profession of faith, by raising one finger, and exclaiming, "La illaha il Allah!" ("There is no God but God"); to which was added, "Mohammed Resoul Allah!" ("Mohammed is the prophet of God").

FAITH IN ANGELS. The beautiful doctrine of angels, or ministering spirits, which was one of the most ancient and universal of oriental creeds, is interwoven throughout the Islam system. They are represented as ethereal beings, created from fire, the purest of elements, perfect in form and radiant in beauty, but without sex; free from all gross or sensual passion, and all the appetites and infirmities of frail humanity; and existing in perpetual and unfading youth. They are various in their degrees and duties, and in their favor with the Deity. Some worship around the celestial throne; others perpetually hymn the praises of Allah; some are winged messengers to execute his orders; and others intercede for the children of men.

The most distinguished of this heavenly host are four Archangels: Gabriel, the angel of revelations, who writes down the divine decrees; Michael, the champion, who fights the battles of the faith; Azraïl, the angel of death; and Israfil, who holds the awful commission to sound the trumpet on the day of resurrection. There was another angel named Azazil, the same as Lucifer, once the most glorious of the celestial band; but he became proud and rebellious. When God commanded his angels to worship Adam, Azazil refused, saying, "Why should I, whom thou hast created of fire, bow down to one whom thou hast formed of clay?" For this offense he was accursed and cast forth from paradise, and his name changed to Eblis, which signifies despair. In revenge of his abasement, he works all kinds of mischief against the children of men, and inspires them with disobedience and impiety.

Among the angels of inferior rank is a class called Moakkibat, two of whom keep watch upon each mortal, one on the right hand, the other on the left, taking note of every word and action. At the close of each day they fly up to heaven with a written report, and are replaced by two similar angels on the following day. According to Moslem tradition, every good action is recorded ten times by the angel on the right; and if the mortal commit a sin, the same benevolent spirit says to the angel on the left, "Forbear for seven hours to record it; peradventure he may repent and pray and obtain forgiveness."

Beside the angelic orders Mohammed inculcated a belief in spiritual beings called Gins or Genii, who, though likewise created of fire, partake of the appetites and frailties of the children of the dust, and like them are ultimately liable to death. By beings of this nature, which haunt the solitudes of the desert, Mohammed, as we have shown, professed to have been visited after his evening orisons in the solitary valley of Al Naklah.

When the angel Azazil rebelled and fell and became Satan or Eblis, he still maintained sovereignty over these inferior spirits, who are divided by Orientalists into Dives and Peri: the former ferocious and gigantic; the latter delicate and gentle, subsisting on perfumes. It would seem as if the Peri were all of the female sex, though on this point there rests obscurity. From these imaginary beings it is supposed the European fairies are derived.

Besides these there are other demi-spirits called Tacwins or Fates, being winged females of beautiful forms, who utter oracles and defend mortals from the assaults and machinations of evil demons.

There is vagueness and uncertainty about all the attributes given by Mohammed to these half-celestial beings, his ideas on the subject having been acquired from various sources. His whole system of intermediate spirits has a strong, though indistinct, infusion of the creeds and superstitions of the Hebrews, the Magians, and the Pagans or Sabeans.

The third article of faith is a belief in the KORAN, as a book of divine revelation. According to the Moslem creed a book was treasured up in the seventh heaven, and had existed there from all eternity, in which were written down all the decrees of God, and all events, past, present, or to come. Transcripts from these tablets of the divine will were brought down to the lowest heaven by the angel Gabriel, and by him revealed to Mohammed from time to time, in portions adapted to some event or emergency. Being the direct words of God, they were all spoken in the first person.

Of the way in which these revelations were taken down or treasured up by secretaries and disciples, and gathered together by Abu Beker after the death of Mohammed, we have made sufficient mention. The compilation, for such in fact it is, forms the Moslem code of civil and penal as well as religious law, and is treated with the utmost reverence by all true believers. A zealous pride is shown in having copies of it splendidly bound and ornamented. An inscription on the cover forbids anyone to touch it who is unclean, and it is considered irreverent, in reading it, to hold it below the girdle. Moslems swear by it, and take omens from its pages, by opening it and reading the first text that meets the eye. With all its errors and discrepancies, if we consider it mainly as the work of one man, and that an unlettered man, it remains a stupendous monument of solitary legislation.

Beside the Koran or written law, a number of precepts and apologues which casually fell from the lips of Mohammed were collected after his death from ear-witnesses, and transcribed into a book called the Sunna or Oral Law. This is held equally sacred with the Koran by a sect of Moslems thenceforth called

Sunnites; others reject it as apocryphal; these last are termed Shiites. Hostilities and persecutions have occasionally taken place between these sects almost as virulent as those which, between Catholics and Protestants, have disgraced Christianity. The Sunnites are distinguished by white, the Shiites by red turbans; hence the latter have received from their antagonists the appellation of Kussilbachi, or Red Heads.

It is remarkable that circumcision, which is invariably practiced by the Moslems and forms a distinguishing rite of their faith, to which all proselytes must conform, is neither mentioned in the Koran nor the Sunna. It seems to have been a general usage in Arabia, tacitly adopted from the Jews, and is even said to have been prevalent throughout the East before the time of Moses.

It is said that the Koran forbids the making likenesses of any living thing, which has prevented the introduction of portrait-painting among Moslems. The passage of the Koran, however, which is thought to contain the prohibition, seems merely an echo of the second commandment, held sacred by Jews and Christians, not to form images or pictures for worship. One of Mohammed's standards was a black eagle. Among the most distinguished Moslem ornaments of the Alhambra at Granada is a fountain supported by lions carved of stone, and some Moslem monarchs have had their effigies stamped on their coins.

Another and an important mistake with regard to the system of Mohammed, is the idea that it denies souls to the female sex, and excludes them from paradise. This error arises from his omitting to mention their enjoyments in a future state, while he details those of his own sex with the minuteness of a voluptuary. The beatification of virtuous females is alluded to in the fifty-sixth sura of the Koran, and also in other places, although from the vagueness of the language a cursory reader might suppose the Houris of paradise to be intended.

The fourth article of faith relates to the PROPHETS. Their number amounts to two hundred thousand, but only six are super-eminent, as having brought new laws and dispensations upon earth, each abrogating those previously received wherever they varied or were contradictory. These six distinguished prophets were Adam, Noah, Abraham, Moses, Jesus, and Mohammed.

The fifth article of the Islamic faith is on the RESURRECTION and the FINAL JUDGMENT. On this awful subject Mohammed blended some of the Christian belief with certain notions current among the Arabian Jews. One of these is the fearful tribunal of the Sepulchre. When Azraïl, the angel of death, has performed his office, and the corpse has been consigned to the tomb, two black angels, Munkar and Nakeer, of dismal and appalling aspect, present themselves as inquisitors, during whose scrutiny the soul is reunited to the body. The defunct, being commanded to sit up, is interrogated as to the two great points of faith, the unity of God and the divine mission of Mohammed, and likewise as to the deeds done by him during life; and his replies are recorded in books against the day of judgment. Should they be satisfactory, his soul is gently drawn forth from his lips, and his body left to its repose; should they be otherwise, he is beaten about the brows with iron clubs, and his soul wrenched forth with racking tortures. For the convenience of this awful inquisition, the Moslems generally deposit their dead in hollow or vaulted sepulchres, merely wrapped in funeral clothes, but not placed in coffins.

The space of time between death and resurrection is called Berzak, or the Interval. During this period the body rests in the grave, but the soul has a foretaste, in dreams or visions, of its future doom.

The souls of prophets are admitted at once into the full fruition of paradise. Those of martyrs, including all who die in battle, enter into the bodies or crops of green birds, who feed on the fruits and drink of the streams of paradise. Those of the great mass of true believers are variously disposed of, but, according to the most received opinion, they hover, in a state of seraphic tranquillity, near the tombs. Hence the Moslem usage of visiting the graves of their departed friends and relatives, in the idea that their souls are the gratified witnesses of these testimonials of affection.

Many Moslems believe that the souls of the truly faithful assume the forms of snow-white birds, and nestle beneath the throne of Allah— a belief in accordance with an ancient superstition of the Hebrews that the souls of the just will have a place in heaven under the throne of glory.

With regard to the souls of infidels, the most orthodox opinion is that they will be repulsed by angels both from heaven and earth, and cast into the cavernous bowels of the earth, there to await in tribulation the day of judgment.

THE DAY OF RESURRECTION will be preceded by signs and portents in heaven and earth. A total eclipse of the moon; a change in the course of the sun, rising in the west instead of the east; wars and tumults; a universal decay of faith; the advent of Antichrist; the issuing forth of Gog and Magog to desolate the world; a great smoke, covering the whole earth: these and many more prodigies and omens affrighting and harassing the souls of men, and producing a wretchedness of spirit and a weariness of life; insomuch that a man passing by a grave shall envy the quiet dead, and say, "Would to God I were in thy place!"

The last dread signal of the awful day will be the blast of a trumpet by the archangel Izrafil. At the sound thereof the earth will tremble; castles and towers will be shaken to the ground, and mountains leveled with the plains. The face of heaven will be darkened; the firmament will melt away, and the sun, the moon, and stars will fall into the sea. The ocean will be either dried up, or will boil and roll in fiery billows.

At the sound of that dreadful trump a panic will fall on the human race; men will fly from their brothers, their parents, and their wives; and mothers, in frantic terror, abandon the infant at the breast. The savage beasts of the forests, and the tame animals of the pasture, will forget their fierceness and their antipathies, and herd together in affright.

The second blast of the trumpet is the blast of extermination. At that sound, all creatures in heaven and on earth and in the waters under the earth, angels and genii and men and animals, all will die; excepting the chosen few especially reserved by Allah. The last to die will be Azraïl, the angel of death!

Forty days, or, according to explantions, forty years of continued rain will follow this blast of extermination; then will be sounded for the third time the trumpet of the archangel Izrafil; it is the call to judgment! At the sound of this blast, the whole space between heaven and earth will be filled with the souls of the dead flying in quest of their respective bodies. Then the earth will open; and there will be a rattling of dry bones, and a gathering together of scattered limbs; the very hairs will congregate together, and the whole body be reunited, and the soul will re-enter it, and the dead will rise from mutilation, perfect in every part, and naked as when born. The infidels will grovel with their faces on the earth, but the faithful will walk erect; as to the truly pious, they will be borne aloft on winged camels, white as milk, with saddles of fine gold.

Every human being will then be put upon his trial as to the manner in which he has employed his faculties, and the good and evil actions of his life. A mighty balance will be poised by the angel Gabriel; in one of these scales, termed Light, will be placed his good actions; in the other, termed Darkness, his evil deeds. An atom or a grain of mustard-seed will suffice to turn this balance; and the nature of the sentence will depend on the preponderance of either scale. At that moment retribution will be exacted for every wrong and injury. He who has wronged a fellow-mortal will have to repay him with a portion of his own good deeds, or, if he have none to boast of, will have to take upon himself a proportionate weight of the other's sins.

The trial of the balance will be succeeded by the ordeal of the bridge. The whole assembled multitude will have to follow Mohammed across the bridge Al Serát, as fine as the edge of a scimitar, which crosses the gulf of Jehennam or Hell. Infidels and sinful Moslems will grope along it darkling and fall into the abyss; but the faithful, aided by a beaming light, will cross with the swiftness of birds and enter the realms of paradise. The idea of this bridge, and of the dreary realm of Jehennam, is supposed to have been derived partly from the Jews, but chiefly from the Magians.

Jehennam is a region fraught with all kinds of horrors. The very trees have writhing serpents for branches, bearing for fruit the heads of demons. We forbear to dwell upon the particulars of this dismal abode, which are given with painful and often disgusting minuteness. It is described as consisting of seven stages, one below the other, and varying in the nature and intensity of torment. The first stage is allotted to Atheists, who deny creator and creation, and believe the world to be eternal. The second for Manicheans and others that admit two divine principles, and for the Arabian idolaters of the era of Mohammed. The third is for the Brahmins of India; the fourth for the Jews; the fifth for Christians; the sixth for the Magians or Ghebers of Persia; the seventh for hypocrites, who profess without believing in religion.

The fierce angel Thabeck, that is to say, the Executioner, presides over this region of terror.

We must observe that the general nature of Jehennam, and the distribution of its punishments, have given rise to various commentaries and expositions among the Moslem doctors. It is maintained by some, and it is a popular doctrine, that none of the believers in Allah and his prophets will be condemned to eternal punishment. Their sins will be expiated by proportionate periods of suffering, varying from nine hundred to nine thousand years.

Some of the most humane among the doctors contend against eternity of punishment to any class of sinners, saying that, as God is all-merciful, even infidels will eventually be pardoned. Those who have an intercessor, as the Christians have in Jesus Christ, will be first redeemed. The liberality of these worthy commentators, however, does not extend so far as to admit them into paradise among true believers; but concludes that, after long punishment, they will be relieved from their torments by annihilation.

Between Jehennam and paradise is Al Araf or the Partition, a region destitute of peace or pleasure, destined for the reception of infants, lunatics, idiots, and such other beings as have done neither good nor evil. For such, too, whose good and evil deeds balance each other; though these may be admitted to paradise through the intercession of Mohammed, on performing an act of adoration, to turn the scales in their favor. It is said that the tenants of this region can converse with their neighbors on either hand, the blessed and the condemned; and that Al Araf appears a paradise to those in hell, and a hell to those in paradise.

AL JANNAT, OR THE GARDEN. When the true believer has passed through all his trials, and expiated all his sins, he refreshes himself at the pool of the Prophet. This is a lake of fragrant water, a month's journey in circuit, fed by the river Al Cauther, which flows from paradise. The water of this lake is sweet as honey, cold as snow, and clear as crystal; he who once tastes of it will never more be tormented by thirst—a blessing dwelt upon with peculiar zest by Arabian writers, accustomed to the parching thirst of the desert.

After the true believer has drunk of this water of life, the gate of paradise is opened to him by the angel Rushvan. The same prolixity and minuteness which occur in the description of Jehennam are lavished on the delights of paradise, until the imagination is dazzled and confused by the details. The soil is of the finest wheaten flour, fragrant with perfumes, and strewed with pearls and hyacinths instead of sands and pebbles.

Some of the streams are of crystal purity, running between green banks enamelled with flowers; others are of milk, of wine and honey; flowing over beds of musk, between margins of camphire, covered with moss and saffron! The air is sweeter than the spicy gales of Sabea, and cooled by sparkling fountains. Here, too, is Taba, the wonderful tree of life, so large that a fleet horse would need a hundred years to cross its shade. The boughs are laden with every variety of delicious fruit, and bend to the hand of those who seek to gather.

The inhabitants of this blissful garden are clothed in raiment sparkling with jewels; they wear crowns of gold enriched with pearls and diamonds, and dwell in sumptuous palaces or silken pavilions, reclining on voluptuous couches. Here every believer will have hundreds of attendants, bearing dishes and goblets of gold, to serve him with every variety of exquisite viand and beverage. He will eat without satiety, and drink without inebriation; the last morsel and the last drop will be equally relished with the first; he will feel no repletion, and need no evacuation.

The air will resound with the melodious voice of Izrafil, and the songs of the daughters of paradise; the very rustling of the trees will produce ravishing harmony, while myriads of bells, hanging among their branches, will be put in dulcet motion by airs from the throne of Allah.

Above all, the faithful will be blessed with female society to the full extent even of oriental imaginings. Beside the wives he had on earth, who will rejoin him in all their pristine charms, he will be attended by the Hûr al Oyûn, or Houris, so called from their large black eyes; resplendent beings, free from every human defect or frailty; perpetually retaining their youth and beauty, and renewing their virginity. Seventy-two of these are allotted to every believer. The intercourse with them will be fruitful or not according to their wish, and the offspring will grow within an hour to the same stature with the parents.

That the true believer may be fully competent to the enjoyments of this blissful region, he will rise from the grave in the prime of manhood, at the age of thirty, of the stature of Adam, which was thirty cubits; with all his faculties improved to a state of preternatural perfection, with the abilities of a hundred men, and with desires and appetites quickened rather than sated by enjoyment.

These and similar delights are promised to the meanest of the faithful; there are gradations of enjoyment, however, as of merit; but, as to those prepared for the most deserving, Mohammed found the powers of description exhausted, and was fain to make use of the text from Scripture, that they should be such things "as eye hath not seen, ear hath not heard, neither hath it entered into the heart of man to conceive."

The expounders of the Islamic law differ in their opinions as to the whole meaning of this system of rewards and punishments, one set understanding everything in a figurative, the other in a literal sense. The former insist that the prophet spoke in parable, in a manner suited to the coarse perceptions and sensual natures of his hearers; and maintain that the joys of heaven will be mental as well as corporeal, the resurrection being of both soul and body. The soul will revel in a supernatural development and employment of all its faculties; in a knowledge of all the arcana of nature; the full revelation of everything past, present, and to come. The enjoyments of the body will be equally suited to its various senses, and perfected to a supernatural degree.

The same expounders regard the description of Jehennam as equally figurative; the torments of the soul consisting in the anguish of perpetual remorse for past crimes, and deep and ever-increasing despair for the loss of heaven; those of the body in excruciating and never-ending pain.

The other doctors, who construe everything in a literal sense, are considered the most orthodox, and their sect is beyond measure the most numerous. Most of the particulars in the system of rewards and punishments, as has been already observed, have close affinity to the superstitions of the Magians and the Jewish rabbis. The Houri, or black-eyed nymphs, who figure so conspicuously in the Moslem's paradise, are said to be the same as the Huram Behest of the Persian Magi, and Mohammed is accused by Christian investigators of having purloined much of his description of heaven from the account of the New Jerusalem in the Apocalypse, with such variation as is used by knavish jewellers, when they appropriate stolen jewels to their own use.

The sixth and last article of the Islamic faith is PREDESTINATION, and on this Mohammed evidently reposed his chief dependence for the success of his military enterprises. He inculcated that every event had been predetermined by God, and written down in the eternal tablet previous to the creation of the world. That the destiny of every individual, and the hour of his death, were irrevocably fixed, and could neither be varied nor evaded by any effort of human sagacity or foresight. Under this persuasion, the Moslems engaged in battle without risk; and, as death in battle was equivalent to martyrdom, and entitled them to an immediate admission into paradise, they had in either alternative, death or victory, a certainty of gain.

This doctrine, according to which men by their own free will can neither avoid sin nor avert punishment, is considered by many Moslems as derogatory to the justice and clemency of God; and several sects have sprung up who endeavor to soften and explain away this perplexlng dogma; but the number of these doubters is small, and they are not considered orthodox.

The doctrine of Predestination was one of those timely revelations to Mohammed that were almost miraculous from their seasonable occurrence. It took place immediately after the disastrous battle of Ohod, in which many of his followers, and among them his uncle Hamza, were slain. Then it was, in a moment of gloom and despondency, when his followers around him were disheartened, that he promulgated this law, telling them that every man must die at the appointed hour, whether in bed or in the field of battle. He declared, moreover, that the angel Gabriel had announced to him the reception of Hamza into the seventh heaven, with the title of Lion of God and of the Prophet. He added, as he contemplated the dead bodies, "I am witness for these, and for all who have been slain for the cause of God, and they shall appear in glory at the resurrection, with their wounds brilliant as vermilion and odoriferous as musk."

What doctrine could have been devised more calculated to hurry forward, in a wild career of conquest, a set of ignorant and predatory soldiers, than this assurance of booty if they survived, and paradise if they fell?[1] It rendered almost irresistible the Moslem arms; but it likewise contained the poison that was to destroy their dominion. From the moment the successors of the prophet ceased to be aggressors and conquerors, and sheathed the sword definitely, the doctrine of predestination began its baneful work. Enervated by peace, and the sensuality permitted by the Koran—which so distinctly separates its doctrines from the pure and self-denying religion of the

Messiah—the Moslem regarded every reverse as preordained by Allah, and inevitable; to be borne stoically, since human exertion and foresight were vain. "Help thyself and God will help thee," was a precept never in force with the followers of Mohammed, and its reverse has been their fate. The crescent has waned before the cross, and exists in Europe, where it was once so mighty, only by the suffrage, or rather the jealousy, of the great Christian powers, probably ere long to furnish another illustration, "that they that take the sword shall perish with the sword."

Religious Practice

The articles of religious practice are fourfold: Prayer, including ablution, Alms, Fasting, Pilgrimage.

ABLUTION is enjoined as preparative to PRAYER, purity of body being considered emblematical of purity of soul. It is prescribed in the Koran with curious precision. The face, arms, elbows, feet, and a fourth part of the head, to be washed once; the hands, mouth, and nostrils, three times; the ears to be moistened with the residue of the water used for the head; and the teeth to be cleaned with a brush. The ablution to commence on the right and terminate on the left; in washing the hands and feet to begin with the fingers and toes; where water is not to be had, fine sand may be used.

PRAYER is to be performed five times every day, namely: the first in the morning before sunrise; the second at noon; the third in the afternoon before sunset; the fourth in the evening between sunset and dark; the fifth between twilight and the first watch, being the vesper prayer. A sixth prayer is volunteered by many between the first watch of the night and the dawn of day. These prayers are but repetitions of the same laudatory ejaculation, "God is great! God is powerful! God is all powerful!"and are counted by the scrupulous upon a string of beads. They may be performed at the mosque, or in any clean place. During prayer the eyes are turned to the Kebla, or point of the heaven in the direction of Mecca, which is indicated in every mosque by a niche called Al Mehrab, and externally by the position of the minarets and doors. Even the postures to be observed in prayer are prescribed, and the most solemn act of adoration is by bowing the forehead to the ground. Females in praying are not to stretch forth their arms, but to fold them on their bosoms. They are not to make as profound inflections as the men. They are to pray in a low and gentle tone of voice. They are not permitted to accompany the men to the mosque, lest the minds of the worshippers should be drawn from their devotions. In addressing themselves to God, the faithful are enjoined to do so with humility, putting aside costly ornaments and sumptuous apparel.

Many of the Moslem observances with respect to prayer were similar to those previously maintained by the Sabeans; others agreed with the ceremonials prescribed by the Jewish rabbis. Such were the postures, inflections and prostrations and the turning of the face towards the Kebla, which, however, with the Jews was in the direction of the temple at Jerusalem.

Prayer, with the Moslem, is a daily exercise, but on Friday there is a sermon in the mosque. This day was generally held sacred among oriental nations as the day on which man was created. The Sabean idolaters consecrated it to Astarte, or Venus, the most beautiful of the planets and brightest of the stars. Mohammed adopted it as his Sabbath, partly perhaps from early habitude, but chiefly to vary from the Saturday of the Jews and Sunday of the Christians.

The *second article* of religious practice is CHARITY, or the giving of alms. There are two kinds of alms, namely: those prescribed by law, called Zakat, like tithes in the Christian church, to be made in specified proportions, whether in money, wares, cattle, corn, or fruit; and voluntary gifts termed Sadakat, made at the discretion of the giver. Every Moslem is enjoined, in one way or the other, to dispense a tenth of his revenue in relief of the indigent and distressed.

The *third article* of practice is FASTING, also supposed to have been derived from the Jews. In each year for thirty days, during the month of Ramadan, the true believer is to abstain rigorously, from the rising to the setting of the sun, from meat and drink, baths, perfumes, the intercourse of the sexes, and all other gratifications and delights of the senses. This is considered a great triumph of self-denial, mortifying and subduing the several appetites, and purifying both body and soul. Of these three articles of practice the Prince Abdul'aziz used to say, "Prayer leads us half way to God, fasting conveys us to his threshold, but alms conducts us into his presence."

PILGRIMAGE is the *fourth grand practical duty* enjoined upon Moslems. Every true believer is bound to make one pilgrimage to Mecca in the course of his life, either personally or by proxy. In the latter case, his name must be mentioned in every prayer offered up by his substitute.

Pilgrimage is incumbent only on free persons of mature age, sound intellect, and who have health and wealth enough to bear the fatigue and expenses of the journey. The pilgrim, before his departure from home, arranges all his affairs, public and domestic, as if preparing for his death.

On the appointed day, which is either Tuesday, Thursday, or Saturday, as being propitious for the purpose, he assembles his wives, children, and all his household, and devoutly commends them and all his concerns to the care of God during his holy enterprise. Then passing one end of his turban beneath his chin to the opposite side of his head, like the attire of a nun, and grasping a stout staff of bitter almonds, he takes leave of his household, and sallies from the apartment, exclaiming, "In the name of God I undertake this holy work, confiding in his protection. I believe in him, and place in his hands my actions and my life."

On leaving the portal he turns his face toward the Kebla, repeats certain passages of the Koran, and adds, "I turn my face to the Holy Caaba, the throne of God, to accomplish the pilgrimage commanded by his law, and which shall draw me near to him."

He finally puts his foot in the stirrup, mounts into the saddle, commends himself again to God, almighty, all wise, all merciful, and sets forth on his pilgrimage. The time of departure is always calculated so as to insure an arrival at Mecca at the beginning of the pilgrim month Dhu'l-hajji.

Three laws are to be observed throughout this pious journey:

1. To commence no quarrel.

2. To bear meekly all harshness and reviling.

3. To promote peace and goodwill among his companions in the caravan.

He is, moreover, to be liberal in his donations and charities throughout his pilgrimage.

When he has arrived at some place in the vicinity of Mecca, he allows his hair and nails to grow, strips himself to the skin, and assumes the Ihram or pilgrim garb, consisting of two scarfs, without seams or decorations, and of any stuff excepting silk. One of these is folded round the loins, the other thrown over the neck and shoulders, leaving the right arm free. The head is uncovered, but the aged and infirm are permitted to fold something round it in consideration of alms given to the poor. Umbrellas are allowed as a protection against the sun, and indigent pilgrims supply their place by a rag on the end of a staff.

The instep must be bare; and peculiar sandals are provided for the purpose, or a piece of the upper leather of the shoe is cut out. The pilgrim, when thus attired, is termed Al Mohrem.

The Ihram of females is an ample cloak and veil, enveloping the whole person, so that, in strictness, the wrists, the ankles, and even the eyes should be concealed.

When once assumed, the Ihram must be worn until the pilgrimage is completed, however unsuited it may be to the season or the weather. While wearing it, the pilgrim must abstain from all licentiousness of language; all sensual intercourse; all quarrels and acts of violence; he must not even take the life of an insect that infests him; though an exception is made in regard to biting dogs, to scorpions, and birds of prey.

On arriving at Mecca, he leaves his baggage in some shop, and, without attention to any worldly concern, repairs straightway to the Caaba, conducted by one of the Metowefs or guides, who are always at hand to offer their services to pilgrims.

Entering the mosque by the Bab el Salam, or Gate of Salutation, he makes four prostrations, and repeats certain prayers as he passes under the arch. Approaching the Caaba, he makes four prostrations opposite the Black Stone, which he then kisses; or, if prevented by the throng, he touches it with his right hand, and kisses that. Departing from the Black Stone, and keeping the building on his left hand, he makes the seven circuits, the three first quickly, tbe latter four with slow and solemn pace. Certain prayers are repeated in a low voice, and the Black Stone kissed, or touched, at the end of every circuit.

The Towaf, or procession, round the Caaba was an ancient ceremony observed long before the time of Mohammed, and performed by both sexes entirely naked. Mohammed prohibited this exposure, and prescribed the Ihram, or pilgrim dress. The female Hajji walk the Towaf generally during the night, though occasionally they perform it mingled with the men in the daytime.[2]

The seven circuits being completed, the pilgrim presses his breast against the wall between the Black Stone and the door of the Caaba and, with outstretched arms, prays for pardon of his sins.

He then repairs to the Makam, or station of Abraham, makes four prostrations, prays for the intermediation of the Patriarch, and thence to the well Zem Zem, and drinks as much of the water as he can swallow.

During all this ceremonial, the uninstructed Hajji has his guide or Metowef close at his heels, muttering prayers for him to repeat. He is now conducted out of the mosque by the gate Bab el Zafa, to a slight ascent about fifty paces distant, called the Hill of Zafa, when, after uttering a prayer with uplifted hands, he commences the holy promenade, called the Saa or Say. This lies through a straight and level street called Al Mesaa, six hundred paces in length, lined with shops like a bazaar, and terminating at a place called Merowa. The walk of the Say is in commemoration of the wandering of Hagar over the same ground, in search of water for her child Ishmael. The pilgrim, therefore, walks at times slowly, with an inquisitive air, then runs in a certain place, and again walks gravely, stopping at times and looking anxiously back.

Having repeated the walk up and down this street seven times, the Hajji enters a barber's shop at Merowa; his head is shaved, his nails pared, the barber muttering prayers and the pilgrim repeating them all the time. The paring and shearing are then buried in consecrated ground, and the most essential duties of the pilgrimage are considered as fulfilled.[3]

On the ninth of the month Al Dhu'l-hajji, the pilgrims make a hurried and tumultuous visit to Mount Arafat, where they remain until sunset; then pass the night in prayer at an Oratory, miled Mozdalifa, and before sunrise next morning repair to the valley of Mena, where they throw seven stones at each of three pillars, in imitation of Abraham, and some say also of Adam, who drove away the devil from this spot with stones, when disturbed by him in his devotions.

Such are the main ceremonies which form this great Moslem rite of pilgrimage; but, before concluding this sketch of the Islamic faith, and closing this legendary memoir of its founder, we cannot forbear to notice one of his innovations, which has entailed perplexity on all his followers, and particular inconvenience on pious pilgrims.

The Arabian year consists of twelve lunar months, containing alternately thirty and twenty-nine days, and making three hundred and fifty-four in the whole, so that eleven days were lost in every solar year. To make up the deficiency, a thirteenth or wandering month was added to every third year, previous to the era of Mohammed, to the same effect as one day is added in the Christian calendar to every leap year. Mohammed, who was uneducated and ignorant of astronomy, retrenched this thirteenth or intercalary month, as contrary to the divine order of revolutions of the moon, and reformed the calendar by a divine revelation during his last pilgrimage. This is recorded in the ninth sura or chapter of the Koran, to the following effect :

"For the number of months is twelve, as was ordained by Allah, and recorded on the eternal tables[4] on the day wherein he created the heaven and the earth.

"Transfer not a sacred month unto another month, for verily it is an innovation of the infidels."

The number of days thus lost amount in 33 years to 363. It becomes necessary, therefore, to add an intercalary year at the end of each thirty-third year to reduce the Moslem into the Christian era.

One great inconvenience arising from this revelation of the prophet is that the Moslem months do not indicate the season, as they commence earlier by eleven days every year. This at certain epochs is a sore grievance to the votaries to Mecca, as the great pilgrim month Dhu'l-hajji, during which they are compelled to wear the Ihram, or half-naked pilgrim garb, runs the round of the seasons, occurring at one time in the depth of winter, at another in the fervid heat of summer.

Thus Mohammed, though according to legendary history he could order the moon from the firmament and make her revolve about the sacred house, could not control her monthly revolutions; and found that the science of numbers is superior even to the gift of prophecy, and sets miracles at defiance.

Endnotes

Introduction

1. Charles Neider, "Introduction" to *The Complete Tales of Washington Irving*, Garden City, N. Y.: Doubleday, 1974, p. xxi.

2. The *Mishkat al-Masabih* was translated by A. N. Matthews, and published in Calcutta in 1809. It has been reprinted several times.

3. Cf. Jean Gagnier, *La Vie de Mahomet traduite et compilée de l'Alcoran, des traditions authentiques de la Sonna, et de meilleurs auteurs Arabes*, Amsterdam: Wetstein & Smith, 1748.

4. Reprinted several times: London, 1911; Lahore, 1975; etc.

5. The Jewish sources of the Koran were the subject of two early studies: Abraham Geiger, *Was hat Mohammed aus dem Judentume aufgenommen?*, 1833, of which Irving seems to have been unaware, and Gustav Weil, *The Bible, the Koran, and the Talmud: or, Biblical Legends of the Musulmans*, 1846, of which Irving owned a copy and which was found in his library, cf. E. N. Feltskog, "Historical Note," in Henry A. Pochmann and E. N. Feltskog (eds.), Washington Irving, *Mahomet and His Successors*, Madison, Wisc.: University of Wisconsin Press, 1970, p. 544.

6. Johann Ludwig Burckhardt, *Notes on the Bedouins and Wahhabis*, 1830; Edward William Lane, *Manners and Customs of the Modern Egyptians*, 1836; Carsten Niebuhr, *Travels through Arabia*, 1792; Sir Austen Henry Layard, *Nineveh and Its Remains*, 1848.

7. Edward Gibbon's *Decline and Fall of the Roman Empire* contains a detailed discussion of the life of Mohammed and the contemporary Arab world, see vol. 5, pp. 332-422 of the London: Methuen, 1911 edition.

8. As quoted by Feltskog, *op. cit.*, pp. 553.

9. Sir William Muir's *Life of Mahomet* (first published in 1861) also closes with a chapter titled "The Person and Character of Mahomet"; cf. 3rd (1894) edition, pp. 494-507.

(The notes which follow are those supplied by Irving himself.)

Chapter 1

1. Besides the Arabs of the peninsula, who were all of the Semitic race, there were others called Cushites, being descended from Cush the son of Ham. They inhabited the banks of the Euphrates and the Persian Gulf. The name of Cush is often given in Scripture to the Arabs generally as well as to their country. It must be the Arabs of this race who at present roam the deserted regions of ancient Assyria, and have been employed recently in disinterring the long-buried ruins of Nineveh. They are sometimes distinguished as the Syro-Arabians. The present work relates only to the Arabs of the peninsula, or Arabia Proper.

2. Haran, Canna, and Aden, ports on the Indian Ocean.

3. In summer the wandering Arabs, according to Burckhardt, seldom remain above three or four days on the same spot. As soon as their cattle have consumed the herbage near a watering place, the tribe moves in search of pasture, and the grass again springing up, serves for a succeeding camp. The encampments vary in the number of tents, from six to eight hundred; when the tents are but few, they are pitched in a circle; but more considerable numbers in a straight line, or a row of single tents, especially along a rivulet, sometimes three or four behind as many others. In winter, when water and pasture never fail, the whole tribe spreads itself over the plain in parties of three or four tents each, with an interval of half an hour's distance between each party. The Sheikh's tent is always on the side on which enemies or guests may be expected. To oppose the former and to honor the latter is the Sheikh's principal business. Every father of a family sticks his lance into the ground by the side of his tent, and ties his horse in front. There also his camels repose at night.—Burckhardt, *Notes on the Bedouins and Wahhabis,* vol. i, p. 33.

The following is descriptive of the Arabs of Assyria, though it is applicable, in a great degree, to the whole race:

"It would be difficult to describe the appearance of a large tribe when migrating to new pastures. We soon found ourselves in the midst of wide-spreading flocks of sheep and camels. As far as the eye could reach, to the right, to the left, and in front, still the same moving crowd. Long lines of asses and bullocks, laden with black tents, huge cauldrons, and variegated carpets; aged women and men, no longer able to walk, tied on the heap of domestic furniture; infants crammed into saddlebags, their tiny heads thrust through the narrow opening, balanced on the animal's back by kids or lambs tied on the opposite side; young girls clothed only in the close-fitting Arab shirt, which displayed rather than concealed their graceful forms; mothers with their children on their shoulders; boys driving flocks of lambs; horsemen armed with their long tufted spears, scouring the plain on their fleet mares; riders urging their dromedaries with their short-hooked sticks, and leading their high-bred steeds by the halter; colts galloping among the throng; such was the motley crowd through which we had to wend our way."—Layard,*Nineveh and Its Remains,* vol. i, chapt. IV, pp. 89-90.

Chapter 2

1. The Beni Sad (or children of Sad) date from the most remote antiquity, and, with the Katan Arabs, are the only remnants of the primitive tribes of Arabia. Their valley is among the mountains which range southwardly from the Taif.—Burckhardt, *op. cit.,* vol. ii, p. 47.

Chapter 4

1. Some assert that these two names indicate two monks who held conversations with Mohammed.

2. *Mishcât-ul-Masâbih,* vol. ii, p. 812.

The conversion of Abraham from the idolatry into which the world had fallen after the deluge is related in the sixth chapter of the Koran. Abraham's father, Azer, or Zerah, as his name is given in the Scriptures, was a statuary and an idolater.

"And Abraham said unto his father Azer, 'Why dost thou take graven images for gods? Verily, thou and thy people are in error.'

"Then was the firmament of heaven displayed unto Abraham, that he might see how the world was governed.

"When night came, and darkness overshadowed the earth, he beheld a bright star shining in the firmament, and cried out to his people who were astrologers: 'This, according to your assertions, is the Lord.'

"But the star set, and Abraham said, 'I have no faith in gods that set.'

"He beheld the moon rising, and exclaimed, 'Assuredly, this is the Lord.' But the moon likewise set, and he was confounded, and prayed unto God, saying, 'Direct me, lest I become as one of these people, who go astray.'

"When he saw the sun rising, he cried out, 'This is the most glorious of all; this of a certainty is the Lord.' But the sun also set. Then said Abraham, 'I believe not, my people, in those things which ye call gods. Verily, I turn my face unto Him, the Creator, who hath formed both the heavens and the earth.'"

Chapter 7

1. Niebuhr (*Travels,* vol. ii.) speaks of the tribe of Harb, which possessed several cities and a number of villages in the highlands of Hedjas, a mountainous range between Mecca and Medina. They have castles on precipitous rocks, and harass and lay under contribution the caravans. It is presumed that this tribe takes its name from the father of Abu Sofian, as did the great line of the Omeyades from his grandfather.

2. By an error of translators, Ali is made to accompany his offer of adhesion by an extravagant threat against all who should oppose Mohammed.

Chapter 8

1. Some etymologists derive Islam from Salem or Aslama, which signifies salvation. The Christians form from it the term Islamism. and the Jews have varied it into Ismailism, which they intend as a reproach, and an allusion to the origin of the Arabs as descendants of Ishmael.

From Islam the Arabians drew the terms Moslem or Muslem, and Musulman, a professor of the faith of Islam. These terms are in the singular number and make Musliman in the dual, and Muslimen in the plural. The French and some other nations follow the idioms of their own languages in adopting or translating the Arabic terms, and form the plural by the addition of the letter *s*;, writing Musulman and Musulmans. A few English writers, of whom Gibbon is the chief, have imitated them, imagining that they were following the Arabian usage. Most English authors, however, follow the idiom of their own language, writing Moslem and Moslems, Musulman and Musulmen. This usage is also the more harmonious.

2. The *Mishnu* of the Jews, like the Sonna or Sunna of the Moslems, is a collection of traditions forming the Oral Law. It was compiled in the second century by Judah Hakkodish, a learned Jewish rabbi, during the reign of Antoninus Pius, the Roman Emperor. The Jerusalem Talmud and the Babylonian Talmud are both commentaries on the Mishnu. The former was compiled at Jerusalem, about three hundred years after Christ, and the latter in Babylonia, about two centuries later. The Mishnu is the most ancient record possessed by the Jews except the Bible.

3. The following words of Mohammed, treasured up by one of his disciples, appear to have been suggested by a passage in Matthew, xxv, 35-45:

"Verily, God will say at the day of resurrection, 'O sons of Adam! I was sick, and ye did not visit me.' Then they will say, 'How could we visit thee? for thou art the Lord of the universe, and art free from sickness.' And God will reply, 'Knew ye not that such a one of my servants was sick, and ye did not visit him? Had you visited that servant, it would have been counted to you as righteousness.' And God will say, 'O sons of Adam! I asked you for food, and ye gave it me not.' And the sons of Adam will say, 'How could we give thee food, seeing thou art the sustainer of the universe, and art free from hunger?' And God will say, 'Such a one of my servants asked you for bread, and ye refused it. Had you given him to eat, ye would have received your reward from me.' And God will say, 'O sons of Adam, I asked you for water, and ye gave it me not.' They will reply, 'O, our supporter! How could we give thee water, seeing thou art the sustainer of the universe, and not subject to thirst?' And God will say, 'Such a one of my servants asked you for water, and ye did not give it to him. Had ye done so, ye would have received your reward from me.'"

4. To exhibit the perplexing maze of controversial doctrines from which Mohammed had to acquire his notions of the Christian faith, we subjoin the leading points of the jarring sects of oriental Christians alluded to in the foregoing chapter, all of which have been pronounced heretical or schismatic.

The *Sabellians*, so called from Sabellius, a Libyan priest of the third century, believed in the unity of God, and that the Trinity expressed but three different states or relations, Father, Son, and Holy Ghost, all forming but one substance, as a man consists of body and soul.

The *Arians*, from Arius, an ecclesiastic of Alexandria in the fourth century, affirmed Christ to be the Son of God, but distinct from him and inferior to him, and denied the Holy Ghost to be God.

The *Nestorians*, from Nestorius, bishop of Constantinople in the fifth century, maintained that Christ had two distinct natures, divine and human; that Mary was only his mother, and Jesus a man; and that it was an abomination to style her, as was the custom of the church, the Mother of God.

The *Monophysites* maintained the single nature of Christ, as their name betokens. They affirmed that he was combined of God and man, so mingled and united as to form but one nature.

The *Eutychians*, from Eutyches, abbot of a convent in Constantinople in the fifth century, were a branch of the Monophysites, expressly opposed to the Nestorians. They denied the double nature of Christ, declaring that he was entirely God previous to the incarnation, and entirely man during the incarnation.

The *Jacobites*, from Jacobus, bishop of Edessa, in Syria, in the sixth century, were a very numerous branch of the Monophysites, varying but little from the Eutychians. Most of the Christian tribes of Arabs were Jacobites.

The *Mariamites*, or worshippers of Mary, regarded the Trinity as consisting of God the Father, God the Son, and God the Virgin Mary.

The *Collyridians* were a sect of Arabian Christians, composed chiefly of females. They worshipped the Virgin Mary as possessed of divinity, and made offerings to her of a twisted cake, called collyris, whence they derived their name.

The *Nazaraeans*, or Nazarenes, were a sect of Jewish Christians, who considered Christ as the Messiah, as born of a Virgin by the Holy Ghost, and as possessing something of a divine nature; but they conformed in all other respects to the rites and ceremonies of the Mosaic law.

The *Ebionites*, from Ebion, a converted Jew, who lived in the first century, were also a sect of judaizing Christians, differing little from the Nazaraeans. They believed Christ to be a pure man, the greatest of the prophets, but denied that he had any existence previous to being born of the Virgin Mary. This sect, as well as that of the Nazaraeans, had many adherents in Arabia.

Many other sects might be enumerated, such as the *Corinthians, Maronites*, and *Marcionites*, who took their names from learned and zealous leaders; and the *Docetes* and *Gnostics*, who were subdivided into various sects of subtle enthusiasts. Some of these asserted the immaculate purity of the Virgin Mary, affirming that her conception and delivery were effected like the transmission of the rays of light through a pane of glass, without impairing her virginity—an opinion still maintained strenuously in substance by Spanish Catholics.

Most of the Docetes asserted that Jesus Christ was of a nature entirely divine; that a phantom, a mere form without substance, was crucified by the deluded Jews; and that the crucifixion and resurrection were deceptive mystical exhibitions at Jerusalem for the benefit of the human race.

The *Carpocratians, Basilidians*, and *Valentinians*, named after three Egyptian controversialists, contended that Jesus Christ was merely a wise and virtuous mortal, the son of Joseph and Mary, selected by God to reform and instruct mankind; but that a divine nature was imparted to him at the maturity of his age, and period of his baptism, by St. John. The former part of this creed, which is that of the Ebionites, has been revived, and is professed by some of the Unitarian Christians, a numerous and increasing sect of Protestants of the present day.

It is sufficient to glance at these dissensions, which we have not arranged in chronological order, but which convulsed the early Christian church and continued to prevail at the era of Mohammed, to acquit him of any charge of conscious blasphemy in the opinions he inculcated concerning the nature and mission of our Saviour.

Chapter 10

1. The miracles here recorded are not to be found in the pages of the accurate historian Abulfeda, nor are they maintained by any of the graver of the Moslem writers. But they exist in tradition, and are set forth with great prolixity by apocryphal authors, who insist that they are alluded to in the fifty-fourth chapter of the Koran. They are probably as true as many other of the wonders related of the prophet. It will be remembered that he himself claimed but one miracle, "the Koran."

Chapter 11

1. The belief in genii was prevalent throughout the East long before the time of Mohammed. They were supposed to haunt solitary places, particularly toward nightfall, a superstition congenial to the habits and notions of the inhabitants of lonely and desert countries. The Arabs supposed every valley and barren waste to have its tribe of genii, who were subject to a dominant spirit, and roamed forth at night to beset the pilgrim and the traveller. Whenever, therefore, they entered a lonely

valley toward the close of evening, they used to supplicate the presiding spirit or lord of the place to protect them from the evil genii under his command.

Those columns of dust raised by whirling eddies of wind, and which sweep across the desert, are supposed to be caused by some evil genius or sprite of gigantic size.

The serpents which occasionally infest houses were thought to be often genii, some infidels and some believers. Mohammed cautioned his followers to be slow to kill a house serpent. "Warn him to depart; if he does not obey, then kill him, for it is a sign that he is a mere reptile or an infidel genius."

It is fabled that in earlier times the genii had admission to heaven, but were expelled on account of their meddling propensities. They have ever since been of a curious and prying nature, often attempting to clamber up to the constellations; thence to peep into heaven, and see and overhear what is going on there. They are, however, driven thence by angels with flaming swords, and those meteors called shooting stars are supposed by Mohammedans to be darted by the guardian angels at these intrusive genii.

Other legends pretend that the earth was originally peopled by these genii, but they rebelled against the Most High and usurped terrestrial dominion, which they maintained for two thousand years. At length, Azazil, or Lucifer, was sent against them and defeated them, overthrowing their mighty king, Gian ben Gian, the founder of the pyramids, whose magic buckler of talismanic virtue fell subsequently into the hands of King Solomon the Wise, giving him power over the spells and charms of magicians and evil genii. The rebel spirits, defeated and humiliated, were driven into an obscure corner of the earth. Then it was that God created man, with less dangerous faculties and powers, and gave him the world for a habitation.

The angels, according to Moslem notions, were created from bright gems, the genii from fire without smoke, and Adam from clay.

Mohammed, when in the seventy-second chapter of the Koran, he alludes to the visitation of the genii in the Valley of Naklah, makes them give the following frank account of themselves:

"We formerly attempted to pry into what was transacting in heaven, but we found the same guarded by angels with flaming darts; and we sat on some of the seats thereof to hear the discourse of its inhabitants; but whoso listeneth now finds a flame prepared to guard the celestial confines. There are some among us who are Moslems, and there are others who swerve from righteousness. Whoso embraceth Islamism seeketh the true direction; but those who swerve from righteousness shall be fuel for the fire of Jehennam."

Chapter 12

1. There are three to which, say the Moslem doctors, God always lends a willing ear: the voice of him who reads the Koran; of him who prays for pardon; and of this cock who crows to the glory of the Most High. When the last day is near, they add, Allah will bid this bird to close his wings and chant no more. Then all the cocks on earth will cease to crow, and their silence will be a sign that the great day of judgment is impending.

The Reverend Dr. Humphrey Prideaux, Dean of Norwich, in his *Life of Mahomet,* accuses him of having stolen this wonderful cock from the tract Bava Bathra of the Babylonish Talmud, " wherein," says he, "we have a story of such a prodigious bird, called Ziz, which, standing with his feet on the earth, reacheth up to the heavens with his head, and with the spreading of his wings darkeneth the whole orb of the sun, and causeth a total eclipse thereof. This bird the Chaldee paraphrast on the Psalms says is a cock, and that he crows before the Lord; and the Chaldee paraphrast on Job tells us of his crowing every morning before the Lord, and that God giveth him wisdom for that purpose."

Chapter 13

1. The renowned and learned Humphrey Prideaux, in his *Life of Mahomet,* confounds this Salman the Persian with Abdallah Ibn Salam, by some called Abdias Ben Salan in the Hebrew dialect, and by others Abdanah Salen, a learned Jew who is accused by Christian writers of assisting Mohammed in fabricating his revelations.

Chapter 17

1. "The Arabs of the desert," says Burckhardt, "are not rich in horses. Among the great tribes on the Red Sea, between Akaba and Mecca, and to the south and southeast of Mecca, as far as Yemen, horses are very scarce, especially among those of the mountainous districts. The settled inhabitants of Hedjaz and Yemen are not much in the habit of keeping horses. The tribes most rich in horses are those who dwell in the comparatively fertile plains of Mesopotamia, on the banks of the river Euphrates, and on the Syrian plains."—Burckhardt, *op. cit.,* vol. ii, p. 50.

2. This miraculous aid is repeatedly mentioned in the Koran, *e.g.*: "God had already given you the victory at Beder, when ye were inferior in number. When thou saidst unto the faithful, Is it not enough for you that your Lord should assist you with three thousand angels, sent down

from heaven? Verily, if ye persevere, and fear God, and your enemies come upon you suddenly, your Lord will assist you with five thousand angels, distinguished by their horses and attire . . .

"O true believers, ye slew not those who were slain at Beder yourselves, but God slew them. Neither didst thou, O Mohammed, cast the gravel into their eyes, when thou didst seem to cast it; but God cast it."—Sale's *Koran*, chap. iii.

3. George Sale (1697?-1736) was a British orientalist. His version of the Koran, which appeared in November 1734, was the first full translation in any modern language.

Chapter 18

1. It is a received law among all the Arabs that whoever sheds the blood of a man owes blood on that account to the famny of the slain person. This ancient law is sanctioned by the Koran: "O true believers, the law of retaliation is ordained to you for the slain; the free shall die for the free." The Blood revenge, or Thar, as it is termed in Arabic, is claimed by the relatives of all who have been killed in open war, and not merely of the actual perpetrator of the homicide, but of all his relations. For those killed in wars between two tribes, the price of blood is required from the persons who were known to have actually killed them.

The Arab regards this Blood revenge as one of his most sacred rights, as well as duties; no earthly consideration could induce him to give it up. He has a proverbial saying, "Were hellfire to be my lot, I would not relinquish the Thar."—See Burckhardt, *op. cit.*, vol.i, p. 314.

Chapter 21

1. This was Mohammed's second wife of the name of Zeinab; the first, who had died some time previous, was the daughter of Chuzeima.

Chapter 25

1. This stupendous feat is recorded by the historian Abulfeda, ch. 24. "Abu Râfe," observes Gibbon, "was an eyewitness; but who will be witness for Abu Râfe?" We join with the distinguished historian in his doubt; yet if we scrupulously question the testimony of an eyewitness, what will become of history?

2. The Jews inhabiting the tract of country called Khaïbar are still known in Arabia by the name of Beni Kheibar. They are divided into three tribes, under independent sheikhs: the Beni Messiad, Beni Schahan, and Beni Anaesse. They are accused of pillaging the caravans.—Niebuhr, *op. cit.*, vol. ii, p. 43.

Chapter 27

1. Maimuna was the last spouse of the prophet and, old as she was at her marriage, survived all his other wives. She died many years after him, in a pavilion at Serif, under the same tree in the shade of which her nuptial tent had been pitched, and was there interred. The pious historian Al Jannabi, who styles himself "a poor servant of Allah, hoping for the pardon of his sins through the mercy of God," visited her tomb on returning from a pilgrimage to Mecca, in the year of the Hegira 963, A. D. 1555. "I saw there," said he, "a dome of black marble erected in memory of Maimuna, on the very spot on which the apostle of God had reposed with her. God knows the truth! and also the reason of the black color of the stone. There is a place of ablution, and an oratory; but the building has fallen to decay."

Chapter 32

1. "The Thakefites continue a powerful tribe to this day, possessing the same fertile region on the eastern declivity of the Hedjas chain of mountains. Some inhabit the ancient town of Taif, others dwell in tents and have flocks of goats and sheep. They can raise two thousand matchlocks [muskets], and defended their stronghold of Taif in the war with the Wahabys."—Burckhardt, *op. cit.*, vol. ii.

Chapter 36

1. One of the funeral rites of the Moslems is for the Mulakken or priest to address the deceased, when in the grave, in the following words: "O servant of God! O son of a handmaid of God! know that, at this time, there will come down to thee two angels commissioned respecting thee and the like of thee; when they say to thee, 'Who is they Lord?' answer them, 'God is my Lord,' in truth; and when they ask thee concerning thy prophet, or the man who hath been sent unto you, say to them 'Mohammed is the apostle of God,' with veracity; and when they ask thee concerning thy religion, say to them 'Islamism is my religion.' And when they ask thee concerning thy book of direction, say to them, 'The Koran is my book of direction, and the Moslems are my brothers;' and when they ask thee concerning they Kebla, say to them, 'The Caaba is my Kebla, and I have lived and died in the assertion that there is no deity but God, and Mohammed is God's apostle;' and they will say, 'Sleep, O servant of God, in the protection of God!'"—See Edward William Lane, *Account of the Manners and Customs of the Modern Egyptians, 1833-35*, London: Charles Knight, 1836, vol. ii, p. 838

Chapter 38

1. The house of Ayesha was immediately adjacent to the mosque, which was at that time a humble edifice with clay walls, and a roof thatched with palm leaves, and supported by the trunks of trees. It has since been included in a spacious temple, on the plan of a colonnade, inclosing an oblong square, 165 paces by 130, open to the heavens, with four gates of entrance. The colonnade, of several rows of pillars of various sizes covered with stucco and gayly painted, supports a succession of small white cupolas on the four sides of the square. At the four corners are lofty and tapering minarets.

Near the southeast corner of the square is an inclosure, surrounded by an iron railing, painted green, wrought with filigree work and interwoven with brass and gilded wire admitting no view of the interior excepting through small windows, about six inches square. This inclosure, the great resort of pilgrims, is called the Hadgira, and contains the tombs of Mohammed and his two friends and early successors, Abu Beker and Omar. Above this sacred inclosure rises a lofty dome surmounted with a gilded globe and crescent, at the first sight of which pilgrims, as they approach Medina, salute the tomb of the prophet with profound inclinations of the body and appropriate prayers. The marvelous tale, so long considered veritable, that the coffin of Mohammed remained suspended in the air without any support, and which Christian writers accounted for by supposing that it was of iron, and dexterously placed midway between two magnets, is proved to be an idle fiction.

The mosque has undergone changes. It was at one time partially thrown down and destroyed in an awful tempest, but was rebuilt by the Soldan of Egypt. It has been enlarged and embellished by various Caliphs, and in particular by Waled I, under whom Spain was invaded and conquered. It was plundered of its immense votive treasures by the Wahabees when they took and pillaged Medina. It is now maintained, though with diminished splendor, under the care of about thirty Agas, whose chief is called Sheikh Al Haram, or Chief of the Holy House. He is the principal personage in Medina. Pilgrimage to Medina, though considered a most devout and meritorious act, is not imposed on Mohammedans, like pilgrimage to Mecca, as a religious duty, and has much declined in modern days.

The foregoing particulars are from Burckhardt, who gained admission into Medina, as well as into Mecca, in disguise and at great peril, admittance into those cities being prohibited to all but Moslems.

Appendix

1. The reader may recollect that a belief in predestination or destiny was encouraged by Napoleon, and had much influence on his troops.

2. Burckhardt's *Travels in Arabia,* vol. i, p. 260 (London, 1829 ed.)

3. The greater part of the particulars concerning Mecca and Medina, and their respective pilgrimages, are gathered from the writings of that accurate and indefatigable traveller, Burckhardt, who, in the disguise of a pilgrim, visited these shrines and complied with all the forms and ceremonials. His work throws great light upon the manners and customs of the East, and practice of the Islamic faith.

The facts related by Burckhardt have been collated with those of other travellers and writers, and many particulars have been interwoven with them from other sources.

4. The eternal tables or tablet was of white pearl, extended from east to west and from earth to heaven. All the decrees of God were recorded on it, and all events past, present, and to come, to all eternity. It was guarded by angels.

Transliteration Equivalents

The purpose of the following list is to aid interested readers in finding more information about individuals, places, events, objects, etc., mentioned in Irving's biography of Mohammed. Since Irving's spelling in English of Arabic names and words was haphazard and inconsistent, a list of equivalent spellings is needed in order to find them in such authoritative sources as the *Encyclopaedia of Islam*. This list contains the Arabic (as well as a few Hebrew and Persian) words appearing in Irving's book, each followed by the transliteration adopted in the *Encyclopaedia of Islam*.

The following four words, listed here with their English translations, appear frequently in Arabic names: *Abu*, "father of"; *banu*, "sons of"; *ibn*, "son of"; and *umm*, "mother of".

I wish to express my thanks to Mr. Gamil Youssef, Arabic expert of the New York Public Library, for his help in compiling this list.

R. P.

Aass: 'Āṣ, al-
Abbas: 'Abbās, al-
Abbas Ibn Mardas: 'Abbās ibn Mirdās
Abdalasis: 'Abd al-'Azīz
Abd al Dar: 'Abd al-Dār
Abdallah: 'Abd Allāh
Abdallah Ibn Jasch: 'Abd Allāh ibn Djahsh
Abdallah Ibn Kawaha: 'Abd Allāh ibn Rawāḥa
Abdallah Ibn Masoud: 'Abd Allāh ibn Mas'ūd
Abdallah Ibn Obba: 'Abd Allāh ibn Ubayy
Abdallah Ibn Obba Solul: 'Abd Allāh ibn Ubayy Ṣalūl

Abdallah Ibn Saad: 'Abd Allāh ibn Sa'd
Abdallah Ibn Salam, - Salen: 'Abd Allāh ibn Salām
Abd al Motâlleb: 'Abd al-Muttalib
Abda'lrahman: 'Abd al-Rahmān
Abdias Ben Salan: 'Abd Allāh ibn Salām
Abd Schems: 'Abd Shams
Abu Afak: Abū 'Afak
Abu Amir: Abū Amīr
Abu Ayub: Abū Ayyūb
Abu Beker: Abū Bakr
Abu Dudjana: Abū Dudjāna
Abu Horaira: Abū Hurayra
Abu Jahl: Abū Jahl
Abu Kasim: Abu 'l-Ḳāsim
Abu Khaitama: Abū Khaythama
Abul Aass: Abu 'l-'Āṣ
Abu Lahab: Abū Lahab
Abu 'lhoen: Abu 'l-Ḥukm
Abulfeda: Abu 'l-Fidā
Abu Musa: Abū Mūsā
Abu Râfe: Abū Rāfi'
Abu Rawaiha: Abū Rawāḥa
Abu Sofian: Abū Sufyān
Abu Taleb: Abū Ṭālib
Abu Yaser: Abū Yāsir
Abwa: Abwā', al-
Achbar: Akbar
Adha, Al: Aḍhā, al-
Adi: 'Adī
Adij: 'Adī
Adites: 'Adites
Aga: Agha
Ahmed: Aḥmad
Ailhala: 'Ayhala
Ajami: 'Ajamī
Akaba, Al: 'Aḳaba, al-
Akrema: 'Ikrima
Ali: 'Alī
Al Lat: Lāt, al-
Amina: Āmina
Amin, Al: Amīn, al-
Amir ibn Tafiel: 'Āmir ibn al-Ṭufayl

Amit! Amit!: Mawt! Mawt!
Amon: 'Ammān
Amru: Imru'
Amru Ibn Hasham: Imru' ibn Hishām
Ansarians: Anṣārians
Araf, Al: 'Uraf, al-
Arafat: 'Arafāt
Asama: Asmā'
Aslam: Aslama
Aswad, Al: Aswad, al-
Autas: Awṭās
Aws, Al: Aws, al-
Ayesha: 'Ā'isha
Azer or Zerah: Āzar
Azazil: 'Azāzīl
Azraïl: 'Izrā'īl

Bab al Salam: Bāb al-Salām
Bab el Zafa: Bāb al-Ṣafā
Bahira: Baḥīrā
Baida: Bayḍā, al-
Balka: Balḳā', al-
Barakat: Barakāt
Basrah: Baṣra, al-
Battar, Al: Battār, al-
Beder: Badr
Beni Amir: Banū Amīr
Beni Kainoka: Banū Ḳaynuḳā'
Beni Kheibar: Banū Khaybar
Beni Koraida: Banū Ḳurayza
Beni Mostalek: Banū Muṣṭaliḳ
Beni Nadher: Banū Naḍīr
Beni Sad: Banū Sa'd
Beni Scheiba: Banū Shaybān
Beni Suleim: Banū Sulaym
Beni Thamud: Banū Thamūd
Berbera: Berberā
Berzak: Barzakh
Bokhari, Al: Bukhārī, al-
Borak, Al: Burāq, al-
Boreida Ibn al Hoseib : Burayda ibn al-Ḥuṣayb
Bosra, Bostra: Baṣra, al-

Caab Ibn Zohair: Ka'b ibn Zuhayr
Caaba: Ka'ba
Cadijah: Khadīdja
Catum, Al: Ḳaṭūm, al-
Cauther, Al: Kawthar, al-
Chuzeima, Chuzima: Kudhīmā
Colthum Ibn Hadem: Kulthūm ibn Hidm

Daldal: Duldul
Dhul Fakar: Dhu 'l-Faḳār
Dhu 'l Holaifa: Dhu 'l-Ḥulayfa
Dhu 'l-hajji: Dhu 'l-Hidjdja
Djasch: Djāḥsh
Doraid: Durayd
Doraid Ibn Simma: Durayd ibn al-Ṣimma
Doul Kaada: Dhu 'l-Ḳa'da
Dsu Huleifa: Dhu 'l-Ḥulayfa
Dhu'l Holaifa: Dhu 'l-Ḥulayfa
Durthur: Dūrthūr

Eblis: Iblīs
Eden or Aden: 'Adan
El Lat: Lāt, al-
Emir or Amir: Amīr
Eyla: Ayla

Fadha, Al: Faḍha, al-
Fadjar, Al: Fidjār, al-
Fatima: Fāṭima
Fazara: Fazāra
Firuz the Dailemite: Fīrūz al-Daylamī

Gassan: Ghassān
Ghatafan: Ghaṭafān
Giafar or Jaafar: Dja'far
Gins: Djinn
Gothreb: Yathrib

Habbar Ibn Aswad: Ḥabbār ibn Aswad
Habid: Ḥabīb
Habib Ibn Malec: Ḥabīb ibn Malik

Hadgira: Ḥadjr
Hadjun: Ḥadjūn
Hajji: Ḥādjdjī
Hafza: Ḥafṣa
Haïdara, Al: Ḥaydar, al-
Haizum: Ḥayzūm
Hajar: Ḥadjar
Hakim: Ḥākim
Halêma: Ḥalīma
Hamza: Ḥamza
Hara: Ḥāra
Harâm, Al: Ḥaram, al-
Harb: Ḥarb
Hareth, Al: Ḥārith, al-
Hareth Ibn Hashem: Ḥārith ibn Hishām
Hasala: Ḥaṣat
Hasan: Ḥasan
Hassan: Ḥasan
Haschem: Ḥāshim
Hateb: Khaṭīb
Hatef: Ḥātif
Hatim: Ḥātim
Hawazan, Hawazin: Hawāzin
Hedjar: Hidjar, al-
Hedjas, Hedjaz: Ḥidjāz
Hegira: Hidjra
Helalite: Hilālite
Hend, Henda: Hind
Hilal Ibn Omeya: Hilāl ibn Umayya
Hobal: Hubal
Hobash: Ḥubaysh
Hodeiba: Ḥudayba
Hodseitites: Hudhayl, Banū
Holagu: Hūlāgū
Honeifa: Ḥunayfa
Honein: Ḥunayn
Hoya Ibn Ahktab: Ḥuyay ibn Akhṭāb
Hûr al Oyûn: Ḥur al-'uyūn
Huram Behest: Hurī beheshtī (Persian)

Ibn al Aass: Ibn al-'Āṣ
Ibn Harb: Ibn Ḥarb

Ibn Omm Mactum: Ibn Umm Maktūm
Ibrahim: Ibrāhīm
Ihram: Iḥrām
Iman: Imām
Iram: Iḥrām
Isa: ʿIsā
Ispahan: Iṣfahān
Izrafil: Isrāfīl

Jaafar ibn Abu Taleb: Djaʿfar ibn Abi Ṭālib
Jadsima: Djadhīma
Jannai, Al: Djannābī, al-
Jannat: Djanna
Jehennam: Djahannam
Joctan: Yoqṭan (Hebrew)
Joddal: Djudda (Djidda)
Johanna Ibn Ruba: Djuhanna ibn Ruʾba
Joshmites: Djusham, Banū
Judah Hakkodish: Judah haQadosh (Hebrew)
Jurham: Djurhum

Kaab Ibn Aschraf: Kaʿb ibn al-Ashraf
Kaab Ibn Malec: Kaʿb ibn Mālik
Kadesia: Ḳādisiyya, al-
Kadhi: Ḳāḍi
Kader, Al: Ḳādir, al-
Kahtan: Ḳaḥṭān
Kaiba: Ḳāybā
Kainoka: Ḳaynuḳaʿ, Banū
Kalb: Kalb, Banū
Kamus, Al: Ḳamūṣ, al-
Kanana: Kināna
Kara: Ḳarā
Karwa, El: Ḳaṣwā, al-
Kasim: Ḳāsim
Kaswa, Al: Ḳaṣwā, al-
Katan: Ḳaḥṭān
Kebla: Ḳibla
Kedaid: Ḳudayd
Kenana: Kināna
Kenana Ibn al Rabi: Kināna ibn al-Rabīʿ
Kenanites: Kināna

Kenda: Kinda
Khaïbar: Khaybar
Khaled: Khālid
Khaled Ibn al Waled: Khālid ibn al-Walīd
Khattab: Khaṭṭāb
Khazradites: Khazradjites
Khazraj, Al: Khazradj, al-
Khosru: Khusraw, Kisrā
Koba: Ḳubā
Kora: Ḳarā
Koraida: Ḳurayẓa
Koreish, -ites: Ḳuraysh
Kubeis: Ḳubays
Kussilbachi: Ḳizil-Bāsh

La illaha il Allah: La ilāha ill' Allāh
Lazlos: Lazzāz

Maalem, Al: Mu'allim, al-
Maimuna: Maymūna
Maïsara: Maysara
Makam: Maḳām
Malec Ibn Auf: Mālik ibn 'Awf
Manna: Mānā
Mansela: Manzila
Marhab: Marḥab
Mariyah: Māriya
Marr Azzahran: Marr al-Ẓahrān
Masroud: Masrūd
Medham: Midham
Mehrab, Al: Miḥrāb, al-
Mena: Minā
Merowa: Marwa
Merwa: Marwa
Merwan: Marwān
Mesjed al Nebi: Masdjid al-Nabī
Metowef: Muṭawwif
Mina: Minā
Mishcat-ul-Masabih: Mishkāt al-Maṣābīḥ
Mishnu: Mishna (Hebrew)
Mistah: Misṭaḥ
Moad Ibn Jabal: Mu'ādh ibn Djabal

Moakkbat: Mu'akkibāt
Moawyah: Mu'āwiya
Modâd: Mudād
Mogheira, Al: Mughīra, al-
Mohadjerins: Muhādjirūn
Mohrem, al: Muhrim, al-
Monthari, al: Muntharī, al-
Monthawi, al: Munthawī, al-
Moraïsi: Muraysī, al-
Mosaab Ibn Omair: Mus'ab ibn 'Umayr
Moseïlma: Musaylima
Moslem: Muslim
Most'-asem Billah, Al-: Musta'ṣim Bi-llāh, al-
Mozdalifa: Muzdalifa
Mukowkis: Mukawkis
Mulakken: Mulakkin
Munkar and Nakeer: Munkar wa-Nakir
Musa: Mūsā
Musab Ibn Omeir: Mus'ab ibn 'Umayr
Mussulman, Musulman: Muslim, -ūn
Muta: Mu'ta
Mutem Ibn Adi: Muṭ'am ibn 'Adī

Naderites: Nadīr, Banū
Nadhar: Nadhr
Nadjed: Nadjd
Najran: Nadjrān
Naklah: Nakhla
Nawfal Ibn Abdallah: Nawfal ibn 'Abd Allāh
Nedja: Nadjd

Obbij Ibn Chalaf: Ubayy ibn Khalaf
Obeidah Ibn al Hareth: 'Ubayda ibn al-Ḥārith
Ocadh: 'Ukāẓ
Ohod: Uḥud
Okaz: 'Ukāẓ
Okba: 'Ukba
Okaider Ibn Malec: Ukaydir ibn Malik
Omar Ibn Al Hareth: 'Umar ibn al-Ḥārith
Omar Ibn al Khattab: 'Umar ibn al-Khaṭṭāb
Omeya: Umayya
Omeyads: Umayyads

Omm Habiba: Umm Ḥabība
Omm Hakem: Umm Ḥakīm
Omm Jemil: Umm Djamīl
Omm Kolthum: Umm Kulthūm
Omm Salma: Umm Salama
Orkham: Orkhān
Osaid Ibn Hodheir: Usayd ibn Ḥudayr
Osmaa Ibn Zeid: Usāma ibn Zayd
Otab: 'Utab
Otba: 'Utba
Otha: 'Utba
Othman: 'Uthmān
Othman Ibn Affan: 'Uthmān ibn 'Affān
Othman Ibn Talha: 'Uthmān ibn Ṭalḥa
Otho: 'Utba

Raab Ibn Malek: Ra'b ibn Malik
Rabi: Rabī'
Rabia Ibn Rafi: Rabī'a ibn Rāfi'
Radjab: Radjab
Radje: Radjī', al-
Rais: Ra'īs
Ramadhan: Ramaḍān
Rehana, Rihana: Rayḥāna
Rokaia: Ruḳayya
Rueim: Ru'aym
Rushvan: Rashwān

Saa, or Say: Sa'y
Saad: Sa'd
Saadia, al-: Ṣudra, al-
Saad Ibn Maad (Moad): Sa'd ibn Mu'ādh
Saadite: Sa'dite
Sabaea, Sabean: Ṣābi'a, al-
Sadakat: Ṣadaḳa
Safa: Ṣafā
Saffana: Saffāna
Safiya: Ṣafiyya
Safwan Ibn al Moattel: Ṣafwān ibn al-Mu'aṭṭal
Saham: Sahm
Salam: Salām
Saleh: Ṣāliḥ

Salem: Salām
Salma: Salmā
Salman al Parsi: Salmān al-Fārisī
Sanaa: Sanʻāʼ
Sara: Sāra
Satiha: Saṭīha
Sawa: Sāwā
Say: Saʻy
Schiites: Shīʻites
Seddek, Al: Saddāḳ, al-
Sedrat: Sidra
Seid: Zayd
Serat: Sirāṭ, al-
Serendib: Sarandīb
Shaiba: Shayba
Shakra: Ṣakhra
Sheikh: Shaykh
Shima, Al: Shaymā, al-
Shiren: Shīrīn
Shorhail: Shuraḥbīl
Siddik: Ṣadīḳ, al-
Soffat: Ṣuffa
Sokran: Sakrān
Soldan: Sulṭān
Solhail: Suhayl
Sonna: Sunna
Sonnites: Sunnites
Soraka Ibn Malec: Surāḳa ibn Malik
Suleimites: Sulaym, Banū

Tabuc, Tabuk: Tabūk
Tacwins: Takwīn
Tai: Ṭāʼī
Takwa, al: Takwā, al-
Talbijah: Talbiya
Talha: Ṭalḥa
Tamim: Tamīm
Tayef: Ṭāʼif, al-
Tehama: Tihāma
Thabeck: Thāḳib
Thabet Ibn Rais: Thābit ibn Ḳays
Thakeef, Thakifites: Thakīf

Thamudites: Tha̲mūd
Thar: Tha̲'r
Thor: Ṭūr
Towaf: Tawāf

Um colthum: Umm Kul<u>th</u>ūm
Uzza: 'Uzzā, al-

Wacksa, Waksa: Wāksā
Wakedi, Al: Wākidī, al-
Walid, Al: Walīd, al-
Waraka: Waraḳa

Yafur: Ya'fur
Yamama: Yamāma
Yarab: Ya'rub
Yathreb: Ya<u>th</u>rib

Zacat: Zakāt
Zaïnab: Zaynab
Zarah, Zerah: Āzar
Zeid: Zayd
Zeid Ibn Horeth: Zayd ibn Ḥāri<u>th</u>a
Zeid Ibn Thabet: Zayd ibn <u>Th</u>ābit
Zeinab: Zaynab
Zem Zem: Zamzam
Zig: Ziz (Hebrew)
Zobier: Zubayr
Zohra: Zuhra

WASHINGTON IRVING was the first American man of letters to achieve international recognition. Lord Byron wrote: "Irving is a genius; and he has something better than genius—a heart....His writings are my delight." And Charles Dickens told a New York audience: "Washington Irving! Why, gentlemen, I don't go upstairs to bed two nights out of the seven ....without taking Washington Irving under my arm." It was during two diplomatic assignments in Spain—the second as U. S. minister, 1842-46—that Irving found time to research and write his biography of the prophet Mohammed. It was published at the end of 1849, and remained more or less continuously in print during the nineteenth century. Translations have appeared in the German, French, Spanish, Italian, Polish, Russian, Greek and Icelandic languages.

RAPHAEL PATAI has taught Middle Eastern anthropology at the University of Pennsylvania and Princeton and Columbia Universities. He is the author of thirty-five books, including *Society, Culture and Change in the Middle East*, *The Arab Mind*, and *The Seed of Abraham*.

COVER: *Halt in the Desert*, oil on panel, Belgian School, 19th Century (private collection).